OXR S10

CIVIL PARTNERSHIP ACT

EXPLANATORY NOTES

INTRODUCTION

1.   These explanatory notes relate to the Civil Partnership Act 2004 which received Royal Assent on 18th November 2004. They have been prepared by the Department of Trade and Industry in order to assist the reader in understanding the Act. They do not form a part of the Act and have not been endorsed by Parliament.

2.   The notes need to be read in conjunction with the Act. They are not, and are not meant to be, a comprehensive description of the Act. So where a section or part of a section does not seem to require any explanation or comment, none is given.

SUMMARY

3.   The purpose of the Civil Partnership Act is to enable same-sex couples to obtain legal recognition of their relationship by forming a civil partnership. They may do so by registering as civil partners of each other provided:

- they are of the same sex;
- they are not already in a civil partnership or lawfully married;
- they are not within the prohibited degrees of relationship;
- they are both aged sixteen or over (and, if either of them is under 18 and the registration is to take place in England and Wales or Northern Ireland, the consent of the appropriate people or bodies has been obtained).

4.   The Act also sets out the legal consequences of forming a civil partnership, including the rights and responsibilities of civil partners.

BACKGROUND

5.   On 30 June 2003 the Government published a consultation paper, 'Civil Partnership: a framework for the legal recognition of same-sex couples', setting out its proposals for civil partnership. After a three-month consultation period, during which over three thousand responses were received, a report summarising the consultation findings was published in November 2003. An intention to bring forward a Civil Partnership Bill was announced in the Queen's Speech on 26 November 2003.

6.   On 10 September 2003, the Scottish Executive announced that in the event that civil partnership registration was introduced in England and Wales, same-sex couples should similarly be able to form a civil partnership in Scotland in order to access a comprehensive package of rights and responsibilities in both reserved and devolved areas. The Scottish Executive therefore proposed seeking the agreement of the Scottish Parliament to the inclusion of Scottish provisions in a future Westminster Civil Partnership Bill. The Scottish Executive published a consultation document on 30 September and an analysis of consultation responses was published on 5 February 2004. The Executive subsequently reaffirmed its intention to introduce civil partnership in Scotland, if it were introduced in

England and Wales. On 3 June 2004 the Scottish Parliament agreed to the inclusion of Scottish provisions in a Westminster Bill.

7.   Northern Ireland Office Ministers set out their policy intentions on civil partnership in their consultation document, published on 19 December 2003. In it they announced that they supported the introduction of civil partnership in Northern Ireland and the inclusion of provisions for Northern Ireland in the Westminster Bill. The consultation period closed on 5 March 2004. Northern Ireland Office Ministers decided to take the proposal forward and establish a civil partnership registration scheme for Northern Ireland by including the necessary provisions in the Civil Partnership Bill.

THE ACT

8.   The Act is in 8 Parts and has 30 Schedules.

9.   Part 1 describes how a civil partnership is formed and how it ends.

10.   Part 2 sets out the arrangements for civil partnerships in England and Wales.

- Chapter 1 makes provision for the formation of a civil partnership by registration.

- Chapter 2 makes provision for the dissolution of a civil partnership, nullity and other proceedings.

- Chapter 3 makes provision for property and financial arrangements.

- Chapter 4 sets out the effect of agreeing to form a civil partnership.

- Chapter 5 covers issues relating to children.

- Chapter 6 covers other miscellaneous provisions.

11.   Part 3 sets out the arrangements for civil partnerships in Scotland.

- Chapter 1 deals with formation and eligibility.

- Chapter 2 makes provision for the formation of a civil partnership by registration.

- Chapter 3 makes provision relating to occupancy rights and tenancies.

- Chapter 4 makes provision for interdicts.

- Chapter 5 makes provision for the dissolution of a civil partnership, separation and nullity.

- Chapter 6 covers other miscellaneous provisions and matters of interpretation.

12.   Part 4 makes provision for civil partnerships in Northern Ireland.

- Chapter 1 makes provision for the formation of a civil partnership by registration.

- Chapter 2 makes provision regarding dissolution, nullity and other proceedings.

- Chapter 3 makes provisions for property and financial arrangements.

- Chapter 4 sets out the effect of agreeing to form a civil partnership.

- Chapter 5 covers issues relating to children.

- Chapter 6 covers other miscellaneous provisions.

13.   Part 5 deals with civil partnerships formed or dissolved abroad.

- Chapter 1 makes provision for registration outside the UK under the provisions of an Order in Council.

- Chapter 2 makes provision for certain overseas relationships to be treated as civil partnerships.

- Chapter 3 sets out the circumstances in which courts in the UK will have jurisdiction in relation to the dissolution or annulment of a civil partnership or the legal separation of civil partners, and makes provision for recognition of dissolutions etc. obtained in other parts of or outside the UK.

- Chapter 4 covers other miscellaneous and supplementary matters.

14. Part 6 deals with relationships arising through civil partnership.

15. Part 7 contains miscellaneous provisions including those relating to social security, child support and tax credits.

16. Part 8 contains supplementary material such as powers to make regulations and orders, commencement and extent.

COMMENTARY ON SECTIONS

Part 1 - Introduction

Section 1: Civil Partnership

17. This section establishes civil partnership as a legal relationship between two people of the same sex. *Subsection (1)* provides for a civil partnership to be formed in either of two ways. The first is when two people register as civil partners of each other, either in the United Kingdom (under the relevant Part of the Act) or under an Order in Council made under section 210 or 211 (which allow for registration overseas at British consulates or by armed forces personnel). The second is where the couple register an "overseas relationship" which is treated as a civil partnership under Chapter 2 of Part 5. "Overseas relationship" is defined in sections 212 to 214. *Subsection (3)* provides that a civil partnership only ends on death, dissolution or annulment.

Part 2 – Civil Partnership: England and Wales

Introduction

18. This Part of the Act, except section 35, extends to England and Wales only.

Chapter 1 – Registration

Section 2: Formation of civil partnership by registration

19. *Subsection (1)* describes the point at which a civil partnership is formed and sets out who is to be present at the registration. Two people are to be regarded as having registered as civil partners of each other once each of them has signed the civil partnership document. "The civil partnership document" is defined in section 7. *Subsection (2)* makes it clear that a civil partnership is formed even if the formalities set out at *subsections (3)* and *(4)* are not complied with. *Subsection (3)* specifies who else must sign the civil partnership document . *Subsection (4)* sets out what is to be recorded in the register once a civil partnership document has been signed and the administrative procedure to be completed following the civil partnership registration.

20. *Subsection (5)* provides that no religious service is to be used while a civil partnership registrar is officiating at the signing of a civil partnership document.

Section 3: Eligibility

21. *Subsection (1)* provides that two people are not eligible to register as civil partners of each other if -

(a) they are not of the same sex,

(b) either of them is already a civil partner or lawfully married,

(c) either of them is under 16, or

(d) they are within prohibited degrees of relationship (set out in Part 1 of Schedule 1).

Section 4: Parental etc. consent where proposed civil partner under 18

22. This section sets out the provisions requiring consent where a person wishing to form a civil partnership is under 18 years of age. Part 1 of Schedule 2 identifies the appropriate person or persons who may give consent. *Subsection (3)* provides an exception to the requirement of consent where a civil partner has been bereaved and wishes to form a subsequent civil partnership before he or she is 18. For the purposes of Part 2 of the Act, *subsection (5)* defines "child" as a person who is under 18 (except where the term is used to express a relationship).

Section 5: Types of pre-registration procedure

23. *Subsection (1)* sets out the various procedures, available in England and Wales, under which two people may register as civil partners of each other. *Subsection (2)* sets out the relevant modifications of those procedures which apply where one of the proposed civil partners lives in Scotland, Northern Ireland or is a member of the armed forces serving abroad, and the other has a usual residence in England and Wales, or where the proposed civil partners are former spouses, one of whom has changed sex. *Subsection (3)* provides for all the procedures to be subject to Schedules 1 and 2 (provisions applicable in connection with prohibited degrees of relationship and where a proposed civil partner is under 18). *Subsection (4)* provides that section 5 is also subject to section 249 and Schedule 23 (provisions relating to the formation of civil partnerships by persons subject to immigration control).

Section 6: Place of registration

24. This section states that the place where the proposed civil partnership is to be registered must be in England and Wales, must not be in religious premises and must be specified in the notice or notices of proposed civil partnership. "Religious premises" is defined in *subsection (2)*. *Subsections (3) and (4)* make it clear that in the case of registration under the standard procedure, the place of registration must be one that is open to anyone wishing to attend and that it must be agreed with the registration authority where the registration is to take place before it is specified in a notice. If the place specified in a notice is not agreed then the notice is void.

Section 7: The civil partnership document

25. This section defines the term "civil partnership document" as a Registrar General's licence in relation to the special procedure and a civil partnership schedule for all other procedures. *Subsection (2)* provides that before a civil partnership registration can take place, the civil partnership document must be delivered to the civil partnership registrar who may

then ask the proposed civil partners for any information required to be recorded in the register.

26.   Sections 8 to 17 set out the standard procedure by which two people may register as civil partners of each other in England and Wales.

Section 8: Notice of proposed civil partnership and declaration

27.   *Subsection (1)* states that for two people to register as civil partners of each other they must each give a notice of proposed civil partnership and have resided in England or Wales for at least 7 days immediately before giving the notice. The information contained in the notice may be prescribed by regulations. *Subsections (3)* and *(4)* state that a notice must include a solemn declaration in writing to be made by the person giving notice. By this declaration the proposed civil partner must confirm that he or she knows of no legal impediments to the formation of the civil partnership and confirm that each proposed civil partner has had a residence in England and Wales for at least 7 days before the notice was given. The declaration must be signed by the person giving the notice and attested by the "authorised person" (as defined by *subsection (6)*). *Subsection (5)* requires the registration authority to record in the register the fact that the notice has been given and the information in it, and that the authorised person attested the declaration.

Section 9: Power to require evidence of name etc.

28.   This section enables a registration authority to request specified evidence to verify certain information contained in a notice of proposed civil partnership. Requests for evidence may only be made before the civil partnership schedule has been issued in accordance with section 14.

Section 10: Proposed civil partnerships to be publicised

29.   This section sets out which registration authority (or authorities), as well as the Registrar General, must publicise "relevant information" during the "waiting period" after a notice has been given. *Subsection (2)* defines "relevant information" as the names of the proposed civil partners and such other information as may be prescribed by regulations.

Section 11: Meaning of the "waiting period"

30.   This section defines the term "waiting period" for the purposes of Chapter 1.

Section 12: Power to shorten the waiting period

31.   This section enables the Registrar General, on an application being made to him, to reduce the waiting period if satisfied there are compelling reasons to do so, because of exceptional circumstances. *Subsections (2)* and *(3)* give the Registrar General the power to make procedural regulations in relation to such applications and to make regulations delegating the power to shorten the waiting period to a registration authority in prescribed cases and making provision for appeals (to the Registrar General) against any decision taken by a registration authority where this power has been delegated.

Section 13: Objection to proposed civil partnership

32.   This section sets out the procedure for any person to make an objection to the issue of a civil partnership schedule. The registration authority which receives an objection must record the fact that the objection has been made and the information it contains in the register as soon as possible.

Section 14: Issue of civil partnership schedule

33.   This section provides for the issue of a civil partnership schedule at the end of the waiting period. *Subsection (2)* confers a power to make provision as to the contents of the civil partnership schedule. The schedule may be issued on the request of one or both of the proposed civil partners, provided the relevant registration authority is satisfied that there is no lawful impediment to the couple forming a civil partnership and that any objections to the proposed civil partnership have been satisfactorily investigated by the relevant registration authority or have been withdrawn. "The relevant registration authority" means the authority which first records that a notice of proposed civil partnership has been given.

Section 15: Appeal against refusal to issue civil partnership schedule

34.   This section provides for an appeal to the Registrar General against the refusal of a registration authority to issue the civil partnership schedule. The Registrar General must either confirm the refusal or direct that a civil partnership schedule be issued.

Section 16: Frivolous objections and representations: liability for costs etc.

35.   This section provides for the Registrar General to deal with frivolous objections made against the issue of the civil partnership schedule. *Subsection (3)* imposes liability on a person who makes a frivolous objection or representation for costs of the proceedings before the Registrar General and for damages payable to the proposed civil partner to whom the objection or representation relates.

Section 17: Period during which registration may take place

36.   This section provides that the proposed civil partners may not form a civil partnership until the waiting period in relation to each notice of proposed civil partnership has expired. It also specifies the period of validity of a civil partnership schedule issued under the standard procedure as being 12 months, running from when notice of proposed civil partnership is recorded, and when notices are not recorded on the same day, from the earlier of the two days. After this period the civil partnership schedule becomes void and cannot be used. Fresh notices of proposed civil partnership would need to be given if the parties still intended to form a civil partnership.

Section 18: House-bound persons

37.   This section caters for people who wish to register as civil partners of each other at the place where one of them is house-bound. A person will be accepted as being house-bound if, in relation to that person, a statement is made by a registered medical practitioner that, in his opinion, because of illness or disability, that person ought not to move from the place where he or she is at the time when the statement is made and that this is likely to be the case for at least the following 3 months. The statement must be made not more than 14 days before the day on which each notice of proposed civil partnership is recorded.

38.   *Subsection* (3) sets out the procedure for a housebound person to register as a civil partner. This is the same as the standard procedure –(see sections 8 – 17) but with the additional requirements that a medical statement must accompany each notice; receipt of the medical statement is recorded in the register; and the applicable period (during which the civil partnership schedule may be signed) is shortened to 3 months.

39.   For the purposes of forming a civil partnership, *subsection (6)* treats a person in relation to whom a medical statement is made as being resident and usually resident at the place where he or she is for the time being, even if this would not otherwise be the case.

Section 19: Detained persons

40.   This section enables two people to register as civil partners of each other at the place where one of them is detained.

41.   *Subsection (2)* defines "detained" as meaning detained as a patient in a hospital (other than as a short-term detainee under the Mental Health Act 1983 (c20)) or in a prison or other place to which the Prison Act 1952 (c. 52) applies.

42.   *Subsection (3)* sets out the procedure for registration in such a case. This is the same as the standard procedure (see sections 8 – 17) with the additional requirements that a supporting statement must accompany each notice; receipt of the supporting statement must be recorded in the register and the applicable period (during which the civil partnership schedule must be signed) is shortened to 3 months.

43.   *Subsection (4)* sets out that a supporting statement is one made by the responsible authority (as defined by *subsection (6)*) identifying the establishment where the person is detained and confirming that the responsible authority has no objection to that place being specified in a notice of proposed civil partnership as the place at which the detained person is to register as a civil partner.

44.   For the purposes of forming a civil partnership, *subsection (8)* treats a detained person as being resident and usually resident at the place where he or she is for the time being, even if this would not otherwise be the case.

Section 20: Modified procedures for certain non-residents

45.   Section 20 modifies the standard procedure and the procedures for house-bound persons and for detained persons where two people wish to register as civil partners of each other in England and Wales and one of them is resident in England and Wales but the other resides in Scotland or in Northern Ireland or is a member of Her Majesty's forces serving overseas.

46.   The modifications are set out in *subsection (5)*. The person resident in England and Wales is required to give a notice of proposed civil partnership but the other person is not required to do so. A registration authority must not issue a civil partnership schedule unless one of the proposed civil partners produces a certificate of no impediment issued under section 97, 150 or 239. In the case of the standard procedure, where one of the proposed civil partners resides in Scotland or Northern Ireland, the applicable period (during which the civil partnership schedule must be signed) is shortened to 3 months.

Section 21: Notice of proposed civil partnership

47.   Sections 21 to 27 deal with "the special procedure". This enables a civil partnership registration to take place very quickly, under a Registrar General's licence, where one of the proposed civil partners is seriously ill and not expected to recover. The licence is the equivalent of a civil partnership schedule but can be issued by a registration authority only on the authority of the Registrar General. It is the document that is signed by the couple to form the civil partnership.

48.   Section 21 relaxes the normal requirement that both proposed civil partners must give notice and allows one of the proposed civil partners to give a notice of proposed civil partnership under the special procedure, as long as that person complies with any requirement made under section 22. *Subsection (3)* applies most of the requirements of subsections (3) to (6) of section 8 relating to the declaration to be made when giving notice. The requirement as to residence (in section 8(4)(b)) is not applied.

Section 22: Evidence to be produced

49. This section sets out the evidence that the Registrar General may require the person giving the notice to produce to the registration authority in order to satisfy the Registrar General that the special procedure should be used.

50. *Subsection (3)* makes it clear that a certificate from a registered medical practitioner is sufficient evidence of the seriousness of a proposed civil partner's medical condition and of that person's ability to understand the nature and purport of signing a Registrar General's licence.

Section 23: Application to be reported to the Registrar General

51. This section requires a registration authority to inform the Registrar General if it receives any notice of proposed civil partnership under the special procedure. The authority must also inform the Registrar General about supporting evidence and comply with any directions that he may give for verifying the evidence.

Section 24: Objection to issue of Registrar General's licence

52. This section sets out the procedure for any person to make an objection to the Registrar General giving authority for the issue of his licence by giving a notice of objection to the Registrar General or any registration authority. A registration authority that receives notice of objection must record the fact that it has been given and the information it contains in the register as soon as possible.

Section 25: Issue of Registrar General's licence

53. This section applies where a notice of proposed civil partnership has been given to a registration authority under the special procedure. The registration authority may issue a Register General's licence only if given authority to do so by the Registrar General. The Registrar General may not give his authority unless he is satisfied that one of the proposed civil partners is seriously ill and not expected to recover. If he is so satisfied, he must give his authority unless he is also satisfied that there is a lawful impediment to the issue of the licence. If an objection has been made to the Registrar General giving his authority, he must not give his authority until he has investigated the objection and has decided whether it ought to obstruct the issue of the licence or the objection has been withdrawn.

Section 26: Frivolous objections: liability for costs

54. This section means that a person who makes a frivolous objection will be liable to costs and damages.

Section 27: Period during which registration may take place

55. This section establishes the period of validity of Registrar General's licences issued under the special procedure as 1 month from the day on which notice is given. After this period the notice of proposed civil partnership and the licence are void.

Section 28: Registration authorities

56. This section defines "registration authority" in relation to England and Wales.

Section 29: Civil partnership registrars

57. This section defines a civil partnership registrar as an individual who is designated by a registration authority as a civil partnership registrar for its area (*subsection (1)*). A registration authority is under a duty to ensure that there are enough registrars for its area

(*subsection (2)*). The Registrar General is required to make a list of civil partnership registrars available to the public (see *subsection (4)*).

Section 30: The Registrar General and the register

58. This section defines "the Registrar General" and places certain responsibilities on him in connection with the maintenance of records that relate to civil partnerships.

Section 31: Offences relating to civil partnership schedule

59. This section creates offences in relation to the civil partnership schedule.

60. *Subsection (3)* sets out the maximum penalty that may be imposed for these offences. *Subsection (4)* specifies the time limit within which a prosecution may be brought.

Section 32: Offences relating to Registrar General's licence

61. This section creates offences in relation to the special procedure.

62. *Subsection (3)* sets out the maximum penalty that may be imposed for these offences. *Subsection (4)* specifies the time limit within which a prosecution may be brought.

Section 33: Offences relating to the recording of civil partnerships

63. This section creates offences in relation to the requirements for recording civil partnerships in the register, and specifies the maximum penalty for each offence. *Subsection (9)* specifies the time limit of 3 years within which a prosecution may be brought for the offences set out in *subsections (5)* and *(7)*.

Section 34: Fees

64. This section enables the Chancellor of the Exchequer to make an order providing for fees to be payable in relation to elements of the different civil partnership registration procedures and other services provided in connection with civil partnership. The section also makes provision, in cases of hardship, for the Registrar General to remit the fee for the issue of his licence under the special procedure.

Section 35: Power to assimilate provisions relating to civil registration

65. *Subsection (1)* gives the Chancellor of the Exchequer the power to make an order to assimilate, if appropriate, the provisions of the Act connected with the formation or recording of a civil partnership to any provision made in relation to civil marriage in England and Wales. Such order may also make appropriate consequential amendments of other legislation.

Section 36: Regulations and orders

66. This section provides that regulations may make provision supplementing the provisions on registration. The section also provides that references to regulations in this Chapter are to regulations made by the Registrar General, with the approval of the Chancellor of the Exchequer. *Subsections (4) to (6)* make provision about the procedure for orders and regulations.

Chapter 2 – Dissolution, Nullity and Other Proceedings

Section 37: Powers to make orders and effect of orders

67. This section sets out the orders that the court can make to bring a civil partnership to an end or to provide for the separation of the parties. These are as follows:

(a) A dissolution order, which when made final will bring a civil partnership to an end.

(b) A nullity order, which when made final will annul a civil partnership which is either void or voidable.

(c) A presumption of death order, which when made final will dissolve the civil partnership on the ground that one of the civil partners is presumed to be dead.

(d) A separation order, which provides for the separation of the civil partners, but will not allow either civil partner to marry or to form another civil partnership.

68. *Subsection (2)* provides that an order for dissolution, nullity or presumption of death will initially be a conditional order and that it may not be made final until the end of the prescribed period defined in section 38.

69. *Subsection (3)* provides that a nullity order made in respect of a civil partnership which is voidable annuls the civil partnership only as respects any time after the order is made final. The civil partnership is to be treated as if it had existed up to that time.

70. The courts which can make these orders are defined in *subsection (4)* as the High Court or a county court with jurisdiction to hear civil partnership proceedings. *Subsection (5)* makes it clear that the powers of the court under this section are subject to the court having jurisdiction under sections 219 to 224 of the Act.

Section 38: The period before conditional orders may be made final

71. This section sets the period which must elapse before a dissolution, nullity or presumption of death order may be made final. By *subsection (1)*, the period is 6 weeks from the making of the conditional order (subject to a slight modification if this period ends on a day when the court office or registry is closed). *Subsection (2)* gives the Lord Chancellor power to make an order substituting a different period not exceeding 6 months. *Subsection (4)* provides that in particular cases the court may reduce the period (this might be relevant, for example, in the case of a deathbed dissolution and formation of a new civil partnership).

Section 39: Intervention of the Queen's Proctor

72. This section provides for the intervention of the Queen's Proctor in proceedings where an application has been made for a dissolution, nullity or presumption of death order. The court may involve the Queen's Proctor where it considers it necessary or expedient to have any question in relation to the case fully argued by counsel appointed by the Queen's Proctor, under the directions of the Attorney General. The Queen's Proctor may also intervene on the basis of information received from any person.

Section 40: Proceedings before order has been made final

73. This section provides for the court to consider the position once a conditional order has been made but before it has been made final. By *subsection (1)*, the section applies where the Queen's Proctor, or anyone who has not been a party to the proceedings, shows that that there is cause (good reason) why the conditional order should not be made final on the ground that material facts were not put before the court. By *subsection (2)*, the court may also consider a case under this section where the civil partner who applied for the conditional order has not taken steps to have this made final within 3 months from the earliest date when such an application could have been made, and the other civil partner applies to the court under this section.

74. Where this section applies, the court may make the order final, rescind the order, direct that further enquiries are to be made, or deal with the case in such other manner as it thinks fit. By *subsection (4),* the court's power to make the order final applies even if the prescribed period under section 38 has not yet expired, but is subject to the restrictions imposed in section 48(4) (relating to financial provision in separation cases) and section 63 (restrictions on the court's powers to make orders affecting children).

Section 41: Time bar on applications for dissolution orders

75. This section states that an application for dissolution of a civil partnership may not be made until at least 1 year after the date of formation of the civil partnership. However, matters which occurred within this 1 year period may be used in support of the application.

Section 42: Attempts at reconciliation of civil partners

76. This section allows the court to adjourn an application for a dissolution or separation order if it appears that the civil partners have a reasonable possibility of achieving a reconciliation. *Subsection (2)* provides that rules of court must make provision requiring the applicant's solicitors to certify whether they have discussed with their client the possibility of reconciliation and to certify whether they have given the applicant details of persons qualified to help with reconciliation.

Section 43: Consideration by the court of certain agreements or arrangements

77. This section provides that rules of court may make provision for civil partners to refer to the court an agreement or arrangement between them in connection with the dissolution of the civil partnership or with their separation. The rules may allow the court to express an opinion about whether the agreement or arrangement is reasonable, or to give directions.

Section 44: Dissolution of civil partnership which has broken down irretrievably

78. *Subsection (1)* sets out the sole ground on which an application for dissolution may be made, namely that the civil partnership has broken down irretrievably.

79. In order to demonstrate the irretrievable breakdown of the civil partnership the applicant must satisfy the court of one or more of the following facts set out in *subsection (5)*:

a) That his or her civil partner (called the respondent for the purposes of the proceedings) has behaved in such a way that the applicant cannot reasonably be expected to live with the respondent;

b) That the applicant and the respondent have lived apart for a continuous period of at least 2 years immediately preceding the application (this is referred to in the Act as "2 years' separation") and that the respondent consents to a dissolution order being made;

c) That the applicant and the respondent have lived apart for a continuous period of at least 5 years immediately preceding the application (this is referred to as "5 years' separation");

d) That the respondent has deserted the applicant for a continuous period of at least 2 years immediately preceding the making of the application.

80. *Subsection (2)* provides that the court must inquire as far as possible into the facts alleged by the applicant and any facts put forward by the respondent. The court may not hold that the civil partnership has broken down irretrievably unless the applicant satisfies the court of one or more of the facts set out in *subsection (5)*. But if the court is satisfied of any of

those facts it must make a dissolution order unless it is satisfied on all the evidence that the civil partnership has not broken down irretrievably.

Section 45: Supplemental provisions as to facts raising presumption of breakdown

81. *Subsections (1) and (2)* provide that where an applicant alleges that the respondent has behaved in such a way that the applicant cannot reasonably be expected to live with the respondent, but following the final incident relied upon in support of this allegation, the civil partners have continued to cohabit for a period or periods of time not exceeding 6 months in total, the court must disregard this time spent living together when determining whether the applicant cannot reasonably be expected to live with their civil partner.

82. *Subsections (3)* and *(4)* provide that, where a civil partner allegedly consents to the making of a dissolution order under the "2 years' separation" head, rules of court must make provision to ensure that he or she is given information which will enable him to understand the consequences of consenting to the order and the steps which must be taken to indicate consent.

83. *Subsection (5)* allows the court to consider a period of desertion as continuing even when the civil partner concerned was incapable of continuing the necessary intention, provided the court would on the evidence have inferred that the period of desertion would have continued if the civil partner had been able to continue the intention. This would cover a situation where one civil partner deserts his or her civil partner for 2 years but is involved in an accident at some time over the 2 years which leads to a temporary loss of consciousness. This break in the "intention to desert" would not stop the 2 years from accruing.

84. *Subsection (6)* provides that when considering whether a period of living apart or desertion is continuous, no account is to be taken of a period or periods of time not exceeding 6 months in total in which the civil partners resumed living together. However (as a separate issue from whether the period of living apart or desertion could be regarded as "continuous") under *subsection (7)* no period during which the civil partners lived together can count as part of the period of living apart or desertion. So for example, desertion or separation for 2 years can be proved, even if the civil partners lived together for, say, 2 months during the relevant period, so long as the total period of desertion or separation adds up to 2 years (excluding those 2 months).

85. *Subsection (8)* provides that civil partners are to be treated as living apart unless they are living with each other in the same household.

Section 46: Dissolution order not precluded by previous separation order etc.

86. This section provides that where a separation order, an order for financial relief in the magistrates' court or an order under sections 33 or 37 of the Family Law Act 1996 (c. 27) has been made, this does not prevent either civil partner from applying to the court for a dissolution order on the basis of the same facts that were relied upon when granting the previous order. Under *subsection (3)* the court may treat the previous order as sufficient proof of the facts by reference to which it was made, but must not make that the dissolution order without receiving evidence from the applicant.

87. *Subsection (4)* applies where an application for a dissolution order is made following a separation order or any order requiring the civil partners to live apart. If there was a period of desertion immediately preceding the application for a separation order, the parties have not resumed living together, and the separation order has been continuously in force since it was made, the period of desertion is to be treated as if it had taken place immediately prior to the

application for the dissolution order. This will mean that the period of desertion can be used to support the application for a dissolution order.

88. Under *subsection (5)* the court may also treat as a period of desertion to support an application for a dissolution order a period during which the respondent was subject to an injunction excluding him or her from the civil partnership home or when an order under sections 33 or 37 of the Family Law Act 1996 (c. 27) was in force prohibiting the civil partner from occupying a dwelling-house used (then or previously) as the civil partnership home.

Section 47: Refusal of dissolution in 5 year separation cases on ground of grave hardship

89. *Subsection (1)* provides that the respondent to an application for a dissolution order in which the applicant alleges 5 years' separation may oppose the making of a dissolution order on the ground that the dissolution of the civil partnership would result in grave financial or other hardship to him or her and that in all the circumstances it would be wrong to make the order. By *subsection (3)* the court must consider all the circumstances, including the conduct of the civil partners and the interests of the civil partners and any children or other persons concerned, and if the court is satisfied that there would be grave hardship it must dismiss the application for the dissolution order. *Subsection (4)* provides that "hardship" includes the loss of the chance of acquiring any benefit which the respondent might acquire if the civil partnership were not dissolved.

Section 48: Proceedings before order made final: protection for respondent in separation cases

90. *Subsection (1)* provides that the court can rescind a dissolution order which has not been made final, where the application was on the basis of 2 years' separation coupled with the other civil partner's consent, if the applicant misled the respondent over any matter which was taken into account when giving that consent.

91. *Subsections (2)* to *(5)* allow the respondent to an application for a dissolution order alleging either 2 years' or 5 years' separation to apply to the court to consider his or her financial position after dissolution of the civil partnership. The court must consider all the relevant circumstances including the age, health, conduct, earning capacity, financial resources and obligations of each civil partner and the position of the respondent on the death of the applicant, assuming the applicant died first. Under *subsection (4)* the court must not make the dissolution order final unless it is satisfied either that the applicant should not be required to make financial provision for the respondent or that the provision made for the respondent is reasonable and fair, or is the best that can be made in the circumstances. Under *subsection (5)* the court may make the dissolution order final if the circumstances make it desirable to do so without delay, provided it has obtained an undertaking from the applicant to make such financial provision for the respondent as the court may approve.

Section 49: Grounds on which civil partnership is void

92. This section sets out the grounds on which a civil partnership will be void (in other words invalid) under the law of England and Wales, where the parties registered as civil partners of each other in England and Wales. (The grounds on which the law of England and Wales will hold civil partnerships formed outside England and Wales to be void are set out in section 54.) A civil partnership that is void may be annulled by an order of the court under section 37.

93.   *Paragraph (a)* provides that the civil partnership will be void if, at the time when the two people registered as civil partners in England and Wales, they were not eligible to register as civil partners of each other under the requirements set out in section 3.

94.   *Paragraph (b)* lists the breaches of formal requirements which will render the civil partnership void, if both civil partners were aware of the breach at the time of the registration. These are failure to give the required notice of proposed civil partnership, the civil partnership document not being duly issued or having expired, the place of registration not being the place specified in the notice(s) of proposed civil partnership and the civil partnership document, or a civil partnership registrar not being present at the registration.

95.   *Paragraph (c)* provides that the civil partnership will be void if the civil partnership document is void because one of the intended civil partners is a child (under the age of 18) and the issue of the civil partnership document has been forbidden by a person whose consent is required for the child to form a civil partnership.

Section 50: Grounds on which civil partnership is voidable

96.   This section sets out the grounds on which an application can be made in England or Wales for an order annulling a civil partnership on the grounds that it is voidable, where the parties registered as civil partners of each other in England and Wales. (The grounds on which the law of England and Wales will hold other civil partnerships to be voidable are set out in section 54.) The grounds are as follows:

a) Either of the civil partners did not validly consent to the formation of the civil partnership, through a mistake, through being put under duress or due to unsoundness of mind or otherwise.

b) At the time of the formation of the civil partnership either of the civil partners, although able to consent to the registration, was suffering from a mental disorder which made them unfitted for civil partnership.

c) At the time of the formation of the civil partnership one of the civil partners was pregnant (other than by the applicant, although that could only be relevant in a case involving a gender change under the Gender Recognition Act 2004). This is subject to section 51(6) which ensures that the court may not make a nullity order unless it is satisfied that the applicant did not know of the pregnancy at the time of the formation of the civil partnership. An application on this ground is subject to the 6 month time limit in section 51(5) (see below).

d) An interim gender recognition certificate under the Gender Recognition Act 2004 has been issued to either civil partner after the time of the formation of the civil partnership.

e) The respondent is a person whose gender at the time of the formation of the civil partnership had become the acquired gender under the Gender Recognition Act 2004. This is subject to section 51(6) which ensures that the court may not make a nullity order unless it is satisfied that the applicant did not know at the time of the formation of the civil partnership that his or her partner had changed gender.

Section 51: Bars to relief where civil partnership is voidable

97.   *Subsection (1)* provides that the court must not make a nullity order on the grounds that a civil partnership is voidable if the respondent satisfies the court that the applicant acted towards the respondent in such a way as to indicate that he or she would not apply for a nullity order, and that it would be unjust to the respondent to make the order now.

14

98.   In most cases an application for a nullity order on the grounds that a civil partnership is voidable must be made within 3 years from the date that the civil partnership was formed (see *subsection (2))*.. *Subsections (3)* and *(4)* permit the court to allow later applications where it is just to do so on the basis that the applicant suffered from mental disorder at some time during the 3-year period.

99.   A shorter time limit applies where the application is made on the ground that an interim gender recognition certificate has been issued under the Gender Recognition Act 2004 after the date of formation of the civil partnership. In this case proceedings must be instituted within 6 months from the date of issue of that certificate.

100. *Subsection (6)* provides that, where the application is made on the grounds of pregnancy at the time of formation of the civil partnership, or a change of gender previous to that date, a nullity order must not be made unless the court is satisfied that the applicant did not know of the relevant facts at the time of formation of the civil partnership.

Section 52: Proof of certain matters not necessary to validity of civil partnership

101. This section provides that where two people have registered as civil partners of each other in England and Wales it is not necessary for them to provide evidence that any consent required under section 4 (consent by parents etc. where one of the intended civil partners is under 18) was actually given, or that the person who officiated at the signing of the civil partnership schedule was a designated civil partnership registrar for the area in which registration took place. No evidence may be given in any nullity proceedings to disprove either of these facts.

102. The issue of consent is subject to the provisions of section 49(c) which provides that a civil partnership involving a person under 18 will be void if the issue of the civil partnership document was forbidden by a person whose consent was required.

Section 53: Power to validate civil partnership

103. *Subsection (1)* provides that the Lord Chancellor may by order validate a civil partnership, where two people register as civil partners of each other in England and Wales, if it appears to him that the civil partnership is or may be void under section 49(b). *Subsection (2)* provides that an order under subsection (1) may include provisions for relieving a person from any liability under sections 31(2), 32(2), 33(5) or 33(7) (offences relating to civil partnership schedule, Registrar General's licence and recording of civil partnerships). *Subsection (3)* provides that the draft of an order under subsection (1) must be advertised not less than one month prior to the order being made. *Subsection (4)* provides that the Lord Chancellor must consider all written objections sent to him during that month and, if it appears necessary to him, direct a local inquiry into the validity of any such objections. *Subsection (5)* provides that an order under *subsection (1)* is subject to the special parliamentary procedure. The special parliamentary procedure is laid down in the Statutory Orders (Special Procedure) Act 1945.

Section 54: Validity of civil partnership registered outside England and Wales

104. This section sets out the rules to be applied when determining whether, under the law of England and Wales, a civil partnership is void or voidable where the parties did not register as civil partners in England and Wales. If the civil partnership is void or voidable, a court in England and Wales which has jurisdiction under sections 219 to 221 may make a nullity order in respect of the civil partnership under section 37.

105. *Subsection (1)* ensures that a civil partnership formed in Scotland is void for the purposes of the law of England and Wales only if it would be void under the Scottish provisions in section 123. The civil partnership will also be voidable if an interim gender recognition certificate is subsequently issued to either party under the Gender Recognition Act 2004. (If the case were being considered in Scotland, this would instead be grounds for dissolution of the civil partnership under section 117(2)(b).)

106. *Subsection (2)* ensures that, where two people registered as civil partners in Northern Ireland, the civil partnership is void for the purposes of the law of England and Wales only if it would be void under the Northern Ireland provisions in section 173. The civil partnership will also be voidable if the circumstances fall within any paragraph of section 50(1) (since these are all circumstances which would equally render the civil partnership voidable in Northern Ireland under section 174).

107. *Subsection (4)* deals with the situation where the parties registered as civil partners outside the United Kingdom under an Order in Council made under section 210 or 211. Orders in Council made under those sections will include provision for determining the relevant part of the United Kingdom for certain purposes. Paragraphs (a)(i) and (b) of subsection (4) ensure that questions of nullity are then dealt with in exactly the same way as would apply under English law if the parties had registered as civil partners in that part of the United Kingdom.

108. In addition the civil partnership will be void if the condition in section 210(2)(a) or 211(2)(a) (whichever is relevant) was not met. Where the parties registered as civil partners of each other at a British consulate etc., the condition is that one party must be a United Kingdom national as defined in section 245. Where the parties registered as civil partners of each other in the armed services, the condition is that one of the proposed civil partners is a member of the armed forces serving in the country or territory where the partnership is registered, or falls within certain other related categories as set out in section 211(2)(a).

109. Finally the civil partnership will also be void if there is a breach of a requirement of the Order in Council which is prescribed for this purpose by the Order itself (this power will be used to define in the Order those requirements which are mandatory in order to ensure the validity of the civil partnership).

110. *Subsection (8)* sets out the rules to be applied in relation to an apparent or alleged overseas relationship. An overseas relationship can be treated as a civil partnership under Chapter 2 of Part 5. But the civil partnership will be void if it transpires that the relationship is in fact not an overseas relationship as defined in sections 212 to 214, or if one of the requirements for the overseas relationship to be treated as a civil partnership under sections 215 to 218 is not met. For example the civil partnership will be void if, under the law of the country where the registration took place, the formalities necessary to enter into the overseas relationship were not fulfilled or there was no capacity to enter into the overseas relationship (see section 215(1)). It will also be voidable if that is the effect of the law of the country where the registration took place (see the definition of "the relevant law" in *subsection (10)*) or on the grounds that an interim gender recognition certificate has been issued under the Gender Recognition Act 2004. But if either party was domiciled in England and Wales then the civil partnership will also be voidable in the other circumstances set out in section 50(1), and the same applies if either party was domiciled in Northern Ireland (since these are all circumstances which would equally render the civil partnership voidable in Northern Ireland under section 174).

111. Where a civil partnership is voidable in accordance with this section the section 51 bars to relief are applied in the usual way. However where the civil partnership is voidable by virtue of the application of foreign law, the bars to relief will only apply in so far as they are applicable in accordance with the foreign law.

Section 55: Presumption of death orders

112. This section gives the court power to make a presumption of death order, on the application of a civil partner, if satisfied that there are reasonable grounds for believing that the other civil partner is dead. The fact that the other civil partner has been absent from the applicant for a continuous period of 7 years or more and that the applicant has no reason to believe that he or she has been living during that time will be accepted as evidence that the other civil partner is dead until the contrary is proved.

Section 56: Separation orders

113. This section allows an application to be made for a separation order on the basis of the same facts as are required for an order for dissolution of a civil partnership. The court must inquire as far as possible into the facts alleged by the applicant and any facts put forward by his or her civil partner (referred to as the respondent for the purpose of the proceedings). If the court is satisfied of the facts alleged it must make a separation order (subject to the provisions of section 63 relating to children). However it is irrelevant whether the civil partnership has broken down irretrievably.

Section 57: Effect of separation order

114. This section provides that, if a civil partner dies without making a will (intestate) at a time when a separation order is in force and the separation is continuing, the rules in respect of the passing of intestate estates shall be applied as if his or her surviving (but separated) civil partner were also dead.

Section 58: Declarations

115. This section provides for people to apply to the High Court or a county court for declarations regarding the status of a civil partnership. These applications cover its validity, that it was or was not in existence on a certain date, and declarations as to whether a dissolution, annulment or legal separation obtained outside England and Wales is or is not entitled to recognition in England and Wales.

116. Under *subsection* (2) if the applicant is not one of the civil partners the court must refuse to hear the application if it considers that the applicant has insufficient interest in the outcome.

Section 59: General provisions as to making and effect of declarations

117. This section provides that where an application is made under section 58 and the truth of the proposition to be declared is proved to the satisfaction of the court, the court must make the declaration requested unless it would be manifestly contrary to public policy to do so. If the court dismisses the application, it must not make any other declaration which has not been applied for. The court cannot make a declaration that a civil partnership was void at its inception. Nothing in this section will prevent the court from being able to make a nullity order in respect of the civil partnership.

Section 60: The Attorney General and proceedings for declarations

118. This section provides that, in any case where an application is made for a declaration under section 58, the court may direct that the appropriate papers in the matter should be sent

to the Attorney General. The Attorney General may in any event intervene in proceedings for a declaration under section 58 as he thinks necessary or expedient, and may argue any question which the court thinks should be fully argued. *Subsection (3)* enables the court to make an order for the parties to the proceedings to pay the costs incurred by the Attorney General if this is justified.

Section 61: Supplementary provisions as to declarations

119. This section provides for rules of court to determine the form of an application under section 58 for a declaration, and of the declaration itself. The rules may provide for the information to be supplied by the applicant and for notice of the application to be served on the Attorney General and on persons who may be affected by the declaration.

120. *Subsection (3)* provides that no proceedings under section 58 will affect any final order or judgment already given. *Subsection (4)* allows the court to hear any application under section 58 (or any part of it) in private (and by *subsection (5)* any application for such a direction must itself be heard in private unless the court directs otherwise).

Section 62: Relief for respondent in dissolution proceedings

121. This section provides that if the respondent in dissolution proceedings alleges and proves any of the facts which the applicant had to satisfy the court of, the court may grant the respondent the relief that would normally be granted to an applicant who had proved such facts, as if it had been the respondent who had made the application.

Section 63: Restrictions on making of orders affecting children

122. This section provides that in any proceedings for a dissolution, nullity or separation order the court must consider whether there are any children for whom the court should exercise its powers under the Children Act 1989 (c. 41) in order to safeguard their welfare and provide for their upbringing. If necessary the court may direct that the dissolution, nullity or separation order is not to be made final until the court has considered whether to exercise those powers. The provisions apply to any child of the family who is under 16 years of age at the date the court considers the position and also to children of the family over 16 if the court directs that they should also be included in its consideration.

Section 64: Parties to proceedings under this chapter

123. This section allows rules of court to be made to allow for parties to be joined to proceedings for dissolution, nullity or separation if they are involved in allegations of improper conduct made in the proceedings. The rules may provide for the court to dismiss from the proceedings any parties whom it has joined. Rules may also make provision as to the persons who are to be parties to an application for a declaration. *Subsection (3)* enables the court to permit a person to intervene if it thinks he or she should be made a party.

Chapter 3 – Property and financial arrangements

Section 65: Contribution by civil partner to property improvement

124. This section provides that where a civil partner has made a substantial contribution in money or money's worth to the improvement of property in which either or both the civil partners have an interest he or she is to be treated as having acquired a share or an enlarged share in that property. The extent of the share will be determined by any agreement made between the parties. Alternatively if there is no agreement, it will be determined by what may seem in all the circumstances just to any court before which the question of the existence or extent of the beneficial interest of either of the civil partners arises. The contributing civil

partner will not be treated as acquiring a share or an enlarged share where there is an express or implied agreement between the parties to the contrary.

Section 66: Disputes between civil partners about property

125. This section enables civil partners to refer disputes over property to court. It provides that civil partners may apply to the High Court or to a county court in respect of any question relating to the title to or the possession of property. The court may make such order with respect to the property as it thinks fit, including an order for the sale of the property.

Section 67: Applications under section 66 where property not in possession etc.

126. This section allows one civil partner (A) to make an application under section 66 where the other civil partner (B) no longer has the money or property concerned or A does not know whether B still has the money or property. The power of the court to make orders under section 66 includes the power to order B to pay to A such sum of money as seems appropriate or to make any other order which it could have made under section 64.

Section 68: Applications under section 66 by former civil partners

127. This section allows a former civil partner to make an application to the court under section 66 in respect of a dispute over property despite the fact that the civil partnership has been dissolved or annulled. The application must be made within 3 years of the date of dissolution or annulment of the civil partnership.

Section 69: Actions in tort between civil partners

128. This section enables the court to stay proceedings in tort brought by one civil partner against the other during their civil partnership if it appears that neither party would substantially benefit from continuation of the proceedings, or where the issue could better be resolved by an application under section 66. It also enables the court to exercise any of the powers it could exercise under section 66 or give any directions as it thinks fit for the disposal, under that section, of any question arising in the proceedings.

Section 70: Assurance policy by civil partner for benefit of other civil partner etc.

129. This section extends the application of section 11 of the Married Women's Property Act 1882 (c.75) to civil partners, so that if a civil partner takes out a life insurance policy to provide for his or her civil partner or children the money payable under the policy is not to form part of the estate of the insured.

Section 71: Wills, administration of estates and family provision

130. This section introduces Schedule 4 which amends legislative provisions relating to wills, the administration of estates and family provision so that civil partners will receive the same treatment as married people.

Section 72: Financial relief for civil partners and children of the family

131. *Subsection (1)* introduces Schedule 5, which makes provision for financial relief for civil partners which corresponds to the relief available to married couples in the High Court or a county court under Part 2 of the Matrimonial Causes Act 1973 when they go through divorce, nullity or judicial separation proceedings.

132. *Subsection (2)* provides that if the effect of rules of law is that provisions for financial relief under Part 2 of the Matrimonial Causes Act 1973 are interpreted as being available in the case of the dissolution of a marriage on the ground of presumed death, then those rules of law will also apply to the corresponding financial provisions in Schedule 5 to the Act for civil

partners, with any necessary modifications. This is to allow case law to be available to civil partners which allows for financial relief to be available if the person who was presumed dead is subsequently proved to be alive.

133. *Subsection (3)* introduces Schedule 6, which provides civil partners with the right to apply for financial relief in magistrates' courts in a way that corresponds to the rights that exist for married people under the Domestic Proceedings and Magistrates Courts Act 1978 (c.22).

134. *Subsection (4)* introduces Schedule 7, which contains provisions for financial relief in England and Wales after a civil partnership has been dissolved or annulled or the civil partners have been legally separated in a country outside the British Islands. "British Islands" is defined in the Interpretation Act 1978 (c. 30) as comprising the United Kingdom, the Channel Islands and the Isle of Man.

Chapter 4 – Civil partnership agreements

Section 73: Civil partnership agreements unenforceable

135. This section provides that an agreement to form a civil partnership ("a civil partnership agreement") does not constitute a contract giving rise to legal rights under the law of England and Wales and will not be enforceable.

136. *Subsection (2)* provides that no action can be taken over any breach of a civil partnership agreement.

137. *Subsection (4)* provides that the section will apply to civil partnership agreements entered into both before and after the section comes into force but it will not affect any legal action which has begun before the section comes into force.

Section 74: Property where civil partnership agreement is terminated

138. This section applies when a civil partnership agreement is terminated. It provides that section 65 (contributions to property improvement by a civil partner) and sections 66 and 67 (disputes between civil partners about property and applications where property is not in possession) will apply in relation to property in which either or both of the parties to the agreement had a beneficial interest while the agreement was in force.

139. An application made using the provisions of sections 66 and 67 must be made within 3 years of the date of termination of the civil partnership agreement.

140. *Subsection (5)* provides that a person who makes a gift to the other person on the understanding that it will be returned if the civil partnership agreement is terminated is not prevented from recovering the property merely because he or she terminated the agreement.

Chapter 5 – Children

141. This Chapter makes various amendments to the Children Act 1989 and the Adoption and Children Act 2002 to reflect the creation of the new relationship of civil partnership.

Section 75: Parental responsibility, children of the family and relatives

142. This section amends various provisions of the Children Act 1989 ("the 1989 Act") to put civil partners on the same footing as married couples.

143. *Subsection (2)* amends section 4A(1) of the 1989 Act to enable a civil partner to acquire parental responsibility of his or her civil partner's child in the same way as a person who is married to the parent of the child (but is not that child's parent).

144. *Subsection (3)* amends the definition of "child of the family" in section 105(1) of the 1989 Act to include a child of both civil partners and any other child who has been treated as a child of the family by both civil partners, unless the child had been placed with the civil partners by a local authority or a voluntary organisation as foster parents.

145. *Subsection (4)* amends the definition of "relative" in section 105 (1) of the 1989 Act to replace "by affinity" with "by marriage or civil partnership".

Section 76: Guardianship

146. This section amends section 6 of the 1989 Act in relation to the revocation and disclaimer of appointments of guardians. Under section 5(3) and (4) of the 1989 Act a parent or guardian may appoint any person to act as the guardian of a child in his or her place. This section inserts a provision into section 6 of the 1989 Act so that where a person appoints his or her civil partner to be the guardian of a child that appointment is revoked if the civil partnership is dissolved or annulled, unless the appointment itself indicates that a dissolution or annulment of the civil partnership should not affect the appointment.

Section 77: Entitlement to apply for a residence or contact order

147. This section amends section 10(5) of the 1989 Act to add a civil partner in a civil partnership to the class of people who are able to apply for a residence or contact order. The amendment enables civil partners to apply for an order whether or not the civil partnership subsists.

Section 78: Financial provision for children

148. This Section amends Schedule 1 to the 1989 Act by adding to the definition of periodical payment orders in paragraph 2(6) of that Schedule orders under the provisions of Parts 1 and 9 of Schedule 5 and under Schedule 6 to this Act. This will enable courts to make orders for periodical payments to be made from one civil partner to the other or to a child of the family, or to a particular person for the benefit of a child of the family.

149. *Subsection (3)* amends Paragraph 15(2) of Schedule 1 to the 1989 Act so that a local authority will not be able to make a contribution towards the maintenance of a child who is subject to a residence order where the person with whom the child is living is a parent of the child, or the husband or wife or civil partner of a parent of the child.

150. *Subsection (4)* extends the meaning of "parent" in paragraph 16(2) of Schedule 1 to the 1989 Act to include any civil partner in a partnership, whether it is still in existence or whether it has been brought to an end, for whom the child concerned is a child of the family.

Section 79: Adoption

151. This section amends the Adoption and Children Act 2002 ("the 2002 Act") to ensure that the relationship of civil partnership is recognised for the purposes of adoption.

152. *Subsection (2)* amends section 21(4)(c) of the 2002 Act to allow a placement order to end when a child forms a civil partnership.

153. *Subsection (3)* inserts an additional subsection in section 47 of the 2002 Act so that an adoption order cannot be made in respect of any person who is in a civil partnership or has been in a civil partnership.

154. *Subsection (4)* amends section 51(1) of the 2002 Act to allow for an adoption order to be made on the application of one person where that person is over the age of 21 years and is not married or is not a civil partner.

155. *Subsection (5)* inserts an additional subsection in section 51 of the 2002 Act to set out the circumstances where one member of a civil partnership may apply for an adoption order on their own and not as a couple. The circumstances are that: the person's civil partner cannot be found; the civil partners have separated and are living apart, and the separation is likely to be permanent; or the person's civil partner is incapable of making an application for an adoption order because of physical or mental ill-health.

156. *Subsection (6)* amends section 64 of the 2002 Act to include a civil partnership. Section 64(5) enables fees to be prescribed in respect of persons who apply to the adoption agency under sections 60, 61 or 62 for information. The exception is amended to provide that the adopted person cannot be charged in respect of any information disclosed to him about any person who but for his adoption would be related to him by blood, including half-blood, marriage or civil partnership.

157. *Subsection (7)* amends section 74(1) of the 2002 Act to ensure that the status conferred as a consequence of an adoption order does not apply for the purposes of either Schedule 1 to the Civil Partnership Act (prohibited degrees of relationship) or Schedule 1 to the Marriage Act 1949.

158. *Subsection (8)* amends section 79(7) of the 2002 Act to ensure that an adopted person who intends to form a civil partnership can apply to the Registrar General for him to check that the person, with whom the applicant intends to form a civil partnership, does not fall within the prohibited degrees.

159. *Subsection (9)* amends section 81 of the 2002 Act to ensure that the meaning of "relative" for the purposes of an entry in the adoption contact register includes a person related by civil partnership.

160. *Subsection (10)* ensures that the meaning of "relative" in section 98 of the 2002 Act includes a person related by civil partnership. Section 98 of the 2002 Act amplifies the regulation-making power in section 9 to provide that the appropriate Minister may make regulations in connection with adoptions made before the commencement of sections 56 to 65. Section 98(1) of the 2002 Act provides that regulations may make provision for assisting adults adopted before the appointed day to obtain information about their adoption and to facilitate contact between them and their relatives.

161. *Subsection (11)* extends the meaning of "relative" in relation to a child in section 144(1) of the 2002 Act to include people related by civil partnership as well as by marriage. Section 144 of the 2002 Act provides general interpretation.

162. *Subsection (12)* amends the definition (for the purposes of that Act) of "couple" in section 144(4) of the 2002 Act to include two people who are civil partners of each other. With the amendment made by the Civil Partnership Act, a couple means a married couple, two people who are civil partners of each other, or two people, whether of different sexes or of the same sex, living as partners in an enduring family relationship.

Chapter 6 – Miscellaneous

Section 80: False statements etc. with reference to civil partnerships

163. *Subsection (1)* makes it an offence knowingly to make certain false statements or representations. For example, a person who signs a declaration under section 8 that he is free to form a civil partnership, knowing that the declaration is false, commits an offence. A person guilty of an offence under *subsection (1)* is liable on conviction on indictment to imprisonment, for a term not exceeding 7 years, or to a fine (or both) and on summary

conviction, to a fine not exceeding the statutory maximum. These provisions are similar to those in section 3(1) of the Perjury Act 1911 under which it is an offence to make false statements or representations with reference to marriage. The effect of *subsection (4)* is that all the other relevant provisions in the Perjury Act 1911 will apply, without having to replicate them in the Civil Partnership Act. So, for example, section 7(1) of the Perjury Act, which applies to people who aid, abet etc offences under that Act, would apply to a person who helps another person to commit an offence under section 80.

Section 81: Housing and tenancies

164. This section introduces Schedule 8, which makes amendments to a range of enactments relating to housing and tenancies.

Section 82: Family homes and domestic violence

165. This section introduces Schedule 9, which amends Part 4 of the Family Law Act 1996 and related enactments so that they apply in relation to civil partnerships as they apply in relation to marriages. The amendments will mean that civil partners have the same rights to occupy the civil partnership home as married persons have to occupy the matrimonial home. In addition civil partners will be able to apply for non-molestation orders and occupation orders. Occupation orders are orders regulating occupation of the home. An occupation order might, for example, exclude the respondent from the home and vicinity of the home or prohibit, terminate or restrict the exercise of the respondent's occupation rights.

Section 83: Fatal accidents claims

166. This section extends the provisions of the Fatal Accidents Act 1976 to include civil partners, so that where a person's death is caused by the wrongful act, neglect or default of another person, a civil partner of the deceased will be able to claim compensation in the same way as a spouse.

167. *Subsections (2)* and *(3)* widen the definition of "dependant" for the purposes of a right of action under the 1976 Act to include a civil partner of the deceased, a person living as the civil partner of the deceased and a former civil partner of the deceased. *Subsection (4)* widens the definition of "dependant" to include any person (not being a child of the deceased) who was treated by the deceased as a child of the family, in relation to any civil partnership to which the deceased was at any time a party.

168. *Subsections (5) to (8)* make consequential provision related to these changes.

Section 84: Evidence

169. *Subsection (1)* of this section provides that enactments or rules of law applying to the giving of evidence by a spouse will apply also to the giving of evidence by a civil partner.

170. However, *subsection (2)* sets out that the general provision in *subsection (1)* is subject to any specific amendment made by or under the Act which relates to the giving of evidence by a civil partner. This takes account of the fact that in some instances it is more appropriate to amend specific provisions in other enactments or rules. A number of the amendments made by Schedule 27 relate specifically to the giving of evidence by a civil partner.

171. *Subsection (5)* provides that any rule of law which makes evidence of family tradition admissible to prove or disprove the existence of a marriage is to apply in a similar way in order to prove or disprove the existence of a civil partnership.

Part 3 - Civil Partnerships: Scotland

Introduction

172. This Part extends to Scotland only (see section 252(2)).

Chapter 1 - Formation and eligibility

Section 85: Formation of civil partnership by registration

173. This section provides that a civil partnership is formed when both persons sign the completed civil partnership schedule before two witnesses aged 16 years or over and an authorised registrar (all being present). Registering as civil partners of each other creates the legal relationship between the two persons, but registration cannot take place unless both persons are eligible to be registered.

Section 86: Eligibility

174. *Subsection (1)* provides that two people are not eligible to register in Scotland as civil partners of each other if –

a) they are not of the same sex,

b) they are related in a forbidden degree

c) either of them is under 16

d) either of them is married or already in a civil partnership

e) either is incapable of

    (i) understanding the nature of a civil partnership

    (ii) validly consenting to its formation

175. *Subsection (2)* defines "forbidden degree" by reference to columns 1 and 2 of Schedule 10.

176. *Subsections (3) and (4)* set out the circumstances in which persons over 21, within the relationships of affinity set out in paragraphs 2 and 3 of Schedule 10, will not be related in a forbidden degree.

177. *Subsections (5) to (7)* apply the provisions of this section and Schedule 10, with appropriate modifications, to the case of a person wishing to form a civil partnership in his acquired gender under the Gender Recognition Act 2004.

178. *Subsections (9)* and *(10)* set out that half blood relationships and adoptive relationships are included within the degrees of relationship specified in paragraph 1 of Schedule 10. In practice, this means for example, that a person could not form a civil partnership with their sibling, whether that sibling was full blood, half blood or adopted.

Chapter 2 - Registration

179. The UK has three Registrars General covering Scotland, Northern Ireland and England and Wales. The law concerning registration in Scotland is devolved to the Scottish Parliament. There is separate legislation covering the functions of the Registrar General for Scotland. Consequently, the provisions on civil partnerships reflect (and are internally consistent with) the legislation and procedures that apply in Scotland.

Section 87: Appointment of authorised registrars

180. This section empowers the Registrar General for Scotland, for the purpose of affording reasonable facilities throughout Scotland for registration as civil partners, to appoint such number of district registrars as he thinks necessary, and for any district with a district registrar, one or more assistant registrars, as persons who may carry out such registration.

Section 88: Notice of proposed civil partnership

181. This section closely follows the procedures for civil preliminaries contained in the Marriage (Scotland) Act 1977. It provides procedures for the completion, by each party, of the notice of proposed civil partnership and for the submission, with the prescribed fee, of the notice to the district registrar. The content of the notice may be prescribed by regulations made by the Registrar General for Scotland with the approval of the Scottish Ministers.

Section 89: Civil partnership notice book

182. This section requires the district registrar to enter into "the civil partnership book" such particulars from the notice of proposed civil partnership may be prescribed by the Registrar General for Scotland. The Registrar General is to prescribe the form and content of the book.

Section 90: Publicisation

183. This section follows similar provisions in the Marriage (Scotland) Act 1977 about making public the intention to form a civil partnership. The section provides that the district registrar must publicise the relevant information (names of intended civil partners and date of intended registration) as soon as practicable and send it to the Registrar General who must also publicise the information. Subject to section 91, the date on which it is intended to sign the civil partnership document should be a date more than 14 days after publicisation by the district registrar. The manner in which the information is to be publicised will be prescribed by the Registrar General.

Section 91: Early registration

184. This section enables an authorised registrar, provided he is authorised to do so by the Registrar General, on receipt of a written request from one or both of the intended civil partners to fix the date for registering as civil partners at a date earlier than 14 days after the publicisation of the intended date of signing the civil partnership register. It is anticipated that this power will be exercised in similar circumstances to its equivalent under the Marriage (Scotland) Act 1977, typically where one of the proposed civil partners is seriously ill and not expected to recover.

Section 92: Objections to registration

185. This section provides procedures for any person to make an objection in writing to the district registrar to the issue of a civil partnership schedule to prevent the registration as civil partners. The objection must relate to a lawful impediment.

Section 93: Place of registration

186. This section provides that a civil partnership document may be signed at a registration office or at any place which the intended civil partners and the local registration authority agree. It also provides that the place of registration may, if the approval of the Registrar General is obtained, be outwith the district of the authorised registrar carrying out the registration. However, the place must not be in religious premises, which are defined in *subsection (2)*.

Section 94: The civil partnership schedule

187. This section provides for the completion by the district registrar of the civil partnership schedule. This may be done providing the relevant district registrar has no concerns over the capacity of the couple to form a civil partnership, that there are no outstanding objections and that the required period of publicisation has expired.

Section 95: Further provision as to registration

188. *Subsection (1)* requires the persons who intend to form a civil partnership to confirm that (to the best of their knowledge) the particulars set out in the civil partnership schedule are correct.

189. *Subsection (2)* also requires the authorised registrar, as soon as practicable after the schedule has been signed, to cause the particulars to be entered into the "civil partnership register". *Subsection (3)* states that the form and content of the register will be prescribed by the Registrar General for Scotland. *Subsection (4)* provides that a prescribed fee will also be paid by the intended civil partners for the registration of their relationship.

Section 96: Civil partnership with former spouse

190. This section provides for the signing of a civil partnership schedule to take place quickly, where the couple were previously married to each other and one of them has changed gender under the provisions of the Gender Recognition Act 2004. The aim is to minimise, as much as possible, the time between the end of the marriage and the creation of the civil partnership where couples wish to recreate their legal relationship.

191. The section sets out the procedure for effecting the signature of the civil partnership document in the circumstances described above. The signing of the civil partnership schedule can take place on any of the 30 days immediately following the day that both notices of proposed civil partnerships are given, or if they are given on different days, on the day the second notice is given.

Section 97: Certificates of no impediment for part 2 purposes

192. This section applies where two people intend to register as civil partners of each other and one ("A") resides in Scotland and the other ("B") resides in England or Wales. *Subsections (1)* and *(2)* would allow "A" to submit a notice of intention to register in Scotland under section 88. Under *subsection (3),* if the district registrar is satisfied that there is no impediment to "A" registering as "B's" civil partner, the district registrar must issue a certificate that there is not known to be any impediment. *Subsection (4)* states that the certificate is not to be issued earlier than 14 days after receipt of the notice, except in circumstances relating to section 96(1) where "A" elects for the certificate to be issued as soon as possible. The form of the certificate is to be prescribed by the Registrar General. *Subsection (5)* allows for an objection to be made to the district registrar in writing by any person before a certificate is issued. *Subsection (6)* states that the district registrar is obliged to take into account any objection when he is deciding whether he is satisfied that there is no legal impediment.

Section 98: Application of certain sections of 1965 Act to civil partnership register

193. This section provides that certain provisions of the Registration of Births, Deaths and Marriages (Scotland) Act 1965 apply to the civil partnership register as they apply in relation to registers of births, deaths and marriages. These provisions enable the examination of the civil partnership register by district examiners, the searching of indexes kept by registrars or

the Registrar General for Scotland and the application to the register of the process of correction.

Section 99: Correction of errors in civil partnership register

194. This section provides that no alteration may be made to the civil partnership register except as authorised by or under an Act (including an Act of the Scottish Parliament). It enables the district registrar to correct a clerical error or an error of a kind prescribed by the Registrar General for Scotland. The Registrar General may also authorise district examiners to correct any specified errors which they discover during an examination under section 34 of the Births, Deaths and Marriages (Scotland) Act 1965.

Section 100: Offences

195. This section provides for certain offences in relation to civil partnerships. *Subsections (1)* and *(2)* set out the offences a person, if they act knowingly, may possibly commit under civil partnership proceedings. *Subsection (3)* sets out the maximum penalties that may be imposed on a person found guilty under *Subsection (1)* or *(2)*. *Subsection (4)* confirms the time limit during which a prosecution may commence.

Chapter 3 – Occupancy Rights and Tenancies

Section 101: Occupancy rights

196. This section sets out the rights that civil partners have to occupy the family home of the civil partnership. The section applies where one of the civil partners is either entitled to occupy the family home, or permitted to do so by a third party, and the other civil partner has no such entitlement or permission. An example of this would be where the family home is owned or leased in the name of one civil partner only. The civil partner who is entitled to occupancy or permitted occupancy by a third party is called the "entitled partner". The civil partner who is not entitled to occupancy or permitted occupancy by a third party is called the "non-entitled partner".

197. *Subsection (1)* sets out that non-entitled partners have the right to continue to occupy the family home (if they are already doing so), or have the right to enter and occupy the family home (if they are not already doing so). If the entitled partner has occupancy rights by virtue of permission of a third party, the non-entitled partner does not require the permission of the third party to exercise the rights conferred by *subsection (1)*.

198. *Subsection (2)* means that this right also extends to any child of the family.

199. *Subsection (3)* covers a situation whereby the entitled partner shares a right of occupancy with another person who is not the civil partner. In this situation, the rights explained in *subsection (1)* only apply if that other person waives their right to occupy the family home in favour of the entitled partner.

200. *Subsection (4)* provides recourse to the court, if the entitled partner refuses to let their civil partner enter the home. The latter can apply to the court for an order, as explained in section 103.

201. *Subsection (5)* allows the non-entitled partner to renounce their rights under this section in writing in certain circumstances. *Subsection (6)* provides that such a statement must be made before a notary public and made without coercion.

202. *Subsection (7)* provides definitions of "child of the family" and "family" and *Subsection (8)* defines what a notary public is.

Section 102: Occupancy: subsidiary and consequential rights

203. This section sets out the rights ancillary to the occupancy rights of a non-entitled partner in relation to the family home. *Subsection (1)(a)* to *(f)* list the duties that a non-entitled partner can undertake without the permission of the entitled partner. *Subsection (2)* details the circumstances in which if an obligation has been performed or enforced by a non-entitled partner, it will be treated in the same way as if it had been made by the entitled partner.

204. *Subsection (3)* provides that, where there is an entitled and non-entitled partner, the court may make an order apportioning costs incurred or to be incurred by either civil partner if they carry out any of the duties in *subsection (1)(a)* to *(d)* without the consent of the other civil partner, or perform any other activity in respect of the family home with the consent of the other civil partner.

205. *Subsection (4)* sets out the situation as it applies to civil partners where both are entitled or permitted by a third party to occupy a family home. This subsection sets out what each civil partner can do and note matters to which the court may have regard in making an order.

206. *Subsection (5)* covers the situation where one civil partner owns or hires goods such as furniture in a family home. The subsection sets out what the other civil partner may do in connection with these goods. It also sets out how the court may treat such goods if making an order to apportion expenditure in respect of these goods.

207. *Subsections (6)* to *(9)* specify additional criteria relevant to previous *subsections* of this section.

Section 103: Regulation by court of rights of occupancy of family home

208. This section sets out the regulation by the court of rights of occupancy of the family home. *Subsections (1)* and *(2)* detail the type of order a civil partner may apply for from the court in connection with occupancy of the family home or possession or use of goods owned or hired by one of the civil partners.

209. *Subsection (3)* sets out the factors that the court will consider in determining an application for an order. *Subsection (4)* gives the court power to make an interim order under certain circumstances. *Subsection (5)* prevents the court from making an order, if the effect of that order would be to exclude the non-applicant civil partner from the family home.

210. *Subsection (6)* allows the court, on the granting of an order under *subsections (3)* or *(4)*, to grant a warrant allowing a messenger-at-arms or sheriff officer to enter the family home or other premises to search for and take possession of the item required to be delivered and to deliver the item in accordance with the order that is granted. *Subsection (7)* provides that such a warrant be executed only after the end of a period specified in the order for delivery.

211. *Subsection (8)* provides that the court can order one civil partner to pay compensation to the other if its appears to the court that the latter has suffered a loss of occupancy rights, impaired occupation of the family home, or impaired use of the items in the civil partner's possession as a consequence of any act or default on the part of the other civil partner.

212. *Subsection (9)* provides for a civil partner to renounce rights to apply under *subsection (2)* for the possession or use of any item as detailed in that *subsection*.

Section 104: Exclusion orders

213. This section provides that either civil partner in the family home can apply to the court for an order which suspends the occupancy rights of the other civil partner in a family home.

Subsection (2) sets out that the court is to make an exclusion order if it appears necessary to protect the applicant or any child of the family from the conduct of the other civil partner. This is subject to *subsection (3)* which sets out where it would appear unjustified or unreasonable to make an exclusion order.

214. *Subsection (4)* sets out the types of exclusion order that the court can grant, where this is necessary. *Subsection (5)* sets out further directions that the court may attach when making an exclusion order. *Subsection (6)* gives the court power to make an interim order and sets out that *subsections (4)* and *(5)* will apply in the same way to an interim order as to an exclusion order. *Subsection (7)* sets out that an interim order can only be made if the non-applicant partner has been given an opportunity to be heard or represented before the court.

215. If both civil partners are entitled or permitted by a third party to occupy the family home, *subsection (8)* makes it incompetent for one civil partner to bring an action to eject the other from the family home. This is without prejudice to *subsections (1)* and *(6)*.

Section 105: Duration of orders under sections 103 and 104

216. This section sets out the duration of orders made under sections 103 and 104. *Subsection (1)* gives the court the power to vary or cancel an order made under these sections, at the request of one of the civil partners. *Subsection (2)* sets out the circumstances where such an order (unless varied or cancelled) will cease to have effect. In addition, *subsection (3)* provides that where an order has been granted under section 103(3) or (4), which grants possession or use of items, this will cease if a third party revokes permission for these possessions to be retained in the family home.

Section 106: Continued exercise of occupancy rights after dealing

217. This section sets out the occupancy rights in relation to dealings with third parties. *Subsection (1)* provides protection for the non-entitled partner with occupancy rights in relation to the entitled partner's dealings with third parties. *Subsection (2)* provides a definition of dealing for the purposes of *subsection (1)*. *Subsection (2)* also provides that a civil partner is not an entitled partner where they are only entitled to occupy the family home by virtue of permission from a third party, or they share entitlement to occupy along with a person who is not the other civil partner, irrespective of whether that person has waived their rights. *Subsections (3)* and *(4)* deal with the circumstances in which this section does not apply.

Section 107: Dispensation with civil partner's consent to dealing

218. This section allows the court to dispense with the non-entitled partner's consent to a dealing which has taken place or is proposed in certain circumstances. *Subsection (1)* sets out the circumstances under which this can occur. *Subsection (2)* defines when a non-entitled partner is to be regarded as having unreasonably withheld consent. *Subsection (3)* places an onus on the court to consider all the circumstances of the case in considering whether to make an order. *Subsection (4)* provides that where the entitled partner makes an application to the court for an order under this section and the non-entitled partner has brought proceedings in court for enforcement of occupancy rights, the non-entitled partner's proceedings will not be decided until the conclusion of the application by the entitled partner.

Section 108: Interests of heritable creditors

219. This section explains the rights that a heritable creditor has where there is an interest in the family home. *Subsection (1)* provides the grounds under which a creditor, who has an interest in the family home, can seek an order from the court for the non-entitled partner to

make a payment, where such a payment is due. *Subsections (2) to (4)* attach conditions and exceptions to this situation.

Section 109: Provisions where both civil partners have title

220. This section covers the situation where both civil partners have title of the property and are entitled to occupy the family home.

Section 110: Rights of occupancy in relation to division and sale

221. This section explains the circumstances that the court must take into account where a civil partner brings an action for the division and sale of a family home owned jointly with the other civil partner. The section allows the court to refuse to grant a decree, to postpone granting a decree or granting a decree with certain conditions applied.

Section 111: Adjudication

222. This section protects the interests and rights of a civil partner where a decree of adjudication has been pronounced by the court on property or furnishing belonging to the other civil partner, which the former uses.

Section 112: Transfer of tenancy

223. This section allows the court to make an order to transfer the tenancy of a family home to the non-entitled partner and provides for the non-entitled partner to make an appropriate payment to the entitled partner in compensation. The section sets out the circumstances under which this can apply and the consideration that the court should give.

Chapter 4 - Interdicts

Section 113: Civil partners: competency of interdict

224. This section means that the Court of Session or the sheriff can grant a relevant interdict in respect of a couple living together in a civil partnership. A relevant interdict for these purposes and for the purposes of section 114, is an interdict which is designed to prevent any inappropriate conduct on the part of one civil partner towards the other or a child of the family, or to prevent a civil partner from returning to the family home or its vicinity.

Section 114: Attachment of powers of arrest to relevant interdicts

225. This section allows the court to attach a power of arrest to any relevant interdict on the application of a civil partner. The section sets out the conditions which apply to this power.

Section 115: Police powers after arrest

226. This section sets out the action that the police may take where a non-applicant civil partner has been arrested as set out in *subsection (4)* of section 114. It also provides that the facts and circumstances that gave rise to the arrest will be reported to the procurator fiscal who will determine whether criminal proceedings should follow.

Section 116: Procedure after arrest

227. This section covers the procedure that arises where the non-applicant civil partner is not released after arrest, but where the procurator fiscal decides that no criminal proceedings should follow.

Chapter 5 – Dissolution, Separation and Nullity

Section 117: Dissolution

228. This section provides that an action for the dissolution of a civil partnership can be brought in the Court of Session or in the sheriff court. It sets out the terms under which a court may grant a decree, and when the irretrievable breakdown of a civil partnership is taken to be established.

Section 118: Encouragement of reconciliation

229. This section provides that if it seems to the court that there is a reasonable prospect of a reconciliation between the civil partners, the court must continue the action for dissolution for as long as it thinks is proper to enable attempts to be made to effect a reconciliation. *Subsection (2)* provides that where a couple still wish to dissolve their civil partnership after a period of living together again (during the court action), that period will not be taken into account for the purposes of the action.

Section 119: Effect of resumption of cohabitation in certain actions

230. *Subsection (1)* provides that the irretrievable breakdown of a civil partnership on grounds of desertion for a continuous two year period will not be taken to be established if, at the end of that two year period, the parties start living together again and do so at any time after the end of the three months which begin from the date the parties resumed living together. *Subsection (2)* provides that this is subject to section 118(2).

231. *Subsection (3)* provides that, when considering whether any period of desertion or non-cohabitation provided for in section 117(3)(b) to (d) is continuous, the court should not take account of any period or periods of time, not exceeding 6 months in total, in which the civil partners resumed cohabiting with one another. However (as a separate issue from whether the period is to be regarded as "continuous") no such period of cohabitation can count as part of the period of non-cohabitation for the purposes of section 117(3). So for example, non-cohabitation for 2 years can be proved, even if the civil partners lived together for, say, 2 months during the relevant period, so long as the total period of non-cohabitation adds up to 2 years (excluding those 2 months).

Section 120: Separation

232. This section provides that an action for the separation of civil partners may be brought in the Court of Session or in the sheriff court. The court may grant such a decree if satisfied that any of the facts listed in section 117(3)(a) to (d) are established.

Section 121: Dissolution following on decree of separation

233. If a couple that has a decree of separation subsequently decide to dissolve their civil partnership, this section provides that they may apply to the court giving the same evidence upon which a decree of separation was based. The court can treat a decree of separation as proof of the facts under which the decree was granted. However, this does not entitle a court to grant a decree of dissolution of a civil partnership without receiving evidence from the civil partner seeking the dissolution.

Section 122: Registration of dissolution of civil partnership

234. This section requires the Registrar General for Scotland to maintain a register of decrees of dissolution of civil partnership (Register of Dissolutions of Civil Partnership). The Registrar General is also required to make and keep an alphabetical index of entries to this register. The form of the register is to be prescribed. On payment of the prescribed fee to the

Registrar General, the index to the register may be searched and an extract of any entry provided. An extract of an entry in the register is sufficient evidence of the decree of dissolution to which it relates. The Registrar General may also delete, amend or substitute an entry in the register. "Prescribed" is defined in section 126.

Section 123: Nullity

235. This section sets out that if a couple register as civil partners of each other in Scotland despite not meeting the eligibility criteria detail in section 86, or in circumstances where either of them did not validly consent to its formation, the civil partnership will be void, meaning that it will be treated as never having taken place. Either of the couple or another interested person may bring an action in the Court of Session to have the civil partnership declared void.

Section 124: Validity of civil partnerships registered outside Scotland

236. This section sets out the rules to be applied when determining whether, under the law of Scotland, a civil partnership which was not formed in Scotland is void or voidable. If the civil partnership is void or voidable, a court in Scotland which has jurisdiction under section 219 or 225 may make a declarator of nullity in respect of the civil partnership under the inherent declaratory power held by the Court of Session.

237. *Subsection (1)* ensures that a civil partnership which was formed in England and Wales is void or voidable for the purposes of the law of Scotland if that would be the effect of the English provisions in sections 49 or 50. (The only exception is where an interim gender recognition certificate under the Gender Recognition Act 2004 has been issued to either civil partner after the formation of the civil partnership, as mentioned in section 50(1)(d). In Scotland this will instead be a ground for dissolution of the civil partnership under section 117(2)(b).)

238. *Subsection (2)* ensures that a civil partnership which was formed in Northern Ireland is void or voidable for the purposes of the law of Scotland if that would be the effect of the Northern Ireland provisions in sections 173 or 174. (Again, the only exception is where an interim gender recognition certificate under the Gender Recognition Act 2004 has been issued to either civil partner after the formation of the civil partnership, as mentioned in section 174(1)(d). In Scotland this will instead be a ground for dissolution of the civil partnership under section 117(2)(b).)

239. *Subsection (4)* deals with the formation of civil partnerships outside the United Kingdom under an Order in Council made under section 210 or 211. Orders in Council made under those sections will include provision for determining the relevant part of the United Kingdom for certain purposes. Paragraphs (a)(i) and (b) of subsection (4) ensure that questions of nullity are then dealt with in exactly the same way as would apply under Scottish law if the civil partnership had actually been formed in that part of the United Kingdom.

240. In addition the civil partnership will be void if the condition in section 210(2)(a) or 211(2)(a) (whichever is relevant) was not met. For a partnership formed at a British consulate etc., the condition is that one party must be a United Kingdom national as defined in section 245. For a partnership formed in the armed services, the condition is that one of the proposed civil partners is a member of the armed forces serving in the country or territory where the partnership is formed, or falls within certain other related categories as set out in section 211(2)(a).

241. Finally the civil partnership will also be void if there is a breach of a requirement of the Order in Council which is prescribed for this purpose by the Order itself (this power will be

used to define in the Order those requirements which are mandatory in order to ensure the validity of the civil partnership).

242. *Subsections (7) and (8)* set out the rules to be applied in relation to an apparent or alleged overseas relationship. An overseas relationship can be treated as a civil partnership under Chapter 2 of Part 5. But subsection (7) sets out that the civil partnership will be void if it transpires that the relationship is in fact not an overseas relationship as defined in sections 212 to 214, or if one of the requirements for the overseas relationship to be treated as a civil partnership under sections 215 to 218 is not met. For example the civil partnership will be void if, under the law of the country where the overseas relationship was registered, the formalities necessary to enter into the overseas relationship were not fulfilled or there was no capacity to enter into the overseas relationship (see section 215(1)). It is also voidable in terms of subsection (8) if that is the effect of the law of the country where the registration took place (see the definition of "the relevant law" in *subsection (10)*). But if either party was domiciled in England and Wales or Northern Ireland, then the civil partnership will also be voidable in the circumstances set out in section 50(1) or 174(1) (except for the grant of an interim gender recognition certificate, which in Scotland will instead be a ground for dissolution of the civil partnership under section 117(2)(b)).

Section 125: Financial provision after overseas dissolution or annulment

243. This section introduces Schedule 11, which relates to applications for financial provision in Scotland after a civil partnership has been dissolved or annulled, in a country or territory outside the British Islands. "British Islands" is defined in the Interpretation Act 1978 (c. 30) as comprising the United Kingdom, the Channel Islands and the Isle of Man.

Chapter 6 – Miscellaneous and Interpretation

Section 126: Regulations

244. This section provides that, in Chapters 2 and 5, "prescribed" means prescribed in regulations made by the Registrar General for Scotland with the approval of the Scottish Ministers. A statutory instrument containing such regulations is subject to annulment in pursuance of a resolution of the Scottish Parliament.

Section 127: Attachment

245. This section protects the interests and rights of a civil partner where an attachment has been made on property or furnishing belonging to the other civil partner, which the former uses.

Section 128 - Promise of agreement to enter into civil partnership

246. This section sets out that if a couple make an agreement to register as civil partners of each other, it will not confer any rights or obligations under Scots law. If the promise or agreement to form a civil partnership is broken, no action can be brought in a court in Scotland and this is irrespective of the law applicable to the promise of agreement.

Section 129: Lord Advocate as party to action for nullity or dissolution of civil partnership

247. This section makes provision for intimation on the Lord Advocate of proceedings for either declarator of nullity or dissolution of a civil partnership. *Subsection (1)* provides that the Lord Advocate can become a party to either of these kinds of proceedings, and conduct his case in such manner as he considers appropriate. *Subsection (2)* allows the court to intimate these proceedings on the Lord Advocate if the court thinks it necessary to assist in

the determination of the proceedings. *Subsection (3)* provides that, in any case where the Lord Advocate does become a party to the proceedings, no expenses can be claimed against him.

Section 130: Civil partner of accused a competent witness

248. This section provides that the civil partner of an accused person may be called as a witness by the accused, a co-accused, or the prosecutor. If a civil partner of an accused is called as a witness, they cannot be forced to give evidence by the co-accused or the prosecutor, and cannot be forced to reveal communications between the civil partners while the civil partnership continues. If a civil partner of an accused person does not give evidence, neither the defence nor the prosecutor can take advantage of this in any submissions to the court.

Section 131: Succession: legal rights arising by virtue of civil partnership

249. This section ensures that civil partners have the same access to legal rights of succession following the death of a civil partner as a spouse would have following the death of a spouse.

Section 132: Assurance policies: Scotland

250. This section ensures that civil partners are recognised in terms of assurance policies in the same way that spouses are at present.

Section 133: Council Tax: liability of civil partners

251. This section adds a section to the Local Government Finance Act 1992 so that civil partners (and persons living together as such) are jointly and severally liable for the payment of council tax on a property in the same way as spouses (and persons living together as such).

Section 134: General provisions as to fees

252. This section enables a district registrar to refuse to comply with any application made under Part 3 until the appropriate fee has been paid to him. For example, this reflects section 19(2) of the Marriage (Scotland) Act 1977 which provides that an authorised registrar should not solemnise a marriage unless the prescribed fee has been paid. The section also enables the Registrar General to remit fees in cases of hardship. That provision follows what is provided in section 54 of the 1965 Act.

Section 135: Interpretation of this Part

253. This section defines certain expressions used in Part 3 (Civil Partnership: Scotland).

Section 136: The expression "relative" in the 1965 Act

254. This section provides that the definition of "relative" in section 56(1) of the 1965 Act should include "a civil partner and anyone related to the civil partner of the person". In practical terms, this would (for instance) enable a civil partner or a relative of a civil partner to act as the informant for the registration of a death under section 23 of the Registration of Births, Deaths and Marriages (Scotland) Act 1965.

Part 4 – Civil Partnership: Northern Ireland

Introduction

255. The sections in this Part (Part 4) of the Civil Partnership Act extend only to Northern Ireland (see section 262(3)).

Chapter 1 - Registration

Section 137: Formation of civil partnership by registration

256. This section provides that a civil partnership is created when both persons sign the completed civil partnership schedule before two witnesses and the registrar (all being present). The civil partnership schedule should then be signed by both witnesses and the registrar.

257. *Subsection (4)* provides that the registrar must record the civil partnership as soon as possible after the signing of the civil partnership schedule.

258. *Subsection (5)* states that no religious service is to be used when the civil partnership schedule is being signed.

Section 138: Eligibility

259. *Subsection (1)* provides that two people are not eligible to register in Northern Ireland as civil partners of each other if –

   a) they are not of the same sex,

   b) either of them is already a civil partner or lawfully married

   c) either of them is under 16

   d) they are within prohibited degrees of relationship (as determined under Schedule 12 –)

   e) either of them is incapable of understanding the nature of a civil partnership

Section 139: Notice of proposed civil partnership

260. This section provides that each party must give the registrar a notice of proposed civil partnership. The notice must be in a prescribed form and accompanied by a prescribed fee and any other information as may be prescribed. In prescribed cases the notice must be given to the registrar in person.

Section 140: Civil partnership notice book and list of intended civil partnerships

261. This section requires the registrar to record in the civil partnership notice book such particulars as may be prescribed, taken from every civil partnership notice received and the date on which each civil partnership notice is received.

262. *Subsection (3)* requires the registrar to publicise a list containing relevant information (names of intended civil partners and date of intended signing of the civil partnership schedule) in relation to each proposed civil partnership for which the registrar has received a civil partnership notice.

263. *Subsection (5)* provides that any person claiming to have reason to object to a proposed civil partnership may inspect any entry relating to the civil partnership in the civil partnership notice book without charge.

Section 141: Power to require evidence of name etc.

264. This section provides for the registrar to request specified evidence from a proposed civil partner to verify certain information contained in a civil partnership notice. This power to request evidence is only exercisable before the civil partnership schedule has been issued.

Section 142: Objections

265. This section provides that any person may make an objection in writing to the registrar to the issue of a civil partnership schedule to prevent a civil partnership from being formed. The objection must relate to a lawful impediment.

Section 143: Civil partnership schedule

266. This section provides for the completion by the registrar of the civil partnership schedule. This may be done providing the registrar is satisfied that there is no legal impediment to the formation of the civil partnership or the Registrar General has directed him to proceed.

Section 144: Place of registration

267. This section provides that a civil partnership schedule may be signed at a registration office or at any place approved for that purpose by the local registration authority. In some cases of serious illness or disability, as supported by a medical statement, the civil partnership may be formed at the place where the person concerned is located.

Section 145: Parental etc. consent where proposed civil partner under 18

268. This section sets out the provisions for consent requirements where a person wishing to form a civil partnership is under eighteen years of age. The section gives effect to Schedule 13 which identifies the appropriate persons or bodies who may give consent and makes provision for orders dispensing with consent and for recording consents.

269. *Subsection (4)* confirms that a ward of court requires the consent of the High Court to register as a civil partner. *Subsection (5)* provides a definition of "young person" as a person who is under eighteen.

Section 146: Validity of registration

270. This section provides that once the formation of a civil partnership has been recorded, its validity must not be questioned in any legal proceedings commenced after that time on the ground of any contravention of a provision of or made under the Act.

Section 147: Corrections and cancellations

271. This section provides that regulations may make provision for the Registrar General or other registrars to make corrections to the records of the formation of a civil partnership and that the formation of a void civil partnership must be cancelled by the Registrar General or by the registrar as directed by the Registrar General.

Section 148: Interpreters

272. This section provides that a registrar may use an interpreter to assist in relation to the formation of a civil partnership.

273. *Subsections (2)* provides that the interpreter must confirm his ability to act as an interpreter in the relevant language by signing a statement prior to the formation of a civil partnership and must sign a certificate after the registration to the effect that he faithfully acted as an interpreter.

Section 149: Detained persons

274. This section provides that a detained person may register as a civil partner at the place where that person is detained provided that the civil partnership notice is accompanied by a supporting statement.

275. *Subsection (2)* sets out that a supporting statement is one made in a prescribed form by a responsible authority (as defined by *subsection (3)*) identifying the establishment where the person is detained and confirming that the responsible authority has no objection to that place being specified in a notice of proposed civil partnership.

276. *Subsection (4)* sets out that the registrar must notify the Registrar General upon receipt of a civil partnership notice and supporting statement, and must not complete a civil partnership schedule until directed to do so by the Registrar General.

Section 150: Certificates of no impediment for Part 2 purposes

277. This section makes provision for a registrar in Northern Ireland to receive notice from a person living in Northern Ireland who wishes to register as a civil partner in England and Wales. Upon receipt of notice of an intended civil partnership, the registrar in Northern Ireland may issue a certificate to the person resident in Northern Ireland stating that there is no impediment under Northern Ireland law to that person registering as a civil partner. Before such a certificate is issued by the registrar any person may submit a written objection to its issue.

Section 151: Registration districts and registration authorities

278. This section provides definitions for registration districts and registration authorities in Northern Ireland. *Subsection (2)* states that local registration authorities shall exercise their powers as agents of the Department of Finance and Personnel.

Section 152: Registrars and other staff

279. This section makes provision for the appointment or removal, by a local registration authority, of a registrar, one or more deputy registrars and other staff as may be required for the signing of civil partnership documents. The powers of appointment and removal are subject to the approval of the Registrar General.

Section 153: Records and documents to be sent to Registrar General

280. This section provides that any person must comply with a request from the Registrar General to provide any record or document relating to a civil partnership.

Section 154: Annual report

281. This section provides that the Registrar General must submit to the Department of Finance and Personnel an annual report of the number of formations of civil partnership in each year. *Subsection (2)* provides that each annual report must then be laid before the Northern Ireland Assembly.

Section 155: Searches

282. This section provides that the Registrar General and other registrars must ensure that indexes to civil partnership formation records are made available for public inspection.

283. *Subsections (2)* and *(3)* provide that such indexes may be searched and documents relating to a civil partnership registration may be requested upon payment of a prescribed fee. *Subsections (4) and (5)* provide that any document produced by the Registrar General must be stamped with the seal of the General Register Office and judicial notice must be taken of it.

Section 156: Proof of civil partnership for purposes of certain statutory provisions

284. This section makes provision for a civil partner, upon application to the Registrar General and payment of a prescribed fee, to obtain a document proving the civil partnership formation for the purposes of any prescribed statutory provision.

Section 157: Fees

285. This section enables the Department of Finance and Personnel to make an order prescribing fees payable in relation to civil partnership registrations. The order must be approved by resolution of the Assembly.

Section 158: Offences

286. This section creates offences and associated penalties in relation to the formation of civil partnerships.

287. *Subsection (1)* creates an offence where a registrar signs the civil partnership schedule in the absence of the civil partners.

288. *Subsection (2)* makes it an offence for a person, other than a duly appointed registrar, to officiate at the signing of the civil partnership schedule by leading the civil partners to believe that he is a registrar.

289. *Subsection (3)* sets out the maximum penalty that may be imposed for these offences.

290. *Subsection (4)* specifies the time-limit (3 years) within which a prosecution may be brought.

Section 159: Regulations

291. This section provides for the Department of Finance and Personnel, by regulations, to make any necessary provision in relation to registration as civil partners in Northern Ireland.

Section 160: Interpretation

292. This section provides definitions of various terms which are used in this Chapter.

Chapter 2 – Dissolution, Nullity and Other Proceedings

Section 161: Powers to make orders and effect of orders

293. This section sets out the orders that the court can make to bring a civil partnership to an end or to provide for the separation of the parties. These are as follows:

   a) A dissolution order, which when made final will bring a civil partnership to an end.

   b) A nullity order, which when made final will annul a civil partnership which is either void or voidable.

   c) A presumption of death order, which when made final will dissolve the civil partnership on the ground that one of the civil partners is presumed to be dead.

   d) A separation order, which provides for the separation of the civil partners, but will not allow either civil partner to marry or to form another civil partnership.

294. *Subsection (2)* provides that an order for dissolution, nullity or presumption of death will initially be a conditional order and that it may not be made final until the end of the prescribed period defined in section 162.

295. *Subsection (3)* provides that a nullity order made in respect of a civil partnership which is voidable annuls the civil partnership only as respects any time after the order is made. The civil partnership is to be treated as if it had existed up to that time.

296. By *subsection (4)* "the court" is ascribed the meaning given in section 188, namely the High Court or a county court designated by the Lord Chancellor as a civil partnership proceedings county court. *Subsection (5)* makes it clear that the powers of the court under this section are subject to the court having jurisdiction under sections 219 and sections 228 to 232.

Section 162: The period before conditional orders may be made final

297. This section sets the period which must elapse before a dissolution, nullity or presumption of death order may be made final. By *subsection (1)*, the period is 6 weeks from the making of the conditional order. *Subsection (2)* provides that in particular cases the court may reduce the period (this might be relevant, for example, in the case of a deathbed dissolution and formation of a new civil partnership).

Section 163: Intervention by the Crown Solicitor

298. This section provides for the intervention of the Crown Solicitor in proceedings where an application has been made for a dissolution, nullity or presumption of death order. The court may involve the Crown Solicitor where it considers it necessary or expedient to have any question in relation to the case fully argued by counsel appointed by the Crown Solicitor, under the directions of the Attorney General. Any person may also give information to the Crown Solicitor on relevant issues at any time before the order has been made final and the Crown Solicitor can take such steps as the Attorney General considers necessary or expedient. The section also gives the court discretion to order the payment of costs by or to the Crown Solicitor.

Section 164: Proceedings before order has been made final

299. This section provides for the court to consider the position once a conditional order has been made but before it has been made final. By *subsection (1)*, the section applies where the Crown Solicitor, or anyone who has not been a party to the proceedings, shows that that there is cause (good reason) why the conditional order should not be made final on the ground that material facts were not put before the court. By *subsection (2)*, the court may also consider a case under this section where the civil partner who applied for the conditional order has not taken steps to have this made final within 3 months from the earliest date when such an application could have been made, and the other civil partner applies to the court under this section.

300. Where this section applies, the court may make the order final, rescind the order, direct that further enquiries are to be made, or deal with the case in such other manner as it thinks fit. By *subsection (4)*, the court's power to make the order final applies even if the minimum period under section 161(2) has not yet expired, but is subject to the restrictions imposed in section 172(4) (relating to financial provision in separation cases) and section 186 (restrictions on the making of orders affecting children).

Section 165: Time bar on applications for dissolution orders

301. This section states that an application for dissolution of a civil partnership may not be made until at least 2 years after the date of formation of the civil partnership. However, matters which occurred within this 2 year period may be used in support of the application.

Section 166: Attempts at reconciliation of civil partners

302. This section allows the court to adjourn an application for a dissolution or separation order if it appears that the civil partners have a reasonable possibility of achieving a reconciliation. *Subsection (3)* provides that if, during any such adjournment, the parties resume living in the same household, no account will be taken of this fact for the purposes of the proceedings.

303. *Subsection (4)* provides that this power to adjourn is additional to any other power of adjournment.

Section 167: Consideration by the court of certain agreements or arrangements

304. This section provides that rules of court may make provision for civil partners to refer to the court an agreement or arrangement between them in connection with the dissolution of the civil partnership or with their separation. The rules may allow the court to express an opinion about whether the agreement or arrangement is reasonable, or give directions.

Section 168: Dissolution of civil partnership which has broken down irretrievably

305. This section establishes the ground on which (provided the 2 year period set out in section 165 has elapsed) an application for the dissolution of a civil partnership may be made, and the four facts which can prove the ground for dissolution.

306. *Subsection (1)* sets out the sole ground on which an application for dissolution may be made, namely that the civil partnership has broken down irretrievably.

307. In order to demonstrate the irretrievable breakdown of the civil partnership the applicant must satisfy the court of one or more of the following facts set out in *subsection (5):*

    a) That his or her civil partner (called the respondent for the purposes of the proceedings) has behaved in such a way that the applicant cannot reasonably be expected to live with him or her;

    b) That the applicant and their civil partner have lived apart for a continuous period of at least 2 years immediately preceding the application (this is referred to as "2 years' separation") and that their civil partner consents to a dissolution order being made;

    c) That the applicant and their civil partner have lived apart for a continuous period of at least 5 years immediately preceding the application (this is referred to as "5 years' separation");

    d) That his or her civil partner has deserted him or her for a continuous period of at least 2 years immediately preceding the making of the application.

308. *Subsection (2)* provides that the court must inquire as far as possible into the facts alleged by the applicant and any facts put forward by the respondent. The court may not hold that the civil partnership has broken down irretrievably unless the applicant satisfies the court of one or more of the facts set out in *subsection (5)*. But if the court is satisfied of any of those facts, it must make a dissolution order unless it is satisfied on all the evidence that the civil partnership has not broken down irretrievably.

309. *Subsection (6)* provides that the court must consider the oral testimony of the applicant before making a dissolution order, unless there are special reasons to dispense with such testimony.

Section 169: Supplemental provisions as to facts raising presumption of breakdown

310. *Subsections (1)* and *(2)* provide that where an applicant alleges that their civil partner has behaved in such a way that they cannot reasonably be expected to live with him or her, but following the final incident relied on in support of this allegation, the civil partners have continued to cohabit for a period or periods of time not exceeding 6 months in total, the court must disregard this time spent living together when determining whether the applicant cannot reasonably be expected to live with their civil partner.

311. *Subsections (3)* and *(4)* provide that where a civil partner allegedly consents to the making of a dissolution order under the "2 years' separation" head, rules of court must make provision to ensure that he or she is given information which will enable him to understand the consequences of consenting to the order and the steps which must be taken to indicate consent.

312. *Subsection (5)* allows the court to consider a period of desertion as continuing even when the civil partner concerned was incapable of continuing the necessary intention, provided the court would on the evidence have inferred that the period of desertion would have continued if the civil partner had been able to continue the intention. This would cover a situation where one civil partner deserts his or her civil partner for 2 years but is involved in an accident at some time over the 2 years which leads to a temporary loss of consciousness. This break in the "intention to desert" would not stop the 2 years from accruing.

313. *Subsection (6)* provides that when considering whether a period of living apart or desertion is continuous, no account is to be taken of a period or periods of time not exceeding 6 months in total in which the civil partners resumed living together. However (as a separate issue from whether the period of living apart or desertion could be regarded as "continuous") under *subsection (7)* no period during which the civil partners lived together can count as part of the period of living apart or desertion. So for example, desertion or separation for 2 years can be proved, even if the civil partners lived together for, say, 2 months during the relevant period, so long as the total period of desertion or separation adds up to 2 years (excluding those 2 months).

314. *Subsection (8)* provides that civil partners are to be treated as living apart unless they are living with each other in the same household.

Section 170: Dissolution order not precluded by previous separation order etc.

315. This section provides that where a separation order, an order for financial relief in a court of summary jurisdiction or an order under Article 11 or 15 of the Family Homes and Domestic Violence (Northern Ireland) Order 1998 has been made, this does not prevent either civil partner from applying to the court for a dissolution order on the basis of the same facts that were relied upon when granting the previous order.

316. Under *subsection (3)* the court may treat the previous order as sufficient proof of the facts by reference to which it was made, but must not make the dissolution order without receiving evidence from the applicant.

317. *Subsection (4)* applies where an application for a dissolution order is made following a separation order or any order requiring the civil partners to live apart. If there was a period of desertion immediately preceding the application for a separation order, the parties have not resumed living together, and the separation order has been continuously in force since it was made, the period of desertion is to be treated as if it had taken place immediately prior to the application for the dissolution order. This will mean that the period of desertion can be used to support the application for a dissolution order.

318. Under *subsection (5)* the court may also treat as a period of desertion to support an application for a dissolution order a period during which the respondent was subject to an injunction excluding him or her from the civil partnership home or when an order under Article 11 or 15 of the Family Homes and Domestic Violence (Northern Ireland) Order 1998 was in force prohibiting the civil partner from occupying a dwelling-house used (then or previously) as the civil partnership home.

Section 171: Refusal of dissolution in 5 year separation cases on ground of grave hardship

319. *Subsection (1)* provides that the respondent to an application for a dissolution order in which the applicant alleges 5 years' separation may oppose the making of a dissolution order on the ground that the dissolution of the civil partnership would result in grave financial or other hardship to him or her and that in all the circumstances it would be wrong to make the order. By *subsection (3)* the court must consider all the circumstances, including the conduct of the civil partners and the interests the civil partners and of any children or other persons concerned, and if the court is satisfied that there would be grave hardship it must dismiss the application for the dissolution order. *Subsection (4)* provides that "hardship" includes the loss of the chance of acquiring any benefit which the respondent might acquire if the civil partnership were not dissolved.

Section 172: Proceedings before order made final: protection for respondent in separation cases

320. *Subsection (1)* provides that the court can rescind a dissolution order which has not been made final, where the application was on the basis of 2 years' separation coupled with the other civil partner's consent, if the applicant misled their civil partner over any matter which was taken into account when giving that consent.

321. *Subsections (2) to (5)* allow the respondent to an application for a dissolution order alleging either 2 years' or 5 years' separation to apply to the court to consider his or her financial position after dissolution of the civil partnership. The court must consider all the relevant circumstances including the age, health, conduct, earning capacity, financial resources and obligations of each civil partner and the position of the respondent on the death of the applicant, assuming the applicant died first. Under *subsection (4)* the court must not make the dissolution order final unless it has, by order, declared that it is satisfied either that the applicant should not be required to make financial provision for the respondent or that the provision made for the respondent is reasonable and fair, or is the best that can be made in the circumstances or that there are circumstances making it desirable to make the order final without delay. *Subsection (8)* provides that if the court will not make an order under subsection (4), it must, on the applicant's application make an order declaring that it is not satisfied as mentioned in that subsection.

322. Under *subsection (5)* the court must not declare it is satisfied that the order should be made final without delay unless it has obtained an undertaking from the applicant to bring the question of financial provision for the respondent before the court within a specified time.

323. *Subsections (6) and (7)* provide that where an application has been made for a dissolution order on the basis of 2 years' separation or 5 years' separation, and the court makes a final order without making an order under *subsection (4)*, the final order is voidable at the instance of the respondent or the court, but no person may challenge the validity of the final order on the grounds that *subsections (4)* and *(5)* were not satisfied.

Section 173: Grounds on which civil partnership is void

324. This section sets out the grounds on which a civil partnership will be void (and therefore invalid) under the law of Northern Ireland, where the parties registered as civil partners of each other in Northern Ireland. (The grounds on which the law of Northern Ireland will hold other civil partnerships to be void are set out in section 177.)

325. Paragraph (a) provides that the civil partnership will be void if, at the time when the two people registered as civil partners in Northern Ireland, they were not eligible to register as civil partners of each other under the requirements set out in section 138.

326. Paragraph (b) lists the breaches of formal requirements which will render the civil partnership void if both civil partners were aware of them at the time of the registration. These are failure to give the required notice of proposed civil partnership, the civil partnership schedule not being duly issued, the place of registration not being the place specified in the civil partnership schedule, or a registrar not being present at the registration.

Section 174: Grounds on which civil partnership is voidable

327. This section sets out the grounds on which an application can be made for an order annulling a civil partnership on the grounds that it is voidable, where the parties registered as civil partners of each other in Northern Ireland. (The grounds on which the law of Northern Ireland will hold other civil partnerships to be voidable are set out in section 177.) The grounds are as follows:

   a) Either of the civil partners did not validly consent to the formation of the civil partnership, through a mistake, through being put under duress or due to unsoundness of mind or otherwise.

   b) At the time of the formation of the civil partnership either of the civil partners, although able to consent to the registration, was suffering from a mental disorder which made them unfitted for civil partnership.

   c) At the time of the formation of the civil partnership one of the civil partners was pregnant (other than by the applicant, although that could only be relevant in a case involving a gender change under the Gender Recognition Act 2004). This is subject to section 175(6) which ensures that the court may not make a nullity order unless satisfied that the applicant did not know of the pregnancy at the time of the formation of the civil partnership.

   d) An interim gender recognition certificate under the Gender Recognition Act 2004 has been issued to either civil partner after the time of the formation of the civil partnership. An application on this ground is subject to the 6 month time limit in section 175(5) (see below).

   e) The respondent is a person whose gender at the time of the formation of the civil partnership had become the acquired gender under the Gender Recognition Act 2004. This is subject to section 175(6) which ensures that the court may not make a nullity order unless it is satisfied that the applicant did not know at the time of the formation of the civil partnership that his or her partner had changed gender.

Section 175: Bars to relief where civil partnership is voidable

328. *Subsection (1)* provides that the court must not make a nullity order on the grounds that a civil partnership is voidable if the respondent satisfies the court that the applicant acted

towards the respondent in such a way as to indicate that he or she would not apply for a nullity order and that it would be unjust to the respondent to make the order now.

329. *Subsection (2)* establishes that an application for a nullity order on the grounds that a civil partnership is voidable (other than in the circumstances dealt with by subsection (5) below) must be made within 3 years of the date of formation of the civil partnership. However *subsections (3)* and *(4)* permit the court to allow later applications where it is just to do so on the basis that the applicant suffered from mental disorder at some time during the 3-year period.

330. Where the application is made on the ground that an interim gender recognition certificate has been issued under the Gender Recognition Act 2004 after the date of formation of the civil partnership, the time limit under *subsection (5)* is 6 months from the date of issue of that certificate.

331. *Subsection (6)* provides that, where the application is made on the grounds of pregnancy at the time of formation of the civil partnership, or a change of gender previous to that date, a nullity order must not be made unless the court is satisfied that the applicant did not know of the relevant facts at the time of formation of the civil partnership.

Section 176: Proof of certain matters not necessary to validity of civil partnership

332. This section provides that that where two people have registered as civil partners in Northern Ireland it is not necessary for them to provide evidence that any consent required under section 145 (consent by parents etc. where one of the intended civil partners is under 18) was actually given, or that the person who officiated at the signing of the civil partnership schedule was a properly appointed registrar. No evidence may be given in any nullity proceedings to disprove either of these facts.

Section 177: Validity of civil partnerships registered outside Northern Ireland

333. This section sets out the rules to be applied when determining whether, under the law of Northern Ireland, a civil partnership is void or voidable where the parties did not register as civil partners in Northern Ireland. If the civil partnership is void or voidable, a court in Northern Ireland which has jurisdiction under sections 219 or 229 may make a nullity order in respect of the civil partnership under section 161.

334. *Subsection (1)* ensures that a civil partnership which was formed in England and Wales is void for the purposes of the law of Northern Ireland if it would be void under the provisions applicable in England and Wales under section 49. The civil partnership will also be voidable if it would be voidable under the provisions applicable in Northern Ireland under section 174(1) (since these are all circumstances which would equally render the civil partnership voidable in England and Wales under section 50).

335. *Subsection (2)* ensures that a civil partnership which was formed in Scotland is void for the purposes of the law of Northern Ireland if it would be void under the Scottish provisions in section 123. The civil partnership will also be voidable if an interim gender recognition certificate is subsequently issued to either party under the Gender Recognition Act 2004.

336. *Subsection (4)* deals with the situation where the parties registered as civil partners outside the United Kingdom under an Order in Council made under section 210 or 211. Orders in Council made under those sections will include provision for determining the relevant part of the United Kingdom for certain purposes. Paragraphs (a)(i) and (b) of subsection (4) ensure that questions of nullity are then dealt with in exactly the same way as

would apply under the law of Northern Ireland if the civil partnership had actually been formed in that part of the United Kingdom.

337. In addition the civil partnership will be void if the condition in section 210(2)(a) or 211(2)(a) (whichever is relevant) was not met. Where the parties registered as civil partners at a British consulate etc., the condition is that one party must be a United Kingdom national as defined in section 245. Where the parties registered as civil partners in the armed services, the condition is that one of the proposed civil partners is a member of the armed forces serving in the country or territory where the partnership is formed, or falls within certain other related categories as set out in section 211(2)(a).

338. Finally the civil partnership will also be void if there is a breach of a requirement of the Order in Council which is prescribed for this purpose by the Order itself (this power will be used to define in the Order those requirements which are mandatory in order to ensure the validity of the civil partnership).

339. *Subsection (8)* sets out the rules to be applied in relation to an apparent or alleged overseas relationship. An overseas relationship can be treated as a civil partnership under Chapter 2 of Part 5. But the civil partnership will be void if it transpires that the relationship is in fact not an overseas relationship as defined in sections 212 to 214, or if one of the requirements for the overseas relationship to be treated as a civil partnership under sections 215 to 218 is not met. For example the civil partnership will be void if, under the law of the country where the registration took place, the formalities necessary to enter into the overseas relationship were not fulfilled or there was no capacity to enter into the overseas relationship (see section 215(1)). It will also be voidable if that is the effect of the law of the country where the registration took place (see the definition of "the relevant law" in *subsection (10)*) or on the grounds that an interim gender recognition certificate has been issued under the Gender Recognition Act 2004. But if either party was domiciled in Northern Ireland or England and Wales then the civil partnership will also be voidable in the other circumstances set out in section 174(1).

340. Where a civil partnership is voidable in accordance with this section the section 175 bars to relief are applied in the usual way. However where the civil partnership is voidable by virtue of the application of foreign law, the bars to relief will only apply in so far as they are applicable in accordance with the foreign law.

Section 178: Presumption of death orders

341. This section gives the court power to make a presumption of death order, on the application of a civil partner, if satisfied that there are reasonable grounds for believing that the other civil partner is dead. The fact that the other civil partner has been absent from the applicant for a continuous period of 7 years or more and that the applicant has no reason to believe that he or she has been living during that time will be accepted as evidence that the other civil partner is dead until the contrary is proved.

Section 179: Separation orders

342. This section allows for an application to be made for a separation order on the basis of the same facts as are required for an order for dissolution of a civil partnership. The court must inquire as far as possible into the facts alleged by the applicant and any facts put forward by his or her civil partner (referred to as the respondent for the purpose of the proceedings.) If the court is satisfied of the facts alleged it must make a separation order (subject to the provisions of section 186 relating to children). However it is irrelevant whether the civil partnership has broken down irretrievably.

Section 180: Effect of separation order

343. This section provides that, if a civil partner dies without making a will (intestate) at a time when a separation order is in force and the separation is continuing, the rules in respect of the passing of intestate estates shall be applied as if his or her surviving (but separated) civil partner were also dead.

Section 181: Declarations

344. This section provides for people to apply to the court for declarations regarding the status of a civil partnership. These applications cover its validity, that it was or was not in existence on a certain date, and declarations as to whether a dissolution, annulment or legal separation obtained outside Northern Ireland is or is not entitled to recognition in Northern Ireland.

345. Under *subsection (2)*, if the applicant is not one of the civil partners the court must refuse to hear the application if it considers that the applicant has insufficient interest in the outcome.

Section 182: General provisions as to making and effect of declarations

346. This section provides that where an application is made under section 181 and the proposition put forward is proved to the satisfaction of the court, the court must make the order requested unless it would be manifestly contrary to public policy for it to do so. If the court dismisses the application, it must not make any other declaration which has not been applied for. The court cannot make a declaration that a civil partnership was void at its inception. Nothing in this section will prevent the court from being able to make a nullity order in respect of the civil partnership.

Section 183: The Attorney General and proceedings for declarations

347. This section provides that, in any case where an application is made for a declaration under section 181, the court may direct that the appropriate papers should be sent to the Attorney General. The Attorney General may in any event intervene in proceedings for a declaration under section 181 as he thinks necessary, and may argue any question which the court thinks should be fully argued. *Subsection (3)* enables the court to make an order for the parties to the proceedings to pay the costs incurred by the Attorney General if this is justified.

Section 184: Supplementary provisions as to declarations

348. This section provides for family proceedings rules (defined in *subsection (8)*) to determine the form of an application for a declaration under section 181, and of the declaration itself. The rules may provide for the information to be supplied by the applicant and for notice of the application to be served on the Attorney General and on persons who may be affected by the declaration, and must make provision for an appeal to the Court of Appeal from any declaration made by a county court under section 181 or the dismissal of an application under that section.

349. *Subsection (3)* provides that no proceedings under section 181 will affect any final order or judgment already given. *Subsection (4)* provides that the court may direct that the whole or part of any application under section 181 may be heard in private (and by *subsection (5)* any application for such a direction must itself be heard in private unless the court directs otherwise).

Section 185: Relief for respondent in dissolution proceedings

350. This section provides that if the respondent in dissolution proceedings alleges and proves any of the facts which the applicant had to satisfy the court of, the court may grant the respondent the relief that would normally be granted to an applicant who had proved such facts, as if it had been the respondent who had made the application.

Section 186: Restrictions on making of orders affecting children

351. This section provides that in any proceedings for a dissolution, nullity or separation order the court must consider whether there are any children for whom the court should exercise its powers under the Children (Northern Ireland) Order 1995 in order to safeguard their welfare and provide for their upbringing. If necessary the court may direct that the dissolution, nullity or separation order is not to be made final until the court has considered whether to exercise those powers. The provisions apply to any child of the family who is under 16 years of age at the date the court considers the position and also to children of the family over 16 if the court directs that they should also be included in its consideration.

Section 187: Parties to proceedings under this chapter

352. This section allows rules of court to be made to allow for parties to be joined to proceedings for dissolution, nullity or separation if they are involved in allegations of improper conduct made in the proceedings. The rules may also provide for the court to dismiss parties whom it has joined to the proceedings, and as to the persons who are to be party to an application for a declaration. *Subsection (3)* enables the court to permit a person to intervene if it thinks he or she should be made a party.

Section 188: The court

353. *Subsection (1)* defines "the court" for the purposes of Chapter 2 as being the High Court or a county court designated by the Lord Chancellor as a civil partnership proceedings county court and *subsection (5)* defines "civil partnership proceedings county court" as any such county court.

354. *Subsection (6)* provides that rules of court may be made to ensure that a civil partnership cause pending in one civil partnership proceedings county court may be heard and determined either partly in that court and partly in another, or in another such court.

355. *Subsection (7)* makes provision for civil partnership county courts to have jurisdiction even where the amount claimed would not normally enable a county court to exercise jurisdiction.

Section 189: Appeals

356. This section provides that rules of court may be made to allow appeals to the Court of Appeal of decisions or dismissals of applications made by a judge in a civil partnership proceedings county court.

357. *Subsection (3)* provides that a person may appeal any order or dismissal of an application made by a county court with jurisdiction under paragraphs 57, 58 or 66 of Schedule 15 (financial relief in the High Court or county court: Northern Ireland) as if the order or dismissal had been made in exercise of the jurisdiction conferred by Part 3 of the County Courts (Northern Ireland) Order 1980.

Section 190: Transfer of proceedings

358. This section provides that rules of court may be made to facilitate the transfer of any civil partnership cause from a civil partnership proceedings county court to the High Court or alternatively from the High Court back to the civil partnership proceedings county court.

359. *Subsection (3)* provides a definition of a "civil partnership cause" for the purposes of this section.

360. *Subsection (4)* provides that rules of court may provide for the transfer or retransfer of a civil partnership cause from either a civil partnership proceedings county court to the High Court or, from the High Court to a civil partnership proceedings county court.

361. *Subsection (5)* provides that the power conferred by subsections (2) and (4) includes the power to provide for the removal of proceedings at the direction of the High Court. Nothing in this subsection affects the High Court's powers of removal and remittal.

Chapter 3 – Property and Financial Arrangements

Section 191: Disputes between civil partners about property

362. This section enables civil partners to refer disputes over property to court. It provides that civil partners may apply to the High Court or to a county court in respect of any question relating to the title to or the possession of property. The court may make such order with respect to the property as it thinks fit, including an order for the sale of the property.

Section 192: Applications under section 191 where property not in possession etc.

363. This section allows one civil partner (A) to make an application under section 191 where the other civil partner (B) no longer has the money or property concerned or A does not know whether B still has the money or property. The power of the court to make orders under section 191 includes the power to order B to pay to A such sum of money as seems appropriate or to make any other order which it could have made under section 191.

Section 193: Applications under section 191 by former civil partners

364. This section allows a former civil partner to make an application to the court in respect of a dispute over property under Section 191 (as extended by Section 192) despite the fact that the civil partnership has been dissolved, annulled or is void (whether or not an order for annulment has been granted). The application must be made within three years of the date of dissolution or annulment of the civil partnership. Where the civil partnership is void but has not been annulled and the parties have ceased to live together, the application must be made within three years of the date on which the parties ceased to live together.

Section 194: Assurance policy by civil partner for benefit of other civil partner etc.

365. This section extends the application of section 4 of the Law Reform (Husband and Wife) Act (Northern Ireland) 1964 to civil partners, so that if a civil partner takes out a life insurance policy to provide for his or her civil partner or children the money payable under the policy is not to form part of the estate of the insured.

Section 195: Wills, administration of estates and family provision

366. This section states that Schedule 14 contains provisions amending enactments relating to wills, administration of estates and family provision to give the same treatment to civil partners as exist for married people.

Section 196: Financial relief for civil partners and children of the family

367. This section introduces Schedule 15, which makes provision for financial relief for civil partners which corresponds to the relief available to married couples in the High Court or a county court under Part 3 of the Matrimonial Causes (Northern Ireland) Order 1978 when they go through divorce, nullity or judicial separation proceedings.

368. *Subsection (2)* provides that if the effect of rules of law is that provisions for financial relief under Part 3 of the Matrimonial Causes (Northern Ireland) Order 1978 are interpreted as being available in the case of the dissolution of a marriage on the ground of presumed death, then those rules of law will also apply to the corresponding financial provisions in Schedule 15 to the Act for civil partners, with any necessary modifications. This is to allow case law to be available to civil partners which allows for financial relief to be available if the person who was presumed dead is subsequently proved to be alive.

369. *Subsection (3)* introduces Schedule 16, which provides civil partners with the right to apply for financial relief in courts of summary jurisdiction in a way that corresponds to the rights that exist for married people under the Domestic Proceedings (Northern Ireland) Order 1980.

370. *Subsection (4)* introduces Schedule 17, which contains provisions for financial relief in Northern Ireland after a civil partnership has been dissolved or annulled or the civil partners have been legally separated in a country outside the British Islands. "British Islands" is defined in the Interpretation Act 1978 (c. 30) as comprising the United Kingdom, the Channel Islands and the Isle of Man.

Chapter 4 – Civil Partnership Agreements

Section 197: Civil partnership agreements unenforceable

371. This section provides that an agreement to form a civil partnership by any of the means outlined in section 1 ("a civil partnership agreement") does not constitute a contract giving rise to legal rights under the law of Northern Ireland and will not be enforceable.

372. *Subsection (2)* provides that no action can be taken over any breach of a civil partnership agreement.

373. *Subsection (4)* provides that the section will apply to civil partnership agreements entered into both before and after the section comes into force but it will not affect any legal action which has begun before the section comes into force.

Section 198: Property where civil partnership agreement is terminated

374. This section applies when a civil partnership agreement is terminated. It provides that sections 191 and 192 (relating to disputes between civil partners about property) will apply in relation to property in which either or both of the parties to the agreement had a beneficial interest while the agreement was in force.

375. An application made using section 191 or 192 must be made within three years of the date of termination of the civil partnership agreement.

376. *Subsection (4)* provides that where a person makes a gift to the other person on the understanding that it will be returned if the civil partnership agreement is terminated, they can recover the property given even if he or she terminated the agreement himself or herself.

Chapter 5 - Children

377. This Chapter makes various amendments to the Children (Northern Ireland) Order 1995 and the Adoption (Northern Ireland) Order 1987 to reflect the creation of the new relationship of civil partnership.

Section 199: Parental responsibility, children of the family and relatives

378. This section amends various provisions of the Children (Northern Ireland) Order 1995 ("the Children Order") to include civil partners in a way that corresponds to the provisions that apply to married couples.

379. *Subsection (2)* amends the definition of "child of the family" in Article 2(2) of the Children Order to include a child of both civil partners and any other child who has been treated as a child of the family by both civil partners, unless the child had been placed with the civil partners - by a local authority or a voluntary organisation - as foster parents.

380. *Subsection (3)* amends the definition of "relative" in Article 2(2) of the Children Order to replace "by affinity" with "by marriage or civil partnership".

381. *Subsection (4)* amends Article 7(1C) of the Children Order to enable a civil partner to acquire parental responsibility of their civil partner's child in the same way as a person who is married to the parent of the child (but is not that child's parent).

Section 200: Guardianship

382. This section amends Article 161 of the Children Order in relation to the revocation and disclaimer of appointments of guardians. Under Article 160 (1) and (2) of the Children Order a parent or guardian may appoint any person to act as the guardian of a child in his or her place. This section inserts a provision into Article 161 of the Children Order so that where a person appoints his or her civil partner to be the guardian of a child that appointment is revoked if the civil partnership is dissolved or annulled, unless the appointment itself indicates that the dissolution or annulment of the civil partnership should not affect the appointment.

Section 201: Entitlement to apply for a residence or contact order

383. This section amends Article 10(5) of the Children Order to add a civil partner in a civil partnership to the class of people who are able to apply for a residence or contact order. The amendment enables civil partners to apply for an order whether or not the civil partnership subsists.

Section 202: Financial provision for children

384. This section amends Schedule 1 to the Children Order.

Subsection (2) extends the meaning of "parent" in paragraph 1(2) of Schedule 1 to the Children Order to include any civil partner in a civil partnership, whether it is still in existence or whether it has been brought to an end, for whom the child concerned is a child of the family.

385. *Subsection (3)* amends Schedule 1 to the Children Order by adding to the definition of periodical payment orders in paragraph 3(6) of that Schedule orders under the provisions of Parts 1 and 8 of Schedule 15 (Financial relief in the High Court or county court etc.) and under Schedule 16 (Financial relief in court of summary jurisdiction etc.) to this Act. This will enable courts to make orders for periodical payments from one civil partner to the other or to a child of the family, or to a particular person for the benefit of a child of the family.

386. *Subsection (4)* amends paragraph 17(2) of Schedule 1 to the Children Order so that a local authority will not be able to make a contribution towards the maintenance of a child who is subject to a residence order where the person with whom the child is living is a parent of the child, or the husband or wife or civil partner of a parent of the child.

Section 203: Adoption

387. This section amends the Adoption (Northern Ireland) Order 1987 ("the 1987 Order") to ensure that the status of civil partnership is recognised for the purposes of adoption.

388. *Subsection (2)* amends the definition of "relative" in relation to a child in Article 2(2) of the 1987 Order to replace "by affinity" with "by marriage or civil partnership".

389. *Subsection (3)* amends Article 12(5) of the 1987 Order so that an adoption order cannot be made in respect of any person who is or has been married or in a civil partnership.

390. *Subsection (4)* amends Article 15(1)(a) of the 1987 Order to allow for an adoption order to be made on the application of one person where that person is over the age of 21 years and is not married or is not a civil partner.

391. *Subsection (5)* amends Article 33(3)(g) of the 1987 Order so that a protected child ceases to be so on his or her marrying or forming a civil partnership.

392. *Subsection (6)* amends Article 40(3)(a) of the 1987 Order so that the status conferred as a consequence of an adoption order does not apply for the purposes of Schedule 12 to the Civil Partnership Act (prohibited degrees of relationship).

393. *Subsection (7)* amends Article 54(2) of the 1987 Order to ensure that an adopted person who intends to enter into a civil partnership can apply to the Registrar General for him to check that the person with whom the applicant intends to enter a civil partnership, does not fall within the prohibited degrees of relationship for the purposes of Schedule 12 to the Civil Partnership Act.

394. *Subsection (8)* amends Article 54A(13)(a) of the 1987 Order to ensure that the meaning of "relative" for the purposes of an entry in the adoption contact register includes a person related by civil partnership.

Chapter 6 – Miscellaneous

Section 204: False statements etc. with reference to civil partnerships

395. This section amends Article 8 of the Perjury (Northern Ireland) Order 1979 to make it an offence for a person to make false statements or representations with reference to marriage or civil partnership formation.

396. *Subsection (2)* inserts a new paragraph (1A) into Article 8 making it an offence to knowingly make certain false statements or representations for the purpose of procuring the formation of a civil partnership or a record being made in any register relating to civil partnerships, or as a means of forbidding the issue of a civil partnership document or a document required by an Order in Council. For example, a person who signs a declaration that he is free to enter into a civil partnership, knowing that the declaration is false, commits an offence.

Section 205: Housing and tenancies

397. This section introduces Schedule 18 (Housing and tenancies: Northern Ireland), which makes amendments to a range of enactments relating to housing and tenancies.

Section 206: Family homes and domestic violence

398. This section introduces Schedule 19 (Family homes and domestic violence), which amends the Family Homes and Domestic Violence (Northern Ireland) Order 1998 and related enactments so that they apply in relation to civil partnerships as they apply in relation to marriages. The amendments will mean that civil partners have the same rights to occupy the matrimonial home. In addition civil partners will be able to apply for non-molestation orders and occupation orders. Occupation orders are orders regulating occupation of the home (which may include excluding the respondent from the home and vicinity of the home and prohibiting, terminating or restricting the exercise of the respondent's occupation rights, as appropriate).

Section 207: Fatal accidents claims

399. This section extends the provisions of the Fatal Accidents (Northern Ireland) Order 1977 to include civil partners, so that where a person's death is caused by the wrongful act, neglect or default of another person, a civil partner of the deceased will be able to claim compensation in the same way as a spouse.

400. *Subsections (2), (3)* and *(4)* widen the definition of "dependant" for the purposes of a right of action under the Order to include civil partners and former civil partners of the deceased; any person who was living with the deceased as if they were a civil partner; and any person (not being a child of the deceased) who was treated by the deceased as a child of the family, in relation to any civil partnership to which the deceased was at any time a party.

401. *Subsection (5)* defines "former civil partner" as a person whose civil partnership with the deceased has been annulled or dissolved.

402. *Subsection (6)* replaces the reference to a relationship by "affinity" in Article 2(3)(b) of the Order with a reference to a relationship "by marriage or civil partnership", for the purposes of clarity.

403. *Subsection (7)(a)* enables a civil partner of the deceased to claim bereavement damages. *Subsection (7)(b)* prevents a parent of a deceased minor from making a claim for bereavement damages where the minor had entered into a civil partnership.

404. *Subsection (8)* provides that upon assessing damages payable to a dependant in respect of the death of a person with whom the dependant was living as a civil partner, the court shall take account of the fact that the dependant had no enforceable right to financial support by the deceased as a result of their living together.

Section 208: Evidence

405. *Subsection (1)* of this section contains a provision that enactments or rules of law applying to the giving of evidence by a spouse will apply also to the giving of evidence by a civil partner.

406. However, *subsection (2)* sets out that the general provision in *subsection (1)* is subject to any specific amendment made by or under the Civil Partnership Act which relates to the giving of evidence by a civil partner. This takes account of the fact that in some instances it is more appropriate to amend specific provisions in other enactments or rules.

<u>407.</u> *Subsection (5)* provides that any rule of law which makes evidence of family tradition admissible to prove or disprove the existence of a marriage is to apply in a similar way in order to prove or disprove the existence of a civil partnership.

Section 209: Restrictions on publicity of reports of proceedings

408. This section extends section 1 of the Matrimonial Causes (Reports) Act (Northern Ireland) 1966 to civil partners. Section 1 of the 1966 Act makes it an offence to publish certain details in connection with judicial proceedings for dissolution or nullity of marriage, judicial separation and any proceedings by one spouse against the other for financial provision or proceedings concerning an order made in connection with any cause or matter. This clause makes it an offence to disclose similar details in relation to civil partners involved in comparable judicial proceedings under the Civil Partnership Act.

Part 5 – Civil partnerships formed or dissolved abroad etc.

Introduction

409. Part 5 of the Act extends to the whole of the United Kingdom, with the exception of sections 220 to 224 which extend only to England and Wales, sections 225 to 227 which extend only to Scotland and sections 228 to 232 which extend only to Northern Ireland (see section 262(4)).

Chapter 1 – Registration outside UK under Order in Council

Section 210: Registration at British consulates etc.

410. This section confers power to make subordinate legislation by Order in Council to make provision for two people to register as civil partners of each other in countries or territories outside the United Kingdom in the presence of an officer of Her Majesty's Diplomatic Service. The officers in whose presence the parties may register as civil partners, and the countries or territories where this may take place, will be set out in the Order in Council (see the definition of "prescribed" in section 244(5)). This power will be used to make provisions for civil partnership corresponding to the provisions of the Foreign Marriage Act 1892 (c.23). Under that Act it is possible for UK nationals to marry in accordance with UK law at a diplomatic post overseas in certain circumstances, so this power will enable civil partnerships likewise to be formed at diplomatic posts overseas.

411. *Subsection (2)* sets out the four conditions which the Diplomatic Service officer must be satisfied are met. These are that at least one of the proposed civil partners is a United Kingdom national, that the civil partners would have been eligible to register in the relevant part of the United Kingdom as determined according to the provisions of the Order in Council, that the authorities in the country or territory in question will not object to the registration, and that there are insufficient facilities for them to enter into an overseas relationship under that country's law. "Overseas relationship" is defined in sections 212 to 214. In addition, by *subsection (3),* the officer is not required to allow the couple to register as civil partners if in his opinion to do so would be inconsistent with international law or the comity of nations, although the Order may include provision for an appeal against any such refusal. "United Kingdom national" is defined in section 245.

Section 211: Registration by armed forces personnel

412. This section enables provision to be made by Order in Council for two people to register as civil partners of each other in countries or territories outside the United Kingdom where one of them is a member of Her Majesty's forces serving in the country or territory in question or falls within certain connected categories set out in *subsection (2)*. The countries

or territories where a such persons may register will be set out in the Order in Council (see the definition of "prescribed" in section 244(5)). "Her Majesty's forces" is defined in section 245(2).

413. This power will be used to make provisions for civil partnership corresponding to section 22 of the Foreign Marriage Act 1892 (c.23). Under that section, members of the armed forces and certain civilians accompanying them can be married outside the UK by a forces chaplain or an officer authorised by the commanding officer. This section allows similar provision to be made by Order in Council for civil partnership registration outside the UK, in the presence of one of the officers responsible for the recording of births, deaths and marriages (and, in future, civil partnerships) among the Service community.

Chapter 2 – Overseas relationships treated as civil partnerships

414. This Chapter defines the term "overseas relationship", and sets out the circumstances in which two people who have registered such a relationship are to be treated as having formed a civil partnership as mentioned in section 1(1)(b). However this Chapter should be read in conjunction with the other provisions of the Act concerning the dissolution or annulment of a civil partnership, or the legal separation of civil partners. Where two people have registered an apparent or alleged overseas relationship, the civil partnership will be treated as void or voidable in the United Kingdom in the circumstances set out in subsections (6) to (11) of section 54 (for England and Wales), 124 (for Scotland) or 177 (for Northern Ireland). The circumstances in which the courts in each part of the United Kingdom will recognise the validity of an overseas dissolution or annulment of a civil partnership, or an overseas legal separation of civil partners, are set out in Chapter 3 of Part 5.

Section 212: Meaning of "overseas relationship"

415. This section defines the overseas relationships which are capable of being treated as civil partnerships if the other requirements of this Chapter are met. An overseas relationship must be either a "specified relationship" (see section 213 and Schedule 20) or must meet "the general conditions" (see section 214). In addition the relationship must have been registered with a responsible authority in a country or territory outside the UK by two people who are of the same sex under the relevant law, and (as a matter of UK law) are not already in a civil partnership or lawfully married. (They are also required to be of the same sex as a matter of UK law – see section 216.) The overseas relationship may have been registered before the enactment of the Civil Partnership Act (but, in such cases, section 215 ensures that the couple will usually be treated as having formed a civil partnership only at the time when that section comes into force). "The relevant law" is defined in *subsection (2)* as the law of the country or territory where the overseas relationship is registered, including its rules of private international law.

Section 213: Specified relationships

416. This section introduces Schedule 20, which lists the relationships which are "specified relationships" for the purposes of section 212. The Schedule lists various types of relationship which exist in other countries, such as civil union in Vermont in the United States of America, registered partnership in Denmark, and so on. It also includes marriage in Belgium and the Netherlands (both countries where marriage is available to same-sex partners). Relationships falling within the descriptions in Schedule 20 can be treated as civil partnerships as set out in sections 215 to 218 only if the other requirements of those sections and section 212 are met. For example, a marriage in Belgium or the Netherlands could be

54

treated as a civil partnership only if it is between two people of the same sex who are not already in a civil partnership or lawfully married.

417. *Subsections (2)* to *(6)* enable the Schedule to be amended by order made by the Secretary of State with the consent of Scottish Ministers and the Department of Finance and Personnel in Northern Ireland.

Section 214: The general conditions

418. If a relationship is not a "specified relationship" listed in Schedule 20, it is nonetheless an "overseas relationship" if it meets the general conditions set out in this section, provided the other requirements of section 212 are also met.

419. The general conditions relate to the following issues:

(a) exclusivity – it must be a requirement of the relevant law that the relationship cannot be entered into if either of the parties is already in a relationship of that kind or is lawfully married;

(b) duration – it must be a requirement of the relevant law that the relationship is indeterminate in duration (this would exclude an arrangement whereby the parties agreed to live together for a fixed period of time); and

(c) effect – the effect of entering into the relationship must be that the parties are either treated as a couple under the relevant law (either generally or for certain specified purposes), or are treated as married. This requirement concerns the treatment of the parties under the legal system of the country or territory where the registration took place (see the definition of the "relevant law" in section 212(2)). For example registration under a local or municipal scheme within a particular city or town, which has no legal effects under the law of the country or territory as a whole, would not be sufficient to meet this requirement.

Section 215: Overseas relationships treated as civil partnerships: the general rule

420. *Subsection (1)* provides that two people are to be treated as having formed a civil partnership as a result of having registered an overseas relationship if under the relevant law they had capacity to enter into the relationship, and met all requirements necessary to ensure its formal validity under that law. "The relevant law" is defined in section 212(2) as the law of the country or territory where the overseas relationship is registered, including its rules of private international law. Section 215 is subject to sections 216 to 218.

421. *Subsection (2)* provides that the civil partnership is treated as having been formed at the time when the overseas relationship is registered as having been entered into. However if the relationship was registered before this section comes into force, then *subsection (3)* provides that the civil partnership is treated as having been formed only at the date when this section comes into force.

422. *Subsections (4) and (5)* deal with the situation where an overseas relationship was dissolved or annulled outside the United Kingdom before this section comes into force. If the dissolution or annulment meets the requirements for recognition under Chapter 3 of Part 5 (see in particular sections 219 and 234 to 237), the parties will be treated as former civil partners who have dissolved or annulled their relationship for the purposes of Schedules 7, 11 and 17 (financial relief in United Kingdom after dissolution or annulment obtained outside the United Kingdom) and for the purposes of any other provision specified by an order made under section 259; but they are not to be treated as having been civil partners for any other purpose.

Section 216: The same-sex requirement

423. *Subsection (1)* provides that both members of the couple must be of the same sex, at the critical time, if the overseas relationship is to be treated as a civil partnership in the UK. "The critical time" is defined in *subsection (5)* to refer back to section 215(2) or (3) (i.e. depending on whether the relationship was entered into before or after the commencement of section 215).

424. *Subsections (2)* to *(4)* provide an exception where the couple was regarded as a same-sex couple under the relevant law because one of the parties was regarded as having changed gender under that law. In this situation the relationship will be treated as a civil partnership once the party who had changed gender under the relevant law has also acquired a full gender recognition certificate under the Gender Recognition Act 2004. But the parties will only be regarded as having formed a civil partnership if no marriage or civil partnership has been entered into in the interim. These provisions are analogous to provisions contained in the Gender Recognition Act 2004, in relation to overseas marriages.

425. *Subsection (6)* adds the proviso that this section is subject to any enforceable Community right. This means that, where a national of another country within the European Union or European Economic Area has been granted legal recognition of their gender change under the law of that country, and has an enforceable right under European Community law to recognition of their acquired gender in the UK, if they subsequently form a same-sex overseas relationship that relationship can be treated as a civil partnership in the UK without the need for them first to obtain a full gender recognition certificate under the Gender Recognition Act 2004. Again this is analogous to provision contained in the Gender Recognition Act in relation to overseas marriages.

Section 217: Person domiciled in a part of the United Kingdom

426. This section ensures that, where an overseas relationship is registered by a person who is domiciled in England and Wales, Scotland or Northern Ireland, it cannot be treated as a civil partnership unless the couple would have been eligible to register as civil partners of each other in that part of the United Kingdom. Thus the overseas relationship will not be treated as a civil partnership if either party was under 16 at the time of registration, or if the parties are within the prohibited degrees of relationship applicable in the relevant part of the United Kingdom. Where either party was domiciled in Scotland, the overseas relationship will also not be treated as a civil partnership if either party was incapable of understanding the nature of civil partnership. These requirements are additional to the requirements that neither party is already a civil partner or lawfully married and that both parties are of the same sex (see sections 212 and 216).

Section 218: The public policy exception

427. This section provides that two people cannot be treated as having formed a civil partnership as a result of their overseas relationship if it would be manifestly contrary to public policy to recognise the capacity of either or both of them to enter into the relationship under the relevant law.

Chapter 3 - Dissolution etc.: jurisdiction and recognition

Section 219: Power to make provision corresponding to EC Regulation 2201/2003

428. *Subsections (1) and (2)* provide powers for the Lord Chancellor or Scottish Ministers to make regulations concerning:

a) the jurisdiction of the courts in England and Wales, Scotland or Northern Ireland in relation to the dissolution or annulment of civil partnerships or the legal separation of civil partners, where one of them is a resident or national of a member State or is domiciled in a part of the United Kingdom or the Republic of Ireland; and

b) the recognition and enforcement of equivalent judgments from other member States.

429. *Subsection (3)* provides that the regulations may, in particular, make provision corresponding to the rules for dissolution, annulment or legal separation in matrimonial matters set out in EC Regulation 2201/2003. This Regulation will come into effect on 1 March 2005.

430. *Subsection (4)* allows the regulations to define "member State" for the purposes of this Part of the Act and for the purposes of the regulations.

431. *Subsection (5)* provides that the regulations may make provision about recognition of overseas dissolutions etc. even if the date of the dissolution etc. preceded the date on which this section comes into force. This will be relevant in the case of an overseas relationship which was dissolved or annulled in a country or territory outside the UK before the Act is brought into force.

432. Under *subsection (6)* regulations under this section for England and Wales or Northern Ireland must be made by statutory instrument under the affirmative resolution procedure in both Houses of Parliament. Under *subsection (7)* equivalent regulations for Scotland must be made by statutory instrument under the affirmative resolution procedure in the Scottish Parliament.

Section 220: Meaning of "the court"

433. Sections 220 to 224 extend only to England and Wales. Section 220 defines "the court" in sections 221 to 224 in the same way as in Chapter 2 of Part 2 (see section 37(4)).

Section 221: Proceedings for dissolution, separation or nullity order

434. *Subsection (1)* governs jurisdiction to hear applications for dissolution or separation orders. The court may entertain such proceedings if it has jurisdiction under section 219 regulations or, in cases where no court has jurisdiction under those regulations, where either civil partner is domiciled in England and Wales on the date the proceedings begin. A further discretionary ground of jurisdiction is made available for those cases where the couple registered as civil partners of each other in England and Wales. This will operate where the section 219 regulations do not give any court jurisdiction and the court decides it is in the interests of justice to assume jurisdiction.

435. *Subsection (2)* gives the court jurisdiction to hear applications for nullity orders in the same circumstances as for dissolution and separation orders and also, in a case where no court has jurisdiction under section 219 regulations, if either civil partner died before proceedings began and was at death domiciled in England and Wales or had been habitually resident there throughout the year ending with the date of death.

436. *Subsection (3)* gives the court jurisdiction, when proceedings are pending under *subsection (1)* or *(2)*, to hear other proceedings for a dissolution, separation or nullity order in respect of the same civil partnership, even if the court would not have jurisdiction to hear the latter proceedings under those subsections.

Section 222: Proceedings for presumption of death order

437. This section gives the court jurisdiction to hear applications for a presumption of death order provided the applicant is domiciled in England and Wales on the date proceedings begin or was habitually resident there throughout the year ending with that date. A further discretionary ground of jurisdiction is made available for those cases where the couple registered as civil partners of each other in England and Wales. This will operate where the court decides it is in the interests of justice to assume jurisdiction.

Section 223: Proceedings for dissolution, nullity or separation order: supplementary

438. This section allows rules of court to make provision corresponding to the provision for marriages made by Schedule 1 to the Domestic and Matrimonial Proceedings Act 1973 (c.45).

Section 224: Applications for declarations as to validity etc.

439. This section gives the court jurisdiction in relation to proceedings under section 58 (declarations in relation to a civil partnership) provided either of the civil partners is domiciled in England and Wales on the date of the application or has been habitually resident there throughout the year ending with that date, or died before that date and was at death domiciled in England and Wales or had been habitually resident there throughout the year ending with the date of death. A further discretionary ground of jurisdiction is made available for those cases where the couple registered as civil partners of each other in England and Wales. This will operate where the court decides it is in the interests of justice to assume jurisdiction.

Section 225: Jurisdiction of Scottish courts

440. Sections 225 to 227 extend only to Scotland. *Subsections (1) and (2)* govern the jurisdiction of the Court of Session and the sheriff court to hear applications for the dissolution of a civil partnership or for separation of civil partners. They may entertain such proceedings if they have jurisdiction under any Scottish regulations made under section 219 or, in cases where no court has jurisdiction under those regulations, where either civil partner is domiciled in Scotland on the date the proceedings begin. Where an action is raised in the sheriff court then an additional test of 40 days residence in the sheriffdom will need to be satisfied. The Court of Session alone will also have jurisdiction where the parties registered as civil partners in Scotland, no court has jurisdiction under section 219 regulations and the court is satisfied that it is in the interests of justice to assume jurisdiction.

441. Under *subsection (3)*, the Court of Session will have jurisdiction in an action for declarator of nullity of a civil partnership in circumstances largely corresponding to those in subsection (1), but with additional provision where one of the ostensible civil partners has died. *Subsection (4)* makes provision for proceedings parallel to an action already raised.

Section 226: Sisting of proceedings

442. This section allows rules of court to make provision corresponding to the provision for marriages made by Schedule 3 to the Domestic and Matrimonial Proceedings Act 1973 (c.45).

Section 227: Scottish ancillary and collateral orders

443. This section confers jurisdiction on any Scottish court to deal with an application relating to children, aliment (maintenance), financial provision or expenses which is ancillary or collateral to an action for dissolution, separation or declarator of nullity. The only

exception is where such jurisdiction would conflict with regulations made under section 219. Section 8 of the Law Reform (Miscellaneous Provisions) (Scotland) Act 1966 (c.19) confers power on sheriffs to vary or recall particular types of order made by the Court of Session, provided no party objects. Where section 227 enables the Court of Session to hear an application for variation or recall of one of its own orders, and the order is one to which section 8 (as amended by this Act) applies, *subsection (4)* ensures that the sheriff will also have power to hear the application under the section 8 procedure.

Section 228: Meaning of "the court"

444. Sections 228 to 232 extend only to Northern Ireland. Section 228 defines "the court" for the purposes of sections 229 to 232 as having the meaning given by section 188.

Section 229: Proceedings for dissolution, separation or nullity order

445. *Subsection (1)* governs jurisdiction to hear applications for dissolution or separation orders. A court may entertain such proceedings if it has jurisdiction under section 219 regulations or, in cases where no court has jurisdiction under those regulations, where either civil partner is domiciled in Northern Ireland on the date the proceedings begin. A further discretionary ground of jurisdiction is made available for those cases where the couple registered as civil partners of each other in Northern Ireland. This will operate where the section 219 regulations do not give any court jurisdiction and the court decides it is in the interests of justice to assume jurisdiction.

446. *Subsection (2)* gives the court jurisdiction to hear applications for nullity orders in the same circumstances as for dissolution and separation orders and also, in a case where no court has jurisdiction under section 219 regulations, if either civil partner died before proceedings began and was at death domiciled in Northern Ireland or had been habitually resident there throughout the year ending with the date of death.

447. *Subsection (3)* gives the court jurisdiction, when proceedings are pending under subsection (1) or (2), to hear other proceedings for a dissolution, separation or nullity order in respect of the same civil partnership, even if the court would not have jurisdiction to hear the latter proceedings under those subsections.

Section 230: Proceedings for presumption of death order

448. This section gives the High Court jurisdiction to hear applications for a presumption of death order provided the applicant is domiciled in Northern Ireland on the date proceedings begin or was habitually resident there throughout the year ending with that date. A further discretionary ground of jurisdiction is made available for those cases where the couple registered as civil partners of each other in Northern Ireland. This will operate where the court decides it is in the interests of justice to assume jurisdiction.

Section 231: Proceedings for dissolution, nullity or separation order: supplementary

449. This section allows rules of court to make provision corresponding to the provision for marriages made by Schedule 1 to the Matrimonial Causes (Northern Ireland) Order 1978.

Section 232: Applications for declarations as to validity etc.

450. This section gives the court jurisdiction in relation to proceedings under section 181 (declarations in relation to a civil partnership) provided either of the civil partners is domiciled in Northern Ireland on the date of the application or has been habitually resident there throughout the preceding year, or died before that date and was at death domiciled in Northern Ireland or had been habitually resident there throughout the year ending with the

date of death. A further discretionary ground of jurisdiction is made available for those cases where the couple registered as civil partners of each other in Northern Ireland. This will operate where the court decides it is in the interests of justice to assume jurisdiction.

Section 233: Effect of dissolution, annulment or separation obtained in the UK

451. *Subsection (1)* provides that no dissolution or annulment of a civil partnership obtained in one part of the United Kingdom can be effective in any part of the United Kingdom unless it has been obtained from a court of civil jurisdiction. The parts of the United Kingdom, for the purposes of sections 233 to 238 are England and Wales, Scotland, and Northern Ireland (see section 237(5)).

452. *Subsection (2)* provides for any dissolution or annulment of a civil partnership or legal separation of civil partners, obtained from a court of civil jurisdiction in one part of the United Kingdom, to be recognised throughout the United Kingdom, subject to subsections (3) and (4).

453. *Subsection (3)* provides that a dissolution, annulment or legal separation obtained from a court of civil jurisdiction in one part of the United Kingdom can be refused recognition in any other part if the dissolution, annulment or separation was obtained at a time when it was irreconcilable with an earlier decision on the existence or validity of the civil partnership, either given by a civil court in the other part of the United Kingdom, or given by a court elsewhere and recognised or entitled to be recognised in the other part.

454. *Subsection (4)* provides that, in relation to a dissolution or legal separation, recognition can be refused if the dissolution or separation was obtained at a time when, according to the law of the other part, there was no civil partnership in existence.

Section 234: Recognition in the UK of overseas dissolution, annulment or separation

455. This section provides that the validity of an overseas dissolution, annulment or legal separation is to be recognised in the United Kingdom if it is entitled to recognition either under regulations made under section 219 or under sections 235 to 237. An overseas dissolution, annulment or legal separation is defined as a dissolution or annulment of a civil partnership or a legal separation of civil partners which was obtained outside the United Kingdom. This includes a dissolution etc. obtained before the date on which this section comes into force. This could be relevant in the case of an overseas relationship which was dissolved or annulled in a country or territory outside the UK.

Section 235: Grounds for recognition

456. *Subsection (1)* provides for recognition of the validity of an overseas dissolution, annulment or legal separation obtained by proceedings if:

  (a) it is effective under the law of the country where it was obtained, and

  (b) at the relevant date (which is defined by *subsection (3)*) either civil partner was habitually resident or domiciled there or was a national of that country.

457. *Subsection (2)* provides for recognition of the validity of an overseas dissolution, annulment or legal separation obtained otherwise than by proceedings if:

  (a) it is effective under the law of the country where it was obtained,

  (b) at the relevant date:

  - both civil partners were domiciled there; or

- either civil partner was domiciled there and the other was domiciled in a country under the law of which the dissolution etc. is recognised as valid, and

(c) neither civil partner was habitually resident in the United Kingdom for the year immediately before the relevant date.

458. *Subsection (3)* defines the "relevant date". In the case of an overseas dissolution etc. obtained by means of proceedings, the relevant date is defined as the date the proceedings were commenced; in the case of an overseas dissolution etc. otherwise than by proceedings, the relevant date is defined as the date the dissolution etc. was obtained.

Section 236: Refusal of recognition

459. *Subsection (1)* provides for the refusal of recognition of the validity of an overseas dissolution, annulment or legal separation in any part of the United Kingdom if it was obtained at a time when it was irreconcilable with an earlier decision on the existence or validity of the civil partnership, either given by a civil court in that part of the United Kingdom, or given by a court elsewhere and recognised or entitled to be recognised in that part.

460. *Subsection (2)* provides for the refusal of recognition of the validity of an overseas dissolution or legal separation in any part of the United Kingdom if it was obtained at a time when according to the law of that part there was at that time no civil partnership in existence.

461. *Subsection (3)* provides for the refusal of recognition of the validity of an overseas dissolution, annulment or separation if, in relation to proceedings, reasonable steps were not taken to give notice to one of the civil partners, or one of the civil partners was for any other reason not given a reasonable opportunity to take part in the proceedings; or in the absence of proceedings, if there is no official documentation regarding the effectiveness and validity of the dissolution etc. in the country where it was obtained (or any other country where either civil partner was domiciled).

462. Recognition may also be refused in either case if recognition of the dissolution etc. would be manifestly contrary to public policy.

463. *Subsection (4)* defines the meaning of "official" in relation to the documents referred to in subsection (3) and " the relevant date" in relation to the domicile of a civil partner also referred to in that subsection. "Proceedings" is defined in section 237(5) as meaning judicial or other proceedings.

Section 237: Supplementary provisions relating to recognition of dissolution etc.

464. *Subsection (1)* provides, for the purposes of sections 235 and 236, that a civil partner is to be treated as domiciled in a country if he was domiciled in that country either according to the law of that country in family matters or according to the law of the part of the United Kingdom where the question of recognition arises.

465. *Subsection (2)* gives the Lord Chancellor or the Scottish Ministers the power to make regulations applying sections 235 and 236 and subsection (1) with modifications for countries whose territories have different systems of law in force in matters of dissolution, annulment or legal separation, or applying sections 235 and 236 with modifications in relation to an overseas dissolution etc. in relation to an overseas relationship or any case where a civil partner is domiciled in a country or territory whose law does not recognise legal relationships between persons of the same sex. Regulations may also make provision: concerning recognition of the validity of an overseas dissolution, annulment or legal separation in cases where there are cross-proceedings, for example where the validity of an order is contested;

with respect to cases where a legal separation is converted under the law of the country or territory where it is obtained into a dissolution effective under the law of that country or territory; and about proof of findings of fact in proceedings outside the UK.

466. *Subsections (3) and (4)* provide that this power is exercisable by statutory instrument, subject to the negative resolution procedure. In the case of regulations made by the Scottish Ministers this will be the negative resolution procedure in the Scottish Parliament.

467. *Subsection (6)* states that nothing in this Chapter requires recognition of any finding of fault made in proceedings for dissolution etc. or recognition of any maintenance, custody or other ancillary order made in those proceedings.

Section 238: Non-recognition elsewhere of dissolution or annulment

468. Under this section, when a court in any part of the United Kingdom has granted a dissolution or annulment of a civil partnership, or a dissolution or annulment has been recognised as valid by virtue of this chapter, the fact that the dissolution or annulment would not be recognised outside the United Kingdom does not prevent either party from entering a later marriage or civil partnership in that part of the United Kingdom or make the later marriage or civil partnership invalid in that part.

Chapter 4 – Miscellaneous and supplementary

Section 239: Commanding officers' certificates for part 2 purposes

469. This section applies to cases where two people wish to register as civil partners of each other in England and Wales and one of them ("A") is a member of the armed forces and the other resides in England and Wales. Her Majesty may by Order in Council make provision for the issue by A's commanding office of a certificate of no impediment in such cases. A certificate of no impediment is needed for the two people to register as civil partners of each other under section 20. The section follows the approach taken in the Marriage Act 1949 (c.76) in relation to persons serving in a naval vessel at sea, but extends it to all members of the armed forces.

Section 240: Certificates of no impediment to overseas relationships

470. This section permits the making of an Order in Council to allow for the issue of a certificate of no impediment where a United Kingdom national (or a Commonwealth national if prescribed in the Order in Council) intends to enter into an overseas relationship with a person who is neither a United Kingdom national nor a Commonwealth national. The Order in Council will also prescribe the countries or territories which are covered. This power will be used to make provision corresponding to the provisions of section 1(1) of the Marriage with Foreigners Act 1906 (c.40). "United Kingdom national" is defined in section 245. "Overseas relationship" is defined in sections 212 to 214.

Section 241: Transmission of certificates of registration of overseas relationships

471. This section permits the making of an Order in Council to provide for the transmission to the Registrar General of foreign certificates in relation to overseas relationships, for the issue of certified copies by the Registrar General, and for these to be received in evidence. This section will be used to make provision for civil partnerships corresponding to the provisions of section 18(2) of the Foreign Marriage Act 1892 (c.23).

Section 242: Power to make provision relating to certain Commonwealth forces

472. This section permits the making of an Order in Council to ensure that, where the law of certain Commonwealth countries makes provision corresponding to section 211 (allowing for

registration by armed forces personnel serving abroad), relationships formed under such provisions can be recognised in the UK. This will enable provision to be made, if necessary, equivalent to that which can be made under section 3(2) of the Foreign Marriage Act 1947 (c.33).

Section 243: Fees

473. *Subsection (1)* provides that the power of the Chancellor of the Exchequer under section 34(1) to make provision for fees may be used to prescribe fees in respect of things done by registration authorities, or by or on behalf of the Registrar General for England and Wales, by virtue of an Order in Council under Part 5 of the Act. This could be used, for example, to set a fee for attesting a notice of intention to register an overseas relationship under an Order in Council made under section 240 (certificates of no impediment to overseas relationships).

474. *Subsections (2)* and *(3)* provide power for the Registrar General for Scotland, with the approval of the Scottish Ministers, to make regulations prescribing fees in respect of things done by virtue of an Order in Council under Part 5 of the Act.

475. *Subsection (4)* provides that the power of the Department of Finance and Personnel in Northern Ireland under section 157(1) to make provision for fees may be used to prescribe fees in respect of things required by virtue of an Order in Council under Part 5 of the Act to be done by or on behalf of the Registrar General for Northern Ireland.

Section 244: Orders in Council: supplementary

476. This section contains supplementary provisions in relation to the powers to make an Order in Council contained in sections 210, 211 and 239 to 242. Statutory instruments containing an Order in Council under those sections are to be subject to the negative resolution procedure. This procedure applies even if other provisions are included which are made by Order in Council under existing legislation on foreign marriages, such as the Foreign Marriage Act 1892. This section also provides that Orders in Council under those sections may make different provision for different cases. This may be necessary, for example, to take account of differing local conditions in different countries. They may in addition include, for example, supplementary, consequential and transitional provisions. *Subsection (2)* makes clear that such provisions may correspond to, or apply with modifications, any provision of or made under this Act or any Act relating to marriage outside the UK

Section 245: Interpretation

477. This section defines the terms "United Kingdom national" and "Her Majesty's forces" for the purposes of this Part of the Act.

Part 6 – Relationships arising through civil partnerships

Introduction

478. The sections in this Part of the Act relate to the interpretation of references to certain familial relationships in legislation including legislation made by the Scottish Parliament and Northern Ireland legislation.

Section 246: Interpretation of statutory references to stepchildren etc.

479. This section provides that references to "step" relationships and "in-laws", in any provision to which the section applies, are to be read as including relationships arising through civil partnership.

Section 247: Provisions to which section 246 applies: Acts of Parliament etc.

480. This section applies section 246 to references in existing legislation as listed in Schedule 21. In addition, this section confers an order-making power to amend Schedule 21 and to apply section 246 to provisions of existing subordinate legislation. This section also applies section 246 to any provision of a future Act (including Acts of the Scottish Parliament) or future subordinate legislation (subject to any indication to the contrary).

Section 248: Provisions to which section 246 applies: Northern Ireland

481. This section applies section 246 to Northern Ireland legislation which is set out in Schedule 22. It confers on the Department of Finance and Personnel an order-making power to amend Schedule 22 and to apply section 246 to existing Northern Ireland subordinate legislation. Section 248 also provides that, except in so far as otherwise provided, section 246 applies to any provision in future Northern Ireland legislation, either primary or secondary.

Part 7 – Miscellaneous

Section 249: Immigration control and formation of civil partnerships

482. This section introduces Schedule 23, which contains provisions relating to the formation of civil partnerships in the United Kingdom by persons subject to immigration control.

Section 250: Gender Recognition where applicant a civil partner

483. This section amends the Gender Recognition Act 2004 to ensure that anyone who applies for recognition of his or her acquired gender under the Gender Recognition Act who is in a civil partnership is treated in the same way as someone who is married, and to make additional consequential amendments to that Act.

484. Initially, an applicant for gender recognition who is a civil partner will only receive an interim gender recognition certificate. If an interim gender recognition certificate has been issued the civil partnership is voidable under section 50(1)(d) in England and Wales or section 174(1)(d) in Northern Ireland and it may be annulled under section 37 or 161. In Scotland the civil partnership may be dissolved under section 117(2)(b). New section 5A of the Gender Recognition Act provides that a court which makes final a nullity order (or in Scotland grant a decree of dissolution) on this ground must, on doing so, issue a full gender recognition certificate. If an interim gender recognition certificate has been issued to a person and his civil partnership comes to an end in any other way, the applicant may apply to the Gender Recognition Panel for a full gender recognition certificate within certain time limits, showing that the civil partnership has ended and that the applicant has not subsequently formed a new civil partnership or married.

Section 251: Discrimination against civil partners in employment field

485. This section amends the Sex Discrimination Act 1975 (SDA) to extend the prohibition of discrimination against married persons to cover civil partners. Section 3 of the SDA explains the meaning of discrimination for the purposes of Part 2 of that Act, which contains a range of provisions prohibiting discrimination in the field of employment. . The section also amends the exception in section 7(2)(h) of the SDA (genuine occupational qualification where job is one of two to be held by a married couple) to include civil partners. Other amendments to the SDA are consequential.

Section 252: Discrimination against civil partners in employment field: Northern Ireland

486. This section amends the Sex Discrimination (Northern Ireland) Order 1976 (SI 1976/1042 (N.I. 15)) and makes provision corresponding to section 251.

Section 253: Civil partners to have an unlimited insurable interest in each other

487. This section provides that two people who are civil partners will be presumed for the purposes of section 1 of the Life Assurance Act 1774 to have an interest in each other's lives and that that interest shall be unlimited.

Section 254: Social security, child support and tax credits

488. This section introduces Schedule 24, which makes amendments to legislation governing social security, child support and tax credits. In general, civil partners will be treated in the same way as spouses and people living together as if they were civil partners will be treated in the same way as people living together as husband and wife.

489. *Subsections (2)* and *(3)* extend the general power to make further provision in connection with civil partnership which is contained in section 259. Legislation which relates to social security, child support or tax credits, and which refers to persons living together as husband and wife, may be amended so as to refer to persons who are living together as if they were civil partners. Although some amendments of this nature could be made under section 259, it was thought that there might be some borderline situations where the power in that section would not be wide enough to do this.

490. *Subsection (4)* provides that, in the same way that section 175(3), (5) and (6) of the Social Security Contributions and Benefits Act 1992 apply to the exercise of the order-making powers under that Act, those sections shall also apply to the exercise of the section 259 power in relation to social security, child support or tax credits. Subsection (3), (5), and (6) clarify, amongst other things, the cases in which the power may be used, the fact that the power may make different provision for different areas etc. There are some exceptions in section 175(3) and (5) but these are not to be taken into account in relation to the exercise of the section 259 power.

491. *Subsection (5)* makes provision for Northern Ireland that corresponds to the provision made by subsection (4) for England and Wales.

Section 255: Power to amend enactments relating to pensions

492. This section confers a power to amend various kinds of legislation relating to pensions, allowances or gratuities for the purpose of (or in connection with) making provision with respect to pensions, allowances or gratuities for surviving civil partners or dependants of deceased civil partners. All orders made under the power will be subject to the affirmative resolution procedure: *subsection (10)*.

493. The power will be used to require contracted-out defined benefit pension schemes to take account of periods of pensionable service from April 1988. Contracted-out defined contribution schemes would be required to provide survivor benefits from the protected rights accrued from April 1988, if the member is in a civil partnership at the point of retirement. Contracted-out schemes are already required to make provision for survivor benefits for legal spouses.

494. In the context of judicial pensions, allowances or gratuities, this power will be used to amend the Judicial Pensions Act 1981 and the Judicial Pensions and Retirement Act 1993 and

associated subordinate legislation in order to make the judicial pensions regime consistent with the Civil Partnership Act. The 1981 Act and the 1993 Act (together with subordinate legislation) make provision for the survivors (children and spouses) of judicial officers who die while in service or after retirement.

495. Specific references to "spouse" or to "marriage" need to be extended to refer in addition to "civil partners" and to "civil partnership". Similarly, references to children will be amended to include children of a civil partnership. Where appropriate, provisions will be extended to other relationships (e.g. step children) created as a consequence of the formation of a civil partnership in the same way as the benefits created by marriage.

Part 8 – Supplementary

Section 258: Regulations and orders

496. This section provides that powers conferred by the Act to make regulations or orders (except court orders) may be exercised so as to make different provision for different cases and different purposes and to make ancillary provision.

Section 259: Power to make further provision in connection with civil partnership

497. *Subsection (1)* confers power (which is not restricted by any other provision of the Act (see *subsection (5)*) to make, by order, supplementary, incidental, consequential, transitory, transitional or saving provision considered appropriate—

- for the general purposes of the Act,

- for any particular purpose of the Act, or

- in consequence of any provision by or under the Act or for giving effect to this Act or any provision of it.

498. This power is exercisable by a Minister of the Crown, by the Scottish Ministers in relation to a provision within the legislative competence of the Scottish Parliament, by a Northern Ireland department in relation to a provision which deals with a transferred matter, and (except in relation to a provision made by virtue of subsection (3)) by the National Assembly for Wales in relation to matters with respect to which functions are exercisable by the Assembly.

499. *Subsections (3) and (4)* provide that the power may be used to amend or revoke various kinds of legislation.

500. The power is exercisable by statutory instrument or, where it is used by a Northern Ireland department, by statutory rule. In most cases an instrument or statutory rule will be subject to the negative procedure. But if it contains any provision made by virtue of subsection (3) (such as an amendment to primary legislation) it is subject to the affirmative procedure

Section 260: Community obligations and civil partners

501. This power allows Ministers to make provision, by regulations or by Order in Council, for persons who are or have been civil partners (or whose civil partnership was void) that is the same or similar to provision made under section 2(2) of the European Communities Act 1972 which relates to persons who are or have been married (or whose marriage was void).

502. This power is available to any person who is exercising the power in section 2(2) of the European Communities Act 1972, or who would have that power if an instrument were being made under section 2(2) at the same time as the exercise of the power in this section. In

appropriate circumstances, the devolved administrations may use the power in section 2(2) of the 1972 Act, and in such circumstances, they will also be able to exercise this power.

503. *Subsection (5)* applies to instruments made under section 260 the same procedural provisions as apply to instruments made under section 2(2) of the 1972 Act.

Section 262: Extent

504. This section deals with extent. Extent is considered elsewhere in these notes.

Section 263: Commencement

505. This section provides for the coming into force of the provisions of the Act. All substantive provisions of the Act are to come into force by commencement orders. These orders will be made by the Secretary of State, except for the Scottish provisions, which will be made by the Scottish Ministers and the Northern Ireland provisions, which will be made by the Department of Finance and Personnel, both after consulting the Secretary of State. The Secretary of State must consult the Scottish Ministers or the Department of Finance and Personnel before commencing provisions in which they have an interest.

Schedules

Schedule 1 – Prohibited degrees of relationship: England and Wales

506. Part 1 of Schedule 1 contains provisions for determining when two people are within prohibited degrees of relationship, for the purposes of section 3. Section 3(1)(d) provides that two people are not eligible to register as civil partners of each other if they are within the prohibited degrees of relationship.

507. *Paragraph 1* of Schedule 1 lists the people who are absolutely prohibited from forming a civil partnership with each other (broadly speaking, blood relationships). *Paragraphs 2* and 3 list the people who are prohibited from forming a civil partnership with each other unless certain conditions are met (broadly speaking, "in-laws").

508. *Paragraph 4* applies *paragraphs 5 to 7* to those relationships set out in paragraph 2 (prohibited unless both are at least 21 and one has not lived as a child in the same household or been treated as a child of the family by the other).

509. *Paragraph 5(1)* provides that a registration authority must not record the fact that a notice of proposed civil partnership has been given unless it is satisfied by the production of evidence of age that both parties have reached 21 and it has received a declaration made by each proposed civil partner as to their affinal relationship and declaring that the younger of them has not at any time before reaching 18 been a child of the family in relation to the other (a "paragraph 5(1)(b) declaration"). *Paragraph 5(4)* requires a registration authority to record the fact that it has received a paragraph 5(1)(b) declaration and *paragraph 5(5)* requires the registration authority to file and keep such declarations.

510. *Paragraph 5(2)* allows for a High Court declaration to be accepted as evidence of no impediment of affinity to the proposed civil partnership in place of a paragraph 5(1)(b) declaration.

511. *Paragraph 5(3)* provides for the content of and the manner of signing and attesting a declaration made under paragraph 5(1)(b) to be prescribed by regulations.

512. *Paragraph 6* provides that if a registration authority receives an allegation that a paragraph 5(1)(b) declaration is false, as shown in the register, the registration authority in

whose area it is proposed the registration take place must not issue a civil partnership schedule unless a High Court declaration is obtained under paragraph 7.

513. *Paragraph 7* provides for either of the proposed civil partners to apply to the High Court to obtain a declaration confirming there is no impediment of affinity, due to the fact that the qualifications which prevent a civil partnership within the degrees of relationship from being prohibited under paragraph 2 are met.

514. *Paragraph 8* provides that an objection under section 13 to the issue of a civil partnership schedule does not apply in relation to a civil partnership to which paragraphs 5 to 7 apply unless it relates to a ground other than the affinity between the proposed civil partners.

515. *Paragraph 9* provides for evidence of age and relevant deaths to be produced where two people, within the degrees of relationship which under paragraph 3 are prohibited unless both are at least 21 and certain relatives have died, intend to register as civil partners of each other.

Schedule 2 – Civil partnerships of persons under 18: England and Wales

516. *Paragraph 1* Schedule 2 sets out in table form the appropriate persons or bodies required to give consent to the civil partnership of a child and *paragraph 2* defines certain terms used in the table. "Child" is defined in section 4(5) to mean a person who is under the age of 18.

517. No consent is required if the child is a surviving civil partner: see section 4(3).

518. *Paragraph 3* deals with the situation where a person's consent to a child registering as a civil partner is unobtainable and sets out the circumstances in which that consent can be dispensed with or an application can be made to the court for consent. "The court" is defined in paragraph 15.

519. *Paragraph 4* enables a court to give consent in cases where the appropriate person's consent has been refused.

520. *Paragraph 5* provides that if one of the proposed civil partners is a child the necessary declaration under section 8 must either state that consent has been obtained or state that there is nobody whose consent is required. The necessary declaration is the declaration that accompanies each notice of proposed civil partnership.

521. *Paragraph 6* enables a person whose consent is required to a child and another person registering as civil partners of each otherto forbid the issue of a civil partnership schedule if a notice of proposed civil partnership in relation to that child has been recorded in the register. If the issue of a civil partnership schedule is forbidden the notice and all proceedings on it are void. However, a person cannot forbid the issue of a civil partnership schedule if the court has given its consent under paragraphs 3 or 4.

522. *Paragraph 7* provides that if a person declares that the consent of a person whose consent is required has been given, the registration authority may nevertheless refuse to issue the civil partnership schedule unless written evidence is produced that consent has in fact been given.

523. *Paragraph 8* provides an exception to the duty in section 14(1) to issue a civil partnership schedule. This duty does not apply if the issue of a civil partnership schedule has been forbidden under paragraph 6.

524. *Paragraph 9* provides that if a civil partnership schedule is issued in relation to a proposed civil partnership between a child and another person, it must contain a statement that its issue has not been forbidden under paragraph 6.

525. *Paragraphs 10 to 14* make broadly corresponding provision in respect of the special procedure.

526. *Paragraph 15* defines "the court" for the purposes of Schedule 2 and provides for rules of court to be made in relation to applications made under the provisions of this Schedule.

Schedule 3 – Registration by former spouses one of whom has changed sex

527. Schedule 3 makes it possible for two parties to a marriage, who wish to stay together when one of them is changing gender, to have their marriage annulled and to register as civil partners of each other on the same day if so desired. Schedule 3 applies if a court makes absolute a decree of nullity granted on the ground that an interim gender recognition certificate has been issued to the party to the marriage (or, in Scotland, after granting a divorce on that ground) and on doing so, issues a full gender recognition certificate (under section 5(1) of the Gender Recognition Act 2004) and the parties wish to register a civil partnership without delay. In order to make use of the provisions in the Schedule, the parties must give notice of proposed civil partnership within "the relevant period".

528. *Paragraph 2* defines "the relevant period" as the period beginning with the issue of the full gender recognition certificate and ending 1 month after the day of issue.

529. *Paragraph 3* provides for Chapter 1 of Part 2 to apply with the modifications set out in *paragraphs 4 to 6* if each of the parties gives notice of proposed civil partnership during the "relevant period" and makes an election under this paragraph.

530. *Paragraph 4* modifies the standard procedure to allow a couple to register as civil partners without the proposed civil partnership being publicised or a waiting period needing to be completed before the civil partnership schedule is issued. The applicable period (during which the signing of the civil partnership schedule may take place) is the period of one month from the day on which notices of proposed civil partnership are given or if given on different days, the earlier of those days (instead of 12 months as in section 17).

531. *Paragraphs 5 and 6* make consequential modifications of the procedure for housebound persons and the procedure for detained persons. In both cases the period during which registration may take is the same as for the standard procedure (see the discussion of *paragraph 4*).

532. *Paragraph 7* extends the provisions of this Schedule to certain non-residents. It applies where two people wish to register as civil partners of each other in England and Wales but one of them ("A") resides in Scotland or Northern Ireland or is a member of the armed forces serving outside the United Kingdom. In such a case A is not required to give a notice of proposed civil partnership. But the civil partnership schedule will not be issued by a registration authority unless one of the proposed civil partners produces a certificate of no impediment issued to A under section 97, 150 or 239.

Schedule 4 – Wills, the administration of estates and family provision

533. Schedule 4 amends legislation relating to wills, the administration of estates and family provision to ensure that civil partners are given the same rights as married people.

534. *Paragraph 2* inserts new sections 18B and 18C in the Wills Act 1837. The effect of these amendments is that, with the same limited exceptions as apply to marriage, a will is

revoked when the testator forms a civil partnership with someone. They will also - once the civil partnership has been dissolved, annulled or made the subject of a presumption of death order - prevent former civil partners, where named as executors in the will, from becoming executors, and former civil partners named as beneficiaries in the will, from inheriting, unless the will provides otherwise.

535. *Paragraph 3* applies the provisions of the Wills Act 1837 and the Wills Act 1968 so as to prevent the passing of gifts to a civil partner who attests the signature of the testator except where the will would have been valid without that signature.

536. *Paragraph 4* amends section 16 of the Wills Act 1837 so that where the civil partner of a creditor of the testator witnesses the will, he or she may be admitted as a witness in proceedings about the will.

537. *Paragraph 5* provides that the deceased's civil partner has priority over the issue of the testator should the testator bequeath the same gift separately to both of them.

538. *Paragraph 6* amends section 6 of the Public Trustee Act 1906 to place surviving civil partners in the same position as surviving spouses in having priority over the Public Trustee in being granted probate or letters of administration.

539. *Paragraph 7* amends section 46 of the Administration of Estates Act 1925 to allow surviving civil partners to inherit the estate of their deceased civil partner under the intestacy rules in the same way as surviving spouses.

540. *Paragraph 8* amends section 47 of the 1925 Act so that an intestate's residuary estate is held on trust for those of his children (or their issue if they predecease the intestate) who reach the age of 18, or marry, or form a civil partnership, under that age.

541. *Paragraph 9* amends section 47A of the 1925 Act so as to provide that surviving civil partners shall have the same right as surviving spouses to redeem their life interest in their share of the intestate's residuary estate.

542. *Paragraph 10* amends section 48 of the 1925 Act so as to provide that a personal representative shall have the same power to raise sums in respect of a surviving civil partner's interest as they do in respect of a surviving spouse's interest.

543. *Paragraph 11* amends section 51 of the 1925 Act so that where a minor who is equitably entitled to property under a trust dies he is deemed to have had a life interest in the property if he has married nor formed a civil partnership.

544. *Paragraph 12* amends section 55(1)(xviii) of the 1925 Act by adding a reference to the formation of a civil partnership to the definition of "valuable consideration".

545. *Paragraph 13* amends section 5 of and Schedule 2 to the Intestates' Estate Act 1952 by allowing the surviving civil partner to acquire the home he or she has shared with the deceased civil partner.

546. *Paragraph 14* amends section 1 of the Family Provision Act 1966 to allow increases in the fixed net sum which a surviving civil partner may receive from the estate of their deceased civil partner.

547. *Paragraph 15* amends section 1 of the Inheritance (Provision for Family and Dependants) Act 1975 by adding civil partners and former civil partners to the class of persons entitled to make an application for reasonable financial provision from the estate of their deceased civil partner. The amendment to section 1 of the 1975 Act also allows an application for financial provision from the deceased's estate to be made by a person, if for

the whole of the period of two years ending immediately before the date when the deceased died the person was living in the same household as the deceased and as if s/he was the civil partner of the deceased. This is done to preserve the effect of the decision in Ghaidan v. Mendoza 2004 UKHL 30.

548. *Paragraph 16* amends section 2 of the 1975 Act by extending the court's powers to enable it to make orders varying any settlement made on the civil partners either during the civil partnership, or in anticipation of one being formed, including any variation in favour of any children of both the civil partners or of any person treated by the civil partners as a child of the family in relation to the civil partnership.

549. *Paragraph 17* amends section 3 of the 1975 Act by providing that the court, when considering an application for reasonable financial provision from the deceased's estate by a civil partner or a former civil partner, shall take into account the duration of the civil partnership and what the applicant might have received had the civil partnership been ended by being dissolved instead of by death.

550. *Paragraph 18* amends section 3(2A) of the 1975 Act. Section 3(2A) of the 1975 Act sets out additional matters to which the court shall have regard when an application for financial provision from a deceased's estate is made by a person who lived as the husband or wife of the deceased. The amendment to section 3(2A) ensures that the court shall also have regard to these additional matters when a person, who lived with the deceased as his or her civil partner, makes an application.

551. *Paragraph 19* amends section 6 of the 1975 Act by adding the formation of a subsequent civil partnership as an exception to the events that can cause an order for periodical payment to cease to have effect.

552. *Paragraph 20* inserts a new section 14A into the 1975 Act. Section 14A provides that if a civil partner dies within a year of the making of a dissolution, nullity or separation order in relation to the civil partnership, and no application for financial provision has been made or determined, the court may treat a surviving civil partner who applies for an order under the 1975 Act as if the dissolution, nullity or separation order had not been made.

553. *Paragraph 21* inserts a new section 15ZA into the 1975 Act. Section 15ZA empowers the court, when making an order to end a civil partnership either by dissolution, or by nullity, or by separation or by presumption of death, (or at any time after making such an order), to order that neither of the civil partners, on the death of the other, shall be allowed to make an application for reasonable financial provision out of the deceased partner's estate.

554. *Paragraph 22* inserts a new section 15B into the 1975 Act. Section 15B extends the powers contained in section 15ZA to civil partnerships that were ended overseas.

555. *Paragraph 23* amends section 16 of the 1975 Act so that a court hearing an application for reasonable financial provision from the deceased's estate can vary or discharge secured periodical payments orders made prior to the death of the deceased under Schedule 4 to the Act.

556. *Paragraph 24* amends section 17 of the 1975 Act to allow for the court hearing an application for reasonable financial provision from the deceased's estate to vary or revoke any maintenance agreement made between civil partners prior to the death of one of them.

557. *Paragraph 25* inserts a new section 18A into the 1975 Act. Section 18A provides that where a civil partner has been ordered by the court to pay a secured periodical payment to their civil partner or has entered into a maintenance agreement with their civil partner, and

then has died, the surviving civil partner's subsequent application to have the payment order or the maintenance agreement varied or discharged, may be treated as though it was accompanied by an application by them for reasonable financial provision from the estate of the deceased civil partner. The court may then make any order that it could have made on an application under the 1975 Act.

558. *Paragraph 26* amends section 19 of the 1975 Act so that its scope covers civil partners, former civil partners and the formation of civil partnerships.

559. *Paragraph 27* amends section 25 of the 1975 Act, the interpretation section, to insert references to civil partners and civil partnership as appropriate.

Schedule 5 – Financial relief in the High Court or a county court etc.

560. Schedule 5 provides for financial relief when a civil partnership is brought to an end and provides corresponding rights to those available to married people.

Part 1 - Financial provision in connection with dissolution, nullity or separation

561. This Part outlines the circumstances in which the High Court or a county court (with jurisdiction) can make an order for financial provision. A court may award financial provision when making a dissolution, nullity or separation order or at any time afterwards. When making financial provision the court has a number of orders available to it. They are listed in *paragraph 2*. The court may, for example, make an order for a lump sum or for periodical payments to be made from one civil partner to the other or to a child of the family, or to a particular person for the benefit of a child of the family. The court can order periodical payments to be secured by means of a charge or other arrangement. Similarly a court may order a lump sum to be paid by instalments and for the instalments to be secured by a charge on property.

Part 2 - Property adjustment on or after dissolution, nullity or separation.

562. This Part allows for property adjustment orders to be made on or after dissolution, nullity or separation. In the case of a dissolution or nullity order the property adjustment can only take effect after the dissolution or nullity order has been made final.

Part 3 - Sale of property orders

563. This Part provides for orders for sale of specified property in which either or both civil partners have a beneficial interest. The sale of property order can contain supplementary or consequential provisions, in particular it can include provision for payments out of the proceeds of the sale or for the property to be offered for sale to a particular person or group of people. In the case of a dissolution or nullity order the sale of property order can only take effect after the dissolution or nullity order has been made final. Where an order for sale of property contains a provision that the sale of the property can be used to secure regular payments, then such an order would cease to have effect on the death, re-marriage of or formation of a subsequent civil partnership by the civil partner in whose favour the order had been made. The court can direct when the order for sale should take place and there are provisions for third parties with interests in the property to make representations.

Part 4 - Pension sharing orders on or after dissolution or nullity order

564. This Part provides for a pension sharing order to be made so that both civil partners share the benefit of the value of a pension that had previously been held by only one of the civil partners. The value of the pension is effectively split and the court specifies the amount (in percentage terms) transferred to the other civil partner. The court can apportion any

charge made by the person responsible for a pension arrangement. A pension sharing order cannot be made in respect of a pension that is, or has already been, the subject of a pension sharing order between the same two civil partners, or where there is already in force an order under Part 6 in relation to the same pension. The order can only take effect after the dissolution or nullity order has been made final. The Lord Chancellor, in regulations, can set a minimum period before a pension sharing order can take effect.

Part 5 - Matters to which the court is to have regard under Parts 1 to 4

565. This Part sets out the matters which the court must consider when deciding whether to exercise its powers to make orders under the preceding four Parts. Whilst all the circumstances of the case have to be considered the first consideration has to be given to any child of the family under 18 years old. The criteria the court must consider under this Part are parallel to those contained in section 25 of the Matrimonial Causes Act 1973 and reflect the relative financial positions of the civil partners, their current and future obligations, their age and the duration of the civil partnership and the contributions each civil partner has made to the welfare of the family, whether in financial terms or by caring or looking after the home. The conduct of each civil partner will be taken into account if it would be unfair to disregard it. When exercising the powers in relation to a child of the family the court has to consider the financial needs and resources of the child in addition to the financial position of the civil partners. Where a child is not a child of one of the civil partners the court needs to look at any responsibility that civil partner had assumed for the child and the duration of such responsibility. The court has to consider the appropriateness of the orders under Parts 1 to 4 in respect of termination of financial dependence or involvement.

Part 6 - Making of Part 1 orders having regard to pension benefits

566. This Part makes further provisions about orders under Part 1 relating to pensions. The effect of this Part may be summarised as follows. When deciding what orders to make the court must take into account pension arrangements. A court may order the person responsible for a pension arrangement to pay a civil partner a percentage of the payments due to the other civil partner. A civil partner with pension rights may be ordered to exercise any right of commutation that he has under a pension arrangement. The court has power to make orders about the payment of lumps sums payable in respect of a civil partner's death.

Part 7 – Pension Protection Fund compensation etc.

567. This Part contains provisions concerning Pension Protection Fund compensation, which apply where financial relief has been applied for or granted in accordance with the Schedule. It provides that:

- when the court is deciding what orders to make in relation to financial provision following a dissolution, nullity or separation order, it is to take into account any compensation from the Pension Protection Fund (PPF) to which a civil partner is or might be entitled;

- the PPF Board is to implement pension sharing orders made before the Board took over responsibility for the pension scheme, including those orders made during the Assessment period (when the pension scheme is being considered for being taken over by PPF);

- the PPF will implement attachment orders made before the PPF took over responsibility for the scheme including those made during the Assessment period, when the pension scheme is being considered for being taken over by the PPF;

- where the court makes a pension sharing order or a pension attachment order and the PPF Board subsequently assumes responsibility for the scheme, that does not affect the powers of the court to vary or discharge the order or to suspend or revive any provision of it. Also, the assumption of responsibility by the PPF Board does not affect, on appeal, the powers of the appeal court to affirm, reinstate, set aside or vary the order;

- where an order under Part 1 of the Schedule includes a provision requiring the civil partner with pension rights to exercise his right of commutation under an occupational pension scheme to any extent and the PPF Board has assumed responsibility for the scheme before the requirement is complied with, then the order has effect with modifications as may be prescribed by regulations;

- it is to be possible for provision to be made in the future for the court to make an order relating to death benefits during the Assessment period which is conditional on the scheme coming out of the Assessment period and the PPF Board not taking over responsibility for it;

- regulations may make such consequential modifications of any provision of Schedule 5 (or of any provision made by virtue of Schedule 5) as appear to the Lord Chancellor necessary or expedient to give effect to the provisions of Part 7;

The court does not have power to make an attachment order or pension sharing order against the PPF.

Part 8 - Maintenance pending outcome of dissolution, nullity or separation proceedings

568. This Part allows for the court to order one of the civil partners to make periodical payments for maintenance for the other civil partner before the final outcome of the dissolution, nullity or separation proceedings has been determined.

Part 9 - Failure to maintain: financial provision (and interim orders)

569. This Part allows either civil partner to apply to the court because the other civil partner has failed to maintain them adequately or has failed to provide for, or make a proper contribution towards, the welfare of any child of the family. The court is empowered to make a range of orders, including orders for periodical payments for a set period of time, a lump sum payment and an order to secure payments. The court may make an order in favour of the other civil partner, the child of the family or another person for the benefit of the child. An order for a lump sum payment can be made to cover reasonable expenses and liabilities incurred in maintaining the applicant or any child of the family before the application was made. Where there is immediate need of financial assistance an interim order can be made. The Part sets out the matters the court must consider when deciding whether proper maintenance has been provided, which are the same as used in other financial provision cases as set out in Part 5 of the Schedule.

Part 10 - Commencement of certain proceedings and duration of certain orders

570. This Part establishes that, subject to any rules of court, applications for financial provision can be commenced at any time after the application for a dissolution, nullity or separation order. The Part also contains provisions about the circumstances when orders will

cease to have effect or are not available, for example when a child of the family reaches the age of 18 and where a civil partner in receipt of periodical payment marries or forms a subsequent civil partnership. It also deals with applications for periodical payments where a maintenance calculation is still in force.

Part 11 - Variation, discharge etc of certain orders for financial relief

571. This Part confers various supplementary powers on a court in respect of an order made under Schedule 5. The court may vary or discharge the order, suspend any provision of it or revive the operation of any suspended provision. It may also remit (cancel) arrears. Part 11 contains a number of further detailed provisions about the exercise of these powers.

Part 12 - Arrears and repayments

572. This Part deals with arrears and repayments and provides that arrears cannot be enforced without the leave of the court. In certain circumstances the court may order repayment of a sum which ought not to have been paid. For example, if a periodical payments order has ceased to have effect because the recipient has married or formed a new civil partnership the court may order the repayment of any money overpaid by mistake.

Part 13 - Consent orders and maintenance agreements

573. In this Part provisions are made for civil partners to reach agreement on the terms of financial orders and for the court to make an order (a consent order) on terms as set out by the parties and presented to the court. There are also provisions for agreements to be altered by the court during the lives of the parties, restrictions on applications to magistrates' courts for maintenance and provisions relating to the duration and limits of periodical and secured periodical payments where those provisions are inserted into an agreement to alter it. This Part also provides for agreements to be altered after the death of one of the parties, if an agreement for maintenance allows for payments after the death of one of the parties.

Part 14 - Miscellaneous and supplementary

574. This Part provides: for the court to make orders overturning transactions carried out in an attempt to defeat financial orders under the Schedule; provisions for a settlement to be overturned on the bankruptcy of the person who made it; for orders for payments made to a person suffering from a mental disorder to be paid to another person and; for appeals when a pension order has taken effect. This Part also defines a number of terms used in the Schedule.

Schedule 6 - Financial relief in magistrates' courts etc.

575. Schedule 6 provides for civil partners to apply to magistrates' courts for maintenance for themselves and children of the family.

Part 1 - Failure to maintain etc: financial provision

576. This Part sets out the circumstances in which an order can be made and the types of orders which can be made. The court can make an order for lump sum payments or periodical payments to be made if it is satisfied that a civil partner has not made reasonable provision to maintain the applicant or a child of the family. A lump sum payment can take into consideration expenses or liabilities reasonably incurred in maintaining the applicant or child prior to the making of the order. The Part sets out the matters the court is to take into account when determining what orders it should make both in respect of civil partners and in respect of children. These include, amongst other things, the financial resources of the applicant and the civil partner concerned and the financial needs, earning capacity and education of the child. Where the child of the family is not the respondent's child the court must also consider

whether anyone else is liable to maintain the child and whether the respondent has assumed any responsibility to maintain the child. Whilst the court must have regard to all the circumstances of the case, the welfare of any child under the age of 18 should be the first consideration. The court can adjourn the proceedings if the civil partners wish to attempt a reconciliation and must refuse to make an order if an application to the High Court (under Part 9 of Schedule 5) is more appropriate.

Part 2 - Orders for agreed financial provision

577. This Part allows civil partners to apply to the court for a financial provision order on the ground that the other civil partner has agreed to make financial provision for them or for a child of the family. The court has power to make alternative orders if both civil partners agree.

Part 3 - Orders of court where civil partners are living apart by agreement

578. This Part allows the court to make orders for periodical payments for maintenance to be made by one civil partner to the other for that civil partner or for a child of the family. Such orders can be made where the civil partners have been living apart for a continuous period exceeding 3 months and one of the civil partners has been making periodical payments during that three-month period. However, the court cannot order the civil partner to make payments which, during any period of three months, would amount to more than he paid over the three months prior to the application. If the court considers that an order under this Part would not provide reasonable maintenance for the civil partner or for a child of the family, the court may treat the application as if it were an application for an order under Part 1. The matters which the court must take into account when making an order under this Part are the same as those in Part 1.

Part 4 - Interim orders

579. This Part allows the court to make interim orders when applications have been made under any of the provisions in Parts 1, 2 and 3. The interim order will require the civil partner to make periodic payments to the applicant or to a child of the family. The court can set the date when payments under the order begin and when the order ceases to have effect. However, the start date cannot be prior to the date of an application for an order under Part 1, 2 or 3. The order will also cease to have effect when the court makes its final decision on the application or 3 months after the date on which the interim order was made, whichever is earlier.

Part 5 - Commencement and duration of orders under Parts 1, 2 and 3

580. This Part makes provision for when orders made under Parts 1, 2 and 3 can begin, age limits for making orders for children (the court cannot make an order in favour of a child over the age of 18 unless the child is in full-time education or undergoing training) and the length of time for which the orders can remain in force. Orders will cease to apply if the civil partners live with each other for a continuous period of 6 months.

Part 6 - Variation etc. of orders

581. This Part sets out the powers the courts have to vary or revoke periodical payment orders and to suspend or revive any provision of the orders. The court has power to order a lump sum payment in place of an order for periodical payments and vary a periodical payment order by specifying when such an order is to come into effect. The Part sets out the procedure for making such an order and the matters which the court is to consider when exercising its powers under this Part. Either civil partner can apply to have an order varied, as

can a child of 16 or over in relation to orders for periodical payments to or in respect of a child.

Part 7 - Arrears and repayments

582. This Part deals with arrears and repayments and provides the court with powers for the enforcement of orders. It also allows for sums paid under an order after it had ceased to have an effect, because the person entitled to receive the sums had married or had formed a subsequent civil partnership, to be refunded. The magistrates' court will have power to enforce the order in the same way as it can enforce any other maintenance order.

Part 8 - Supplementary

583. This Part ensures that the interests of children are taken into account before a decision is made on an application, and applies various ancillary provisions of the Domestic Proceedings and Magistrates' Court Act (such as those relating to appeals). It also stipulates that the jurisdiction of the magistrates' court under this Schedule be exercisable even if one of the parties is not domiciled in England and Wales.

Schedule 7 - Financial relief in England and Wales after overseas dissolution etc. of a civil partnership

584. This Schedule provides for applications in courts in England and Wales for financial relief following the dissolution, annulment or legal separation of civil partners as a result of legal proceedings in an overseas country. The provisions correspond to those available for overseas divorces etc in Part 3 of the Matrimonial and Family Proceedings Act 1984. Regulations made under section 219 will deal with the validity of overseas dissolutions, annulments and legal separations in member States as defined in section 219, subsection (4).

Part 1 Financial relief

585. Part 1 provides that the Schedule will apply where a civil partnership has been dissolved or annulled or the civil partners have been legally separated in an overseas country and the dissolution etc is entitled to be recognised as valid in England and Wales. For the circumstances in which an overseas dissolution, annulment or legal separation is entitled to be recognised in England and Wales see sections 234 to 237 (and note section 234(2) and the power to make regulations under section 219 for the recognition of orders made in an EU member State).

586. Under *paragraph 2* either civil partner may apply to the court for orders under *paragraph 9* or *13* of the Schedule. However, under *paragraph 3* no application will be possible if the applicant has subsequently formed a new civil partnership or married. *Paragraph 4* provides that the courts' permission is required for an application to be made.

587. Under *paragraph 5* where it appears to the court that the applicant or a child of the family is in need of immediate assistance, an interim order for maintenance may be made in favour of the applicant or the child.

588. *Paragraph 7* sets out the circumstances in which the court has jurisdiction to hear an application under the Schedule. One of the civil partners must be domiciled or have been habitually resident in England and Wales for a period of one year when the application is made or when the civil partnership was dissolved or annulled or the order for legal separation was made. Alternatively either or both of the civil partners must have an interest in a dwelling-house in England and Wales on the date of application for leave to apply which was at some time during the civil partnership a civil partnership home of the civil partners.

589. *Paragraph 8* provides that the court must consider whether England and Wales is the appropriate venue for the application, and outlines the criteria the court is to take into account when considering this. If the court is not satisfied that England and Wales is the appropriate venue it must dismiss the application.

590. *Paragraph 9* describes the orders that the court is able to make on applications under this Schedule. The court may make the same orders for financial provision as are available under Part 1, 2 and 4 of Schedule 5 to the Act for civil partnerships formed in England and Wales, including orders for property adjustment and pension sharing if the civil partnership has been dissolved or annulled. If the civil partners are legally separated the court may make orders for financial provision and property adjustment as provided in Parts 1 and 2 of Schedule 5 to the Act.

591. *Paragraph 10* sets out the matters to which the court must have regard when exercising its powers under this Schedule, which are the same as those to be considered when making financial provision following a dissolution, annulment or legal separation order made in England and Wales.

592. *Paragraph 11* restricts the court's powers when its jurisdiction to deal with the application arises only from the fact that the civil partnership home is situated in England and Wales.

593. *Paragraph 12* provides for the court to make an order on terms agreed by the civil partners (a consent order).

594. *Paragraph 13* provides for the court to order transfer of tenancies of dwelling houses.

595. *Paragraph 14* applies certain provisions of Schedule 5 to interim orders or orders for financial provision, property adjustment and pension sharing made under paragraphs 5 and 9 of this Schedule.

596. *Paragraph 15* provides for the avoidance of transactions designed to defeat claims under paragraphs 5 and 9. Where one of the civil partners (A) is granted leave to make an application for an order under paragraph 9 and the court is satisfied that the other civil partner (B) is, with the intention of defeating a claim by A, about to deal with any property, it may make an order restraining B from doing so. Paragraph 15 also provides that where one civil partner (A) is granted leave to make an application under paragraph 9 or where an order has been made under paragraph 5 or 9 and the other civil partner (B) has, with the intention of defeating a claim by A, made a disposition, then the court may in certain circumstances set aside the disposition.

597. *Paragraph 16* provides circumstances in which it can be presumed, for the purposes of paragraph 15, that the person who disposed of or is about to dispose of property did so, or is about to do so, with the intention of defeating the other civil partner's claim.

Part 2 - Steps to prevent avoidance prior to application for leave under paragraph 4

598. Part 2 provides the court with powers to make such orders as it thinks fit restraining a party from making any disposition or transfer out of the jurisdiction intended to defeat the other party's prospective claim. The court may only make an order under this Part where the applicant intends to apply for leave to make an application for an order under paragraph 9 as soon as he or she has been habitually resident in England and Wales for one year.

Part 3 - Supplementary

599. Part 3 defines various terms for the purposes of this Schedule and provides that the provisions relating to avoidance and prevention of transactions are without prejudice to any power of the High Court to grant injunctions under section 37 of the Supreme Court Act 1981.

Schedule 8 – Housing and tenancies

600. Schedule 8 amends a range of enactments relating to housing and tenancies, in order to ensure equality of treatment between spouses and civil partners. In addition, where these enactments refer to two persons living together as husband and wife, they are amended to refer also to two persons living together as civil partners. This is done to preserve the effect of the decision in Ghaidan v Mendoza 2004 UKHL 30 that such references to persons living together as husband and wife should be interpreted, consistently with the Human Rights Act 1998, as including same-sex couples who live together. Schedule 8 extends only to England and Wales.

601. *Paragraph 1* extends section 149(6) of the Law of Property Act 1925 so as to apply to civil partnership as it does to marriage. It provides that where a lease, underlease or contract to enter into a lease is expressed to be determinable on the formation of a civil partnership, the arrangement will take effect as a lease for a term of 90 years determinable after the formation of the civil partnership by notice in writing.

602. *Paragraph 2* amends paragraph 1(e) of Schedule 3 to the Landlord and Tenant Act 1954. The 1954 Act provides security of tenure for residential tenants on the termination of long tenancies at low rents. Landlords can only seek possession on specified grounds, i.e. those specified in Schedule 3. One of the grounds is that the premises are required by the landlord as a residence for him or for specified members of his family, including his or her spouse's father or mother. This ground is amended so that the father or mother of the landlord's civil partner is included.

603. *Paragraphs 3 to 7* amend the Leasehold Reform Act 1967. This Act enables tenants of houses held on long leases at low rents to acquire the freehold or an extended lease.

604. *Paragraph 3* amends section 1(1ZC), which excludes tenancies under Part 2 of the Landlord and Tenant Act 1954 (business tenancies) from the definition of long lease, unless one of the specified exceptions applies. One of the specified exceptions is that the tenancy is a tenancy taking effect under section 149(6) of the Law of Property Act 1925 (leases terminable after a death or marriage). Paragraph 3 amends the parenthetical words to include a reference to formation of a civil partnership.

605. *Paragraph 4* amends section 1B, which provides that tenancies terminable by notice after death or marriage carry the right to enfranchisement only, not the right to an extension of the lease. Section 1B is amended to refer also to tenancies terminable by notice after the formation of a civil partnership.

606. *Paragraph 5* amends section 3, which governs the meaning of "long tenancy" for Part 1 of the Act. The term includes leases terminable after a death or marriage, and this is amended to add a lease terminable after the formation of a civil partnership, consequential upon the change made by paragraph 1 to section 149(6) of the Law of Property Act 1925. A tenancy terminable by notice after a death or marriage is not to be treated as a long tenancy in certain circumstances - a change is made to refer also to tenancies terminable by notice after the formation of a civil partnership.

607. *Paragraph 6* amends section 7). Section 7 governs the rights of a family succeeding to a tenancy on the death of the tenant. Subsection (7) defines the members of a family who are entitled to succeed to a tenancy. Subsection (8) permits a surviving spouse, in certain circumstances, to appropriate a tenancy in satisfaction of his or her interest in their deceased spouse's estate. Both subsections include several references to "wife or husband". The amendment substitutes "spouse or civil partner".

608. *Paragraph 7* amends section 18(3). Section 18 empowers the landlord to apply for a declaratory order that he may resume possession of the property on the ground that it is required by him for occupation as his residence, or as a residence for an adult member of his family. The definition of member of the family in subsection (3) includes numerous references to "wife or husband". The amendment substitutes "spouse or civil partner".

609. *Paragraph 8* amends the Caravan Sites Act 1968. Section 3 of the 1968 Act concerns the protection of persons occupying caravans under residential contracts against eviction or harassment. Section 3 is amended so that surviving civil partners are entitled to the same protection as widows and widowers.

610. *Paragraphs 9* and *10* amend sections 3 and 4 of the Rent (Agriculture) Act 1976 to give surviving civil partners of a tenant of a protected or statutory tenancy of agricultural land the same rights as a surviving spouse. The amendment to section 4(5A) provides that, for the purposes of section 4(3) of the 1976 Act, a person who was living with the original occupier as if they were civil partners shall be treated as the civil partner of the occupier.

611. *Paragraph 11* amends the right of the Secretary of State in England and the National Assembly for Wales to obtain information about certain tenancies of agricultural land so that the right applies in relation to a civil partner of a person who has been employed in agriculture as it applies in relation to a spouse of such a person.

612. *Paragraph 12* amends one of the grounds for possession applicable to protected occupancies or statutory tenancies of agricultural land. Landlords can only seek possession on specified grounds, i.e. those specified in Schedule 4 of the 1976 Act. One of the grounds is that the premises are required by the landlord as a residence for him or for specified members of his family, including his or her spouse's father, mother or grandparents. This ground is amended so that the father, mother and grandparents of the landlord's civil partner are included.

613. *Paragraphs 13* and *14* amend the Rent Act 1977. Paragraph 13 gives surviving civil partners the same right to succeed to a statutory tenancy as surviving spouses. For these purposes, cohabitants who were living together as if they were civil partners are treated in the same way as civil partners. Paragraph 14 amends the grounds for possession applicable to Rent Act tenancies to equalise the position of spouses and civil partners.

614. *Paragraph 15* amends the Protection from Eviction Act 1977. This amendment extends the protection from eviction from agricultural land afforded to a spouse to a surviving civil partner of an agricultural worker. The provisions apply where an agricultural worker occupied premises under the terms of his employment but his tenancy or licence was not a statutory tenancy under the Rent (Agriculture) Act 1976.

615. *Paragraph 16* amends section 54 of the Housing Act 1980. Section 54 provides that a protected shorthold tenancy may not be assigned except under the terms of a court order in matrimonial or family proceedings. This amendment adds orders in connection with civil partnership proceedings to the list of relevant proceedings.

616. *Paragraph 17* makes consequential amendments to the Housing Act 1980 to reflect the amendments made to the Rent (Agriculture) Act 1976.

617. *Paragraphs 18 to 35* amend the Housing Act 1985 ("the 1985 Act").

618. *Paragraph 18* amends the definition of an "exempted disposal" of land in section 39. Where a local authority has voluntarily disposed of land under section 32 of the 1985 Act in certain areas, including National Parks, the conveyance, assignment or grant may include limitations on any subsequent disposal other than an exempted disposal. Section 39 defines an exempted disposal as including a disposal to a qualifying person. Paragraph 18 adds civil partners and former civil partners to the list of qualifying persons.

619. *Paragraph 19* provides further that disposals made under a property adjustment order or orders for the sale of property in connection with civil partnership proceedings will count as exempt disposals.

620. *Paragraphs 20 to 22* amend sections 87 to 89 of the 1985 Act, which concern succession to a secure tenancy. A person is only qualified to succeed to a secure tenancy if he meets the requirements of section 87 and the tenant did not himself succeed to the tenancy. The amendment to section 87 ensures that a civil partner has the same rights to succeed to a secure tenancy as a spouse. The amendment to section 88 adds court orders for the assignment of a tenancy in connection with civil partnership to the list of assignments which do not count as a succession. Section 89 sets out the procedure to follow if there is more than one person qualified to succeed to a periodic secure tenancy. The amendment to subsection (2)(a) means that civil partners, like spouses, will be given preference over other classes of qualifying successors. Subsection (3)(a) states that if there is no person qualifying to succeed to the tenancy then that tenancy ceases to be a secure tenancy unless a disposal is made in accordance with certain court orders. The amendment to subsection 3(a) adds property adjustment orders made in connection with civil partnership proceedings.

621. *Paragraph 23* amends section 90(3), which concerns devolution of a fixed term secure tenancy on the death of the tenant. Such a tenancy ceases to be a secure tenancy unless it passes to a person qualified to succeed or an assignment is made in pursuance of certain court orders. This paragraph adds disposals made under a property adjustment order in connection with civil partnership proceedings to that list of court orders.

622. *Paragraph 24* amends section 91 which prevents the assignment of a secure tenancy unless the assignment falls within one of the exceptions listed in subsection (3). These include an exception for any assignment made in pursuance of a court order in matrimonial or family proceedings. This amendment adds to the list of exceptions, any assignment made under a property adjustment order in connection with civil partnership proceedings.

623. *Paragraph 25* amends section 99B of the 1985 Act. Section 99A confers power on the Secretary of State to make regulations requiring tenants to be paid compensation for improvements when a secure tenancy comes to an end. This applies only if certain conditions are met. Section 99B sets out the people who qualify for compensation. The amendment adds to the list of qualifying persons any person to whom the tenancy was assigned by the improving tenant in pursuance of a property adjustment order under this Act.

624. *Paragraph 26* amends section 101(3)(c) of the 1985 Act. Section 101 states that the rent on a property should not be increased on account of the improvements the tenant has made under section 99. This includes raising the rent of any qualifying successor. This amendment ensures that people who have been assigned the tenancy, in pursuance of a property adjustment order in connection with civil partnership proceedings, are qualifying successors.

625. *Paragraph 27* amends the definitions of "member of a person's family" in Parts 3 and 4 of the 1985 Act to include references to civil partner or civil partnership alongside references to spouse or to marriage. The amendment also extends the definition to couples who are living together as if they were civil partners as well as people who are living together as husband and wife.

626. *Paragraph 28* amends the definition in section 123 of family members with whom the right to buy under Part 5 of the Housing Act 1985 may be exercised, to include civil partners. The right to buy is a statutory scheme enabling secure tenants to buy the homes that they live in, at a discount, from their landlord.

627. *Paragraph 29* amends section 130 of the 1985 Act. Section 130 allows deductions to be made from the discount applicable to a right to buy purchase where one of the purchasers or their spouse (or deceased spouse) has previously purchased a property and received a discount under the right to buy. The amendment adds a reference to any previous discount received by a civil partner or deceased civil partner.

628. *Paragraph 30* amends section 160 of the 1985 Act. Section 160 exempts certain disposals from the repayment provisions in relation to the discount obtained when the right to buy was exercised. The amendment adds a disposal in pursuance of a property adjustment order or an order for sale of property in connection with civil partnership proceedings.

629. *Paragraph 31* amends section 171B of the Housing Act 1985 which defines qualifying tenants and properties for the purposes of the preserved right to buy. The preserved right to buy gives certain tenants who were secure tenants at the point when their property was transferred to a private sector landlord or their successors a continuing right to buy their property at a discount. The amendment ensures that a person who obtains a secure tenancy from a qualifying tenant as a result of a property adjustment order in civil partnership proceedings will count as a qualifying successor.

630. *Paragraph 32* amends section 554(2A) of the Housing Act 1985. Section 554(2A) requires a registered social landlord other than a co-operative to grant or arrange for the grant of a secure tenancy to certain occupiers of dwellings it has acquired. The amendment allows a civil partner of a former owner-occupier, who was previously a secure tenant, to obtain a tenancy on the same terms as a spouse.

631. *Paragraph 33* amends the domestic violence ground for possession of a secure tenancy to include domestic violence by or against a civil partner. It also provides that the ground for possession applies where two people have been living together as if they were civil partners of each other.

632. *Paragraph 34* amends paragraphs 2, 5 and 5A of Schedule 4 to the Housing Act 1985 so that time spent by a civil partner as a public sector tenant or occupying forces accommodation will be counted towards the qualifying period for the right to buy and discount entitlement. It also ensures that civil partners are included as qualifying persons for the preserved right to buy.

633. *Paragraph 35* amends schedule 6A to the Housing Act 1985 to equalise the treatment of spouses and civil partners in respect of the terms of a purchase made under the right to acquire a property on rent to mortgage terms in section 150 of the Housing Act 1985. The "rents to mortgage" scheme introduced by the Housing Act 1985 allows a tenant to buy his property by turning his existing rent payments into mortgage repayments supporting a capital sum borrowed and paid over to the landlord. The outstanding amount is secured by a charge on the property in favour of the landlord.

634. *Paragraphs 36 to 39* amend the Agricultural Holdings Act 1986 ("the 1986 Act").

635. *Paragraph 36* extends the definition of "close relative" in sections 35(2) and 49(3) of the 1986 Act to civil partners for the purposes of statutory succession to an agricultural tenancy. The amendment also extends the definitions of "close relative" to include any person who, in the case of any civil partnership to which the deceased was at any time a party, was treated by the deceased as a child of the family in relation to that civil partnership.

636. *Paragraphs 37* and *38* relate to the criteria for satisfying the livelihood test for succession to an agricultural tenancy, which requires that for 5 out of the 7 years prior to the date of the death or retirement of the previous tenant, a potential successor has derived their livelihood from agricultural work on the holding. They insert new sections 36(4A) and 50(3A) and provide that in the case of a civil partner, the reference to agricultural work shall be read as a reference to agricultural work carried out by either the civil partner or the deceased/retiring tenant, or the civil partner and the deceased/retiring tenant.

637. *Paragraph 39* amends Schedule 6 to the 1986 Act in relation to the "occupancy condition" for succession to an agricultural tenancy i.e. that a potential successor is not already the occupier of a commercial unit of agricultural land.

638. *Paragraph 39(2)* amends paragraph 1(2) of Schedule 6 to the 1986 Act so that, for the purposes of the occupancy condition, a body corporate will be treated as having been controlled by a close relative of the deceased, where it has been controlled by the deceased or his civil partner or by the deceased and his civil partner together. .

639. *Paragraph 39(3)* inserts a new sub-paragraph into paragraph 1 of schedule 6 to the 1986 Act. The new sub-paragraph provides that any reference in schedule 6 to the civil partner of a close relative of the deceased does not apply in relation to any time when the relative's civil partnership is subject to a dissolution order, nullity order or presumption of death order (that is a conditional order), or a separation order.

640. *Paragraph 39(4)* amends paragraph 6(2) of Schedule 6 to the 1986 Act in respect of situations where occupation is to be disregarded for the purposes of the occupancy condition. The amendment extends the situation in which the disregard does not apply to the case of a tenancy or licence granted to a close relative of the deceased by the civil partner as well as by his spouse.

641. *Paragraph 39(5)* amends paragraph 9(1)(a) of Schedule 6 to the 1986 Act for the purposes of the occupancy condition and joint occupation and provides that occupation by the civil partner of the close relative of the deceased shall be treated as occupation by the relative.

642. *Paragraph 39(6)* amends paragraph 9(2) of Schedule 6 to the 1986 Act so that where, by virtue of paragraph 9(1) of Schedule 6, joint occupation of land by the civil partner of a relative, amounts to occupation by the civil partner, the provisions as to joint occupation in paragraphs 7(2) and (3) will apply to the relative of the civil partner as if he were the holder of the interest.

643. *Paragraph 39(7)* amends paragraph 10(3) of Schedule 6 to the 1986 Act so that, the definition of a "connected person" in relation to a close relative of the deceased includes a close relative's civil partner, as well as a close relative's spouse.

644. *Paragraph 40* amends section 4 of the Landlord and Tenant Act 1987. Part 1 of the 1987 Act gives qualifying tenants a right of first refusal in some circumstances if their landlord chooses to dispose of his interest in their property. Section 4 protects landlords, by

allowing them to make some disposals without triggering the right of a tenant to first refusal. Paragraph 40 ensures that a disposal to a civil partner or a member of their family will be dealt with in the same way as a disposal to a spouse or a member of their family and that a disposal following a property adjustment order or order for sale in connection with civil partnership proceedings will be treated in the same way as a disposal following matrimonial or family proceedings.

645. *Paragraphs 41 to 45* amend the Housing Act 1988.

646. *Paragraph 41* amends section 17 to give civil partners the same rights to succeed to an assured tenancy as spouses. The amendment also states that people who are living together as civil partners have the same rights to succeed to an assured tenancy as people who are living together as husband and wife.

647. *Paragraph 42* amends section 82(1)(b) to allow the Housing Corporation or the National Assembly for Wales the power to provide legal assistance to a surviving civil partner of a former secure or introductory tenant of a housing action trust (HAT) on the same basis as they may assist a surviving spouse. This power only arises in connection with a dispute between the tenant or surviving spouse or civil partner and a new landlord who has acquired the property following a disposal by the HAT under section 79 of the 1988 Act.

648. *Paragraph 43* amends the grounds for possession applicable to assured tenancies to ensure that spouses and civil partners are treated equally and to provide that couples who are living together as if they were civil partners and people that are living together as husband and wife should be treated equally.

649. *Paragraph 44* ensures that civil partners or surviving civil partners have the same rights in relation to an agricultural occupancy as spouses and surviving spouses. It also states that people who are living together as if they were civil partners and people that are living together as husband and wife should be treated equally.

650. *Paragraph 45* amends Schedule 11 to the 1988 Act to ensure that disposals by a housing action trust to a civil partner or former civil partner of a tenant or in pursuance of an order in connection with civil partnership proceedings are treated in the same way as a disposal to a spouse or former spouse or a disposal in connection with matrimonial or family proceedings.

651. Unless a disposal is exempted, Schedule 11 to the 1988 Act allows the housing action trust to reclaim an amount equal to the discount (reduced by one third for each complete year) given to a purchaser under section 79 if the purchaser further disposes of the property before three years has elapsed. Paragraph 45 adds civil partners and former civil partners to the list of qualifying persons for exempted disposal and adds orders in connection with civil partnership proceedings or dissolution to be eligible for exempted disposal.

652. *Paragraph 46* amends the grounds for possession for long residential tenancies in the Local Government and Housing Act 1989. The amendment will equalise the position of spouses and civil partners so as to allow the court to grant a possession order where premises are required as a residence for the father or mother of a landlord's civil partner.

653. *Paragraphs 47* and *48* amend the Leasehold Reform, Housing and Urban Development Act 1993, which confers rights to collective enfranchisement on tenants of flats.

654. *Paragraph* 47 amends section 7 of the 1993 Act, which contains the definition of "long lease" for the purposes of the Chapter on collective enfranchisement. A consequential amendment is made to *subsection (1)(b)* of section 7, as it contains a reference to section

149(6) of the Law of Property Act 1925 (leases terminable after a death or marriage), to reflect the changes made to that provision (see the notes to *paragraph 1* above). The definition of long lease will now also include leases terminable after the formation of a civil partnership.

655. Section 7(2) provides that a lease terminable by notice after a death or marriage is not a long lease if certain criteria apply, including that the notice is capable of being given at any time after the death or marriage. Section 7(2) is amended to ensure that leases terminable by notice after the formation of a civil partnership are treated in the same way.

656. *Paragraph 48* amends section 10(5), which contains the definition for an adult member of another's family, for the purposes of the resident landlord exception. Certain premises are exempt from enfranchisement if the landlord, or an adult member of his family, is resident there. The amendment ensures that civil partners and their close relations are treated in the same way as spouses and their close relations.

657. *Paragraph 49* amends section 7(3) of the Agricultural Tenancies Act 1995 and provides that in the case of a notice to quit, the exemption for tenancies subject to section 149 of the Law of Property Act 1925 (lease for life or lives or for a term determinable with life or lives or on the marriage of the lessee) is extended to the formation of a civil partnership by the lessee.

658. *Paragraphs 50 to 61* amend the Housing Act 1996.

659. *Paragraph 50* amends section 15, which defines exempted and relevant disposals for the purposes of sections 11 to 14 of the 1996 Act. Where a tenant has purchased his home from a registered social landlord at a discount, paragraph 50 ensures that a disposal to a civil partner or former civil partner or in connection with civil partnership proceedings will not trigger repayment of the discount.

660. *Paragraph 51* amends the definition of "member of a person's family" in Part 1 and Chapter 1 of Part 5 to include civil partners, people living together as if they were civil partners and relationships by civil partnership.

661. *Paragraphs 52 to 54* amend the rules relating to succession and to the assignment of introductory tenancies to ensure that civil partners have the same rights as spouses. They also ensure that a property adjustment order in connection with civil partnership proceedings will have the same effect in respect of an introductory tenancy as an order in matrimonial or family proceedings.

662. *Paragraphs 55 to 59* amend the rules relating to succession and to the assignment of demoted tenancies to ensure that civil partners have the same rights as spouses. They also ensure that a property adjustment order in connection with civil partnership proceedings will have the same effect in respect of a demoted tenancy as an order in matrimonial or family proceedings.

663. *Paragraph 59* amends the definition of "member of another's family" to include civil partners and relationships by civil partnership. The definition applies to demoted tenancies under Chapter 1A of the 1996 Act.

664. *Paragraph 60* amends section 160 of the 1996 Act, which provides that the rules regarding local authority housing allocations shall not apply in certain circumstances. Paragraph 60 ensures that the rules do not apply to assignments or disposals of property as a result of property adjustment orders in connection with civil partnership proceedings.

665. *Paragraph 61* amends the definition of "associated persons" in section 178 to include civil partners, former civil partners and relationships resulting from a civil partnership. The definition applies for the purposes of the homelessness provisions in Part 7 of the 1996 Act. Paragraph 61 also ensures that the definition of "associated persons" extends to two people of the same-sex who, although not civil partners of each other, are living together as if they were civil partners.

666. *Paragraphs 62 and 63* amend the Housing Grants, Construction and Regeneration Act 1996.

667. *Paragraph 62* confers power to provide for the financial resources of a civil partner to be taken into account when an application is made for a disabled facilities grant. This mirrors the existing situation in relation to the financial resources of a spouse.

668. *Paragraph 63* amends the repealed section 54 to ensure that a property adjustment order or an order for sale of a property in connection with civil partnership proceedings does not trigger the repayment of a renovation, common parts or Houses in Multiple Occupation grant which was approved before section 54 was repealed.

669. *Paragraphs 64 to 66* amend the Commonhold and Leasehold Reform Act 2002 ("the 2002 Act") which established a new right to enable leaseholders of flats to take over the management of their building without the need to prove shortcomings on the part of the landlord.

670. *Paragraph 64* amends section 76(2)(c) of the 2002 Act. Section 76(2)(c) refers to a tenancy which takes effect under section 149(6) of the Law of Property Act 1925. These tenancies are those that flow from leases, which are terminable after a death or a marriage. Paragraph 64 amends that section so that it refers to leases terminable after a death, marriage or a civil partnership

671. *Paragraph 65* amends section 77(1) of the 2002 Act. Section 77(1) provides that a lease terminable by notice after death or marriage is not a long lease in certain circumstances. Paragraph 65 amends section 77(1) to include leases terminable by notice after the formation of a civil partnership.

672. *Paragraph 66* amends paragraph 3(8) of Schedule 6 to the 2002 Act which excludes certain premises which are occupied by a resident landlord or an adult member of his family from the right to manage introduced by Chapter 1 of Part 2 of the 2002 Act. Paragraph 66 ensures that a civil partner will count as a member of a freeholder's family for these purposes.

Schedule 9 - Family homes and domestic violence

673. This Schedule is discussed in the notes on section 82.

Schedule 10 – Forbidden degrees of relationship: Scotland

674. *Paragraph 1* of Schedule 10 lists the relationships connecting people that absolutely forbid the registration of a civil partnership between them. *Paragraphs 2 and 3* list the relationships connecting people that forbid the registration of a civil partnership between them, unless the requirements specified in section 86 are met.

675. The prohibitions in Schedule 10 closely follow those that are set out in the Marriage (Scotland) Act 1977.

Schedule 11 – Financial provision in Scotland after overseas proceedings

676. This Schedule explains the circumstances under which a Scottish court may consider an application for financial provision following the dissolution or annulment of a civil partnership overseas.

Part 1- Introductory

677. This Part states that the provisions of Schedule 11 will apply wherever a civil partnership has been dissolved or annulled after judicial or other proceedings overseas, and the dissolution or annulment is entitled to recognition in Scotland. Dissolutions or annulments granted before the commencement of Schedule 11 are included. "Overseas" is defined as meaning outside the British Islands.

Part 2- Circumstances in which court may entertain application for financial provision

678. This Part provides that the Scottish court may entertain an application by one of the former (or former ostensible) civil partners following the overseas dissolution or annulment if the criteria specified in paragraphs 2(2) and (3) are satisfied. The application must be made by the party who did not initiate the overseas proceedings, and must be made within five years of the overseas dissolution or annulment taking effect. Both former partners must be alive when the application is made. The other criteria are designed to ensure a substantial connection between the civil partnership and Scotland, and between the parties and both Scotland and the jurisdiction of the relevant court. Paragraph 2(4) gives priority to the jurisdictional standards set out in Part 1 of the Civil Jurisdiction and Judgements Act 1982 and in Council Regulation (EC) No 44/2001, which will supersede the criteria in *paragraph 2(2)* where they apply.

Part 3 - Disposal of applications

679. Under this Part, Scots law will generally apply to the disposal of the application. In particular, the court is to endeavour to place the parties in the position they would have been in had the application for financial provision been disposed of by the Scottish court as part of a Scottish action for dissolution or annulment and on the date when the overseas dissolution or annulment took effect. The court is to have regard to the resources of the parties and to any order for financial provision already made overseas in or in connection with the foreign dissolution or annulment proceedings. An interim periodical allowance may be ordered where appropriate to relieve hardship. However, where the Scottish court's jurisdiction is based solely on the presence of a former family home of the parties in which the respondent has an interest, any order made must relate to the family home, its contents or their capital value.

Part 4 - The expression "order for financial provision"

680. This Part defines the term "order for financial provision" with reference to section 8(1) of the Family Law (Scotland) Act 1985 (as amended by this Act), and to section 109.

Schedule 12 – Prohibited degrees of relationship: Northern Ireland

681. This Schedule sets out the degrees of relationship between persons who may not register as civil partners of each other. It deals with both absolute prohibitions and qualified prohibitions and corresponds to prohibitions to marriage.

682. *Paragraph 1* contains the list of absolute prohibitions. No civil partnership between two persons who stand in relation to each other as described in *paragraph 1* is ever valid.

683. *Paragraphs 2* and *3* deal with qualified prohibitions. A civil partnership between two persons who stand in relation to each other as described in *paragraph* 2(1) and 3 is not valid unless certain conditions apply.

684. *Paragraph 2* deals with what may be referred to as "step-relationships". For example, a civil partnership between a woman and the child of her former husband or civil partner will not be valid unless both have reached the age of 21 and the younger of the two persons has not at any time before reaching the age of 18 been a child of the family in relation to the other person.

685. *Paragraph 2(1)* defines "child of the family" to mean a person who (a) has lived in the same household as the other person and (b) has been treated by that other person as a child of the family.

686. *Paragraph 3* deals with civil partnerships between what may be referred to as "in-laws". For example, a civil partnership between a man and the husband or former civil partner of his child will not be valid unless both have reached the age of 21 and both the man's child and that child's other parent are dead.

Schedule 13 – Civil partnerships of persons under 18: Northern Ireland

687. This Schedule deals with the issue of "consent" where a person under the age of 18 wishes to register a civil partnership with another person.

688. *Paragraphs 1* and *2* list the persons or bodies whose consent is needed to the civil partnership of a person between the age of 16 and 18 and the circumstances in which their consent is required.

689. *Paragraph 3* provides a county court in Northern Ireland with power to make an order dispensing with the consent of any person required by *paragraph 1* if the court is satisfied that the registration of the civil partnership is in the best interests of the young person. This jurisdiction is exercisable by the county court in three circumstances: (1) it is not reasonably practicable to obtain the consent of the person whose consent is required; (2) that person has refused or withheld consent to the civil partnership; or (3) there is uncertainty as to whose consent to the civil partnership is required.

690. *Paragraphs 4 to 7* provide that details of consents to the civil partnership of a young person are to be sent to and recorded by the registrar. *Paragraph 7* applies section 140(5) to the record of consents under this Schedule and a person claiming to have reason to object to the proposed civil partnership may inspect any entry relating to the proposed civil partnership free of charge.

Schedule 14: Wills, administration of estates and family provision: Northern Ireland

691. Schedule 14 makes provision for amending the Wills and Administration Proceedings (Northern Ireland) Order 1994, Administration of Estates Act (Northern Ireland) 1955 and Inheritance (Provision for Family and Dependants) (Northern Ireland) Order 1979 so that civil partners are given the same rights as those that exist for married people.

692. *Paragraph 2* amends Article 4(1) of the Wills and Administration Proceedings (Northern Ireland) Order 1994 so that a will made by a person who is under eighteen years shall be valid if that person is or has been in a civil partnership.

693. *Paragraph 3* amends Article 8(1) and (3) of the Wills and Administration Proceedings (Northern Ireland) Order 1994 so as to prevent the passing of property to a civil partner who

attests to the signature of the testator except where the will would have been valid without that signature.

694. *Paragraph 4* amends Article 9 of the Wills and Administration Proceedings (Northern Ireland) Order 1994 so that where the civil partner of a creditor of the testator witnesses the will, he or she may be admitted as a witness in proceedings about the will.

695. *Paragraph 5* inserts new Articles 13A and 13B in the Wills and Administration Proceedings (Northern Ireland) Order 1994. The effect of these amendments is that, with the same limited exceptions as apply to marriage, a will is revoked when the testator forms a civil partnership with someone. They will also - once the civil partnership has been dissolved, annulled or made the subject of a presumption of death order - prevent former civil partners, where named as executors in the will, from becoming executors, and former civil partners named as beneficiaries in the will, from inheriting, unless the will provides otherwise.

696. *Paragraph 6* amends Article 14 of the Wills and Administration Proceedings (Northern Ireland) Order 1994 to recognise a will is revocable by a marriage or formation of a civil partnership.

697. *Paragraph 7* amends Article 23 of the Wills and Administration Proceedings (Northern Ireland) Order 1994 so that the deceased's civil partner has priority over the issue of the testator should the testator bequeath the same gift separately to both of them.

698. *Paragraph 8* amends Article 27(3) of the Wills and Administration Proceedings (Northern Ireland) Order 1994 so that its scope includes issue who are in civil partnerships as well as those who are married.

699. *Paragraph 9* amends section 6A of the Administration of Estates Act (Northern Ireland) 1955 so that where an intestate dies leaving a civil partner and that civil partner dies within 28 days of the intestate's death, the provisions relating to the distribution of property on intestacy shall have effect as regards the intestate as if the civil partner had not survived the intestate.

700. *Paragraph 10* amends section 7 of the Administration of Estates Act (Northern Ireland) 1955 to allow surviving civil partners to inherit the estate of their deceased civil partner under the intestacy rules in the same way as surviving spouses, and so that the fact that an intestate person does not leave a surviving civil partner is taken into account in the same way as the fact that there is no surviving spouse in determining the succession to his real and personal estate.

701. *Paragraph 11* amends section 8 of the Administration of Estates Act (Northern Ireland) 1955 so that the distribution of an intestate's property to his/her issue shall be subject to the rights of a surviving civil partner.

702. *Paragraph 12* amends section 9 of the Administration of Estates Act (Northern Ireland) 1955 so that the rights of an intestate's parents to the property of an intestate who leaves no issue, shall be subject to the rights of a surviving civil partner or spouse.

703. *Paragraph 13* amends section 10 of the Administration of Estates Act (Northern Ireland) 1955 so that the rights of an intestate's siblings to the property of an intestate who leaves neither issue nor parent, shall be subject to the rights of a surviving civil partner or spouse.

704. *Paragraph 14* amends section 11 of the Administration of Estates Act (Northern Ireland) 1955 so as to provide that the rights of the intestate's next-of-kin to the intestate's

property shall be subject to the rights of a surviving civil partner in the same way as they would be subject to the rights of a surviving spouse.

705. *Paragraph 15* amends section 38 of the Administration of Estates Act (Northern Ireland) 1955 so that an intestate's residuary or whole estate may be held on trust for those of his children (or their issue if they predecease the intestate) who reach the age of 18, or marry, or form a civil partnership, under that age.

706. *Paragraph 16* amends Article 2 of the Inheritance (Provision for Family and Dependants) (Northern Ireland) Order 1979, the interpretation section, to insert references to civil partners and civil partnership as appropriate.

707. *Paragraph 17* amends Article 3 of the 1979 Order by adding civil partners and former civil partners to the class of persons entitled to make an application for reasonable financial provision from the estate of their deceased civil partner. Article 3 is also amended to provide that a person who lived in the same household as the deceased as if they were civil partners (for the two year period immediately preceding the date of death of the deceased) is entitled to make an application for reasonable financial provision.

708. *Paragraph 18* amends Article 4 of the 1979 Order by extending the court's powers to enable it to make orders varying any settlement made on the civil partners either during the civil partnership, or in anticipation of one being formed, including any variation in favour of any children of both the civil partners or of any person treated by the civil partners as a child of the family in relation to the civil partnership.

709. *Paragraph 19* amends Article 5 of the 1979 Order by providing that the court, when considering an application for reasonable financial provision from the deceased's estate by a civil partner or a former civil partner, shall take into account the duration of the civil partnership and what the applicant might have received had the civil partnership been ended by being dissolved instead of by death.

710. *Paragraph 20* amends Article 5(2A) of the 1979 Order by providing that the court, when considering an application for reasonable financial provision from the deceased's estate by any person who was living in the same household as the deceased as a civil partner, shall take into account the age of the applicant, the length of time during which the applicant lived as a civil partner with the deceased and the contribution made by the applicant to the welfare of the family of the deceased.

711. *Paragraph 21* amends Article 8(3) and (10) of the 1979 Order by adding the formation of a subsequent civil partnership as an exception to the events that can cause an order for periodical payment to cease to have effect.

712. *Paragraph 22* inserts a new Article 16A into the 1979 Order. Article 16A provides that if a civil partner dies within a year of the making of a dissolution, nullity or separation order in relation to the civil partnership, and no application for financial provision has been made or determined, the court may treat a surviving civil partner who applies for an order under the 1979 Order as if the dissolution, nullity or separation order had not been made.

713. *Paragraph 23* inserts a new Article 17ZA into the 1979 Order. Article 17ZA empowers the court, when making an order to end a civil partnership either by dissolution, or by nullity, or by separation or by presumption of death, (or at any time after making such an order), to order that neither of the civil partners, on the death of the other, shall be allowed to make an application for reasonable financial provision out of the deceased partner's estate.

714. *Paragraph 24* inserts a new Article 17B into the 1979 Order. Article 17B extends the powers contained in section 17ZA to civil partnerships that were ended overseas.

715. *Paragraph 25* amends Article 18(1) of the 1979 Order so that a court hearing an application for reasonable financial provision from the deceased's estate can vary or discharge secured periodical payments orders made prior to the death of the deceased under Schedule 15 (Financial relief in the High Court or a county court: Northern Ireland) to the Act.

716. *Paragraph 26* amends Article 19(4) of the 1979 Order to allow for the court hearing an application for reasonable financial provision from the deceased's estate to vary or revoke any maintenance agreement made between civil partners prior to the death of one of them.

717. *Paragraph 27* inserts a new Article 20A into the 1979 Order. Article 20A provides that where a civil partner has been ordered by the court to pay a secured periodical payment to their civil partner or has entered into a maintenance agreement with their civil partner, and then has died, the surviving civil partner's subsequent application to have the payment order or the maintenance agreement varied or discharged, may be treated as though it was accompanied by an application by them for reasonable financial provision from the estate of the deceased civil partner. The court may then make any order that it could have made on an application under the 1979 Order.

718. *Paragraph 28* amends Article 21 of the 1979 Order so that its scope covers civil partners, former civil partners and the formation of civil partnerships.

Schedule 15: Financial relief in the High Court or a county court etc.: Northern Ireland

719. This Schedule provides for adjustment of financial provision and property rights of civil partners when a civil partnership is brought to an end and provides corresponding rights to those available to married people on divorce.

Part 1 - Financial provision in connection with dissolution, nullity or separation

720. This Part outlines the circumstances in which the High Court or a county court (with jurisdiction) can make an order for financial provision relating to dissolution, nullity or separation orders in connection with a civil partnership. It states that the court may make an order for a lump sum or for periodical payments to be made from one civil partner to the other or to a child of the family, or to a particular person for the benefit of a child of the family. The court can order periodic payments to be made for a specified time only and can order the civil partner paying to secure the payments by means of a charge or other arrangement. Part 1 also provides for special provisions to be made for lump sum orders either to be paid in instalments or to be secured by a charge on property. Lump sums payments can take account of liabilities or reasonable expenses incurred before the application was made. Where a lump sum order is deferred or ordered to be paid in instalments provision can be made for interest. Where an order is for periodical payments or a lump sum solely to the other civil partner in dissolution or nullity proceedings the order or settlement does not take effect until the dissolution or nullity order has been made final.

Part 2 - Property adjustment on or after dissolution, nullity or separation

721. This Part allows for property adjustment orders to be made on or after dissolution, nullity or separation. This provides for property to be transferred from one civil partner to the other or to a child of the family or to another person for the benefit of a child of the family. It also allows for a settlement of specified property to be made for the benefit of the other civil partner and/or children of the family. An order for a relevant settlement can be varied and the

interest extinguished or reduced. Variation of a property adjustment order may be made even if there are no children of the family. In the case of a dissolution or nullity order the property adjustment or settlement can only take effect after the dissolution or nullity order has been made final.

Part 3 - Pension sharing orders on or after dissolution or nullity order

722. The Part provides for a pension sharing order to be made so that both civil partners share the benefit of the value of a pension that had previously been held by only one of the partners. The value of the pension is effectively split and the court specifies the amount (in percentage terms) transferred to the other civil partner. The Court can apportion any charge from the cost of making pension sharing arrangements. A pension sharing order cannot be made on a pension that is, or has already been, the subject of a pension sharing order between the same two civil partners, or where there is already in force an order under Part 5 in relation to the same pension. The order can only take effect after the dissolution or nullity order has been made final. The Lord Chancellor, in regulations, can set a minimum period before a pension order can take effect.

Part 4 - Matters to which the court is to have regard under Parts 1 to 3

723. This Part sets out the matters which the court must consider when exercising its powers to make orders under the preceding three Parts. Whilst all the circumstances of the case have to be considered the first consideration has to be given to the welfare of any child of the family under 18 years old. The criteria the court must consider under this Part are parallel to those contained in Article 27 of the Matrimonial Causes (Northern Ireland) Order 1978 and reflect the relative financial positions of the civil partners, their current and future obligations, their age and the duration of the civil partnership and the contributions each civil partner has made to the welfare of the family, whether in financial terms or by caring or looking after the home. The conduct of each civil partner will be taken into account if it would be unfair to disregard it. When exercising the powers in relation to a child of the family the court has to consider the financial needs and resources of the child in addition to the financial position of the civil partners. Where a child is not a child of one of the civil partners the court needs to look at any responsibility that civil partner had assumed for the child and the duration of such responsibility. The court has to consider the appropriateness of the orders under Parts 1 to 3 in respect of termination of financial dependence or involvement.

Part 5 - Making of Part 1 orders having regard to pension benefits

724. This Part describes the matters the court must have regard to when taking into account the considerations in Part 4 where a pension arrangement exists and the procedure for making orders in relation to a pension benefit of one civil partner when it becomes due to make payments (in terms of an amount or percentage) for the benefit of the other civil partner. Any such payment discharges the civil partner's liability under the order. Where no pension sharing order has been made on the pension arrangement and that pension includes a lump sum payable on death the court can order that the other civil partner receives the whole or part of that sum. The Lord Chancellor can make regulations addressing: payment from a pension arrangement to be made for the benefit of the other civil partner, the terms on which payment is made, payments made under a mistaken belief, discharges from requirements imposed by this Part, calculation and verification of the valuation of the pension.

Part 6 – Pension Protection Fund compensation etc.

725. This Part ensures that the provisions for financial relief in Northern Ireland reflect the creation of the Pension Protection Fund. It allows the court to include PPF compensation as financial resources of the parties to the civil partnership to which it can have regard to when it is exercising its powers to make financial provision on dissolution or nullity of a civil partnership or separation. This Part also ensures that an attachment order, commutation order or pension sharing order made as a result of dissolution or nullity of a civil partnership, and in certain cases as a result of separation continues to have effect if the pension scheme enters the PPF. Where the court exercises its powers of variation under paragraph 46 of Schedule 15, the PPF shall be bound by any variations made by the court to existing pension attachment orders and pension sharing orders. The Lord Chancellor may, by regulations make necessary and expedient consequential modifications to Schedule 15 as a result of the PPF assuming responsibility for pension sharing orders and attachment orders.

Part 7 - Maintenance pending outcome of dissolution, nullity or separation proceedings

726. This Part allows for the court to order one of the civil partners to make periodic payments for maintenance for the other civil partner before the final outcome of the proceedings has been determined.

Part 8 - Failure to maintain: financial provision (and interim orders)

727. This Part allows either civil partner to apply to the court because the other civil partner has failed to maintain them adequately or has failed to provide for, or make a proper contribution towards, the welfare of any child of the family. The court is empowered to make a range of orders, including orders for periodic payments for a set period of time, a lump sum payment and an order to secure payments. The court may make an order in favour of the other civil partner, the child of the family or another person for the benefit of the child. An order for a lump sum payment can be made to cover reasonable expenses and liabilities incurred in maintaining the applicant or any child of the family before the application was made. Where there is immediate need of financial assistance an interim order can be made. The Part sets out the matters the court must consider when deciding whether proper maintenance has been provided, which are the same as used in other financial provision cases as set out in Part 4.

Part 9 - Commencement of certain proceedings and duration of certain orders

728. This Part establishes that, subject to any rules of court, applications for financial provision can be commenced at any time after the application for a dissolution, nullity or separation order. The Part also establishes provisions for the circumstances when orders will cease to have effect or cannot be applied for, for example when a child of the family reaches the age of 18 and where a civil partner in receipt of periodic payment marries or forms a subsequent civil partnership. It also deals with applications for periodical payments where a maintenance calculation is still in force.

Part 10 - Variation, discharge etc of certain orders for financial relief

729. This Part establishes conditions for the court to vary financial orders made and includes powers to vary orders, discharge orders, suspend or revive suspended provisions of an order, remit (cancel) arrears and to vary property adjustment and pension sharing orders. Where a court discharges or varies a periodical payments order the court can make additional provision through one of the other orders. The Part gives the circumstances in which a child who is sixteen or over can apply for the variation of a periodical payments order. The court may vary periodic payments which are secured when the person liable has died and deal with

the liability within the context of the deceased person's estate. The court will also have power to direct when the variation or other order will take effect.

Part 11 - Arrears and repayments

730. This Part deals with arrears and repayments and provides that arrears cannot be enforced without the leave of the court. The court can order repayment of various sums paid under certain circumstances, for example sums paid by mistake when an order had already ceased to have effect because the recipient had married or formed another civil partnership.

Part 12 - Consent orders and maintenance agreements

731. In this Part provisions are made for civil partners to reach agreement on the terms of financial orders and for the court to make an order (a consent order) on terms as set out by the parties and presented to the court. There are also provisions for agreements to be altered by the court during the lives of the parties, restrictions on applications to magistrates' courts for maintenance and provisions relating to the duration and limits of periodical and secured periodical payments where those provisions are inserted into an agreement to alter it. This Part also provides for agreements to be altered after the death of one of the parties, if an agreement for maintenance allows for payments after the death of one of the parties.

Part 13 - Miscellaneous and supplementary

732. This Part provides: for the court to make orders overturning transactions carried out in an attempt to defeat financial orders under the Schedule provisions; for a settlement to be overturned on the bankruptcy of the person who made it; for orders for payments made to a person suffering from a mental disorder to be paid to another person and; for appeals when a pension order has taken effect. This Part also defines a number of terms used in the Schedule.

Schedule 16: Financial relief in court of summary jurisdiction etc.: Northern Ireland

733. This Schedule provides for civil partners to apply to courts of summary jurisdiction for maintenance for themselves and children of the family.

Part 1 - Failure to maintain etc: financial provision

734. This Part sets out the circumstances in which an order can be made and the types of orders which can be made. The court can make an order for either lump sum payments or periodical payments to be made if it is satisfied that the civil partner has not made reasonable provision to maintain the applicant or a child of the family. A lump sum payment can take into consideration expenses or liabilities reasonably incurred in maintaining the applicant or child prior to the making of the order. The Part sets out the matters the court is to take into account when determining what orders it should make both in respect of civil partners and in respect of children. These include, amongst other things, the financial resources of the applicant and the civil partner concerned and the financial needs, earning capacity and education of the child. Where the child of the family is not the respondent's child the court must also consider whether anyone else is liable to maintain the child and whether the respondent has assumed any responsibility to maintain the child. Whilst the court must have regard to all the circumstances of the case, the welfare of any child under the age of 18 should be the first consideration. The court can adjourn the proceedings if the civil partners wish to attempt a reconciliation and must refuse to make an order if an application to the High Court (under Part 8 of Schedule 15 (Financial relief in the High Court or a county court etc.: Northern Ireland)) is more appropriate.

Part 2 - Orders for agreed financial provision

735. This Part allows civil partners to apply to the court for a financial provision order on the ground that the other civil partner has agreed to make financial provision for them or for a child of the family. The court has power to make alternative orders if both civil partners agree.

Part 3 - Orders of court where civil partners living apart by agreement

736. This Part allows the court to make orders for periodical payments for maintenance to be made by one civil partner to the other for that civil partner or for a child of the family. Such orders can be made where the civil partners have been living apart for a continuous period exceeding three months and one of the civil partners has been making periodical payments during that three-month period. However, the court cannot order the civil partner to make payments which, during any period of three months, would amount to more than he paid over the three months prior to the application. If the court considers that an order under this Part would not provide reasonable maintenance for the civil partner or for a child of the family, the court may treat the application as if it were an application for an order under Part 1. The matters which the court must take into account when making an order under this Part are the same as those in Part 1.

Part 4 - Interim orders

737. This Part allows the court to make interim orders when applications have been made under any of the provisions in Parts 1, 2 and 3. The interim order will require the civil partner to make periodic payments to the applicant or to a child of the family. The court can set the date when payments under the order begin and when the order ceases to have effect. However, the start date cannot be prior to the date of an application for an order under Parts 1, 2 or 3. The order will also cease to have effect when the court makes its final decision on the application or three months after the date on which the interim order was made, whichever is earliest.

Part 5 - Commencement and duration of orders under Parts 1, 2 and 3

738. This Part makes provision for when orders made under Parts 1, 2 and 3 can begin, age limits for making orders for children (the court cannot make an order in favour of a child over the age of 18 unless the child is in full-time education or undergoing training) and the length of time for which the orders can remain in force. Orders will cease to apply if the civil partners live with each other for a continuous period of six months.

Part 6 - Variation etc. of orders

739. This Part sets out the powers the courts have to vary or revoke periodical payment orders and to suspend or revive any provision of the orders. The court has power to order a lump sum payment in place of an order for periodical payments and vary a periodical payment order by specifying when such an order is to come into effect. The Part sets out the procedure for making such an order and the matters which the court is to consider when exercising its powers under this Part. Either civil partner can apply to have an order varied, as can a child of 16 or over in relation to orders for periodical payments to or in respect of a child.

Part 7 - Arrears and repayments

740. This Part deals with arrears and repayments and provides the court with powers for the enforcement of orders. It also allows for sums paid under an order after it had ceased to have an effect, because the person entitled to receive the sums had married or had formed a

subsequent civil partnership, to be refunded. The magistrates' court will have power to enforce the order in the same way as it can enforce any other maintenance order.

Part 8 - Supplementary

741. This Part provides certain supplementary provisions. For instance, it applies to orders made under the appropriate Schedule to the Domestic Proceedings (Northern Ireland) Order 1980 so as to provide for appeals, the constitution of the court and the powers of the High Court and the county court in relation to certain orders, so as to match the provisions available for married people. It also stipulates that the jurisdiction of the magistrates' court under this Schedule be exercisable even if one of the parties is not domiciled in Northern Ireland.

Schedule 17: Financial relief in Northern Ireland after overseas dissolution etc. of a civil partnership

742. This Schedule provides for applications in courts in Northern Ireland for financial relief following the dissolution, annulment or legal separation of civil partners as a result of legal proceedings in an overseas country. The provisions correspond to those available for overseas divorces etc in Part IV of the Matrimonial and Family Proceedings (Northern Ireland) Order 1989.

Part 1 - Financial relief

743. Part 1 provides that the Schedule will apply where a civil partnership has been dissolved or annulled or the civil partners have been legally separated in an overseas country and the dissolution etc. is entitled to be recognised as valid in Northern Ireland. Sub-paragraph 2 of paragraph 1 provides that for the purposes of application for financial relief, the dissolution, annulment or separation may have taken place before the Civil Partnership Act is brought into force. Sub-paragraph 3 of paragraph 1 defines an overseas country as a country or territory outside the United Kingdom, the Channel Islands and the Isle of Man. Sub-paragraph 4 defines a child of the family and sub-paragraph 5 defines "authority" and "voluntary organisation" as per the Children (Northern Ireland) Order 1995.

744. Under *paragraph 2* either civil partner may apply to the court for orders under *paragraph 9* or *13* of the Schedule. However, under *paragraph 3* no application will be possible if the applicant has subsequently formed a new civil partnership or married. *Paragraph 4* provides that leave of the court is required for an application to be made.

745. Under *paragraph 5* where it appears to the court that the applicant or a child of the family is in need of immediate assistance, an interim order for maintenance may be made in favour of the applicant or the child.

746. *Paragraph 7* sets out the criteria the court will use to determine whether it has jurisdiction to deal with an application for financial relief following an overseas dissolution etc. One of the civil partners must be domiciled or have been habitually resident in Northern Ireland for a period of one year when the application is made or when the civil partnership was dissolved or annulled or the order for legal separation was made. Alternatively either or both of the civil partners must have an interest in a dwelling-house in Northern Ireland on the date of application for leave to apply which was at some time during the civil partnership a civil partnership home of the civil partners.

747. *Paragraph 8* provides that the court must consider whether Northern Ireland is the appropriate venue for the application, and outlines the criteria the court is to take into account when considering this.

748. *Paragraph 9* describes the orders that the court is able to make on applications under this Schedule. The court may make the same orders for financial provision as are available for civil partnerships formed in Northern Ireland under Part 1, 2 and 3 of Schedule 15 (Financial relief in the High Court or a county court etc.: Northern Ireland) of the Act including orders for property adjustment and pension sharing if the civil partnership has been dissolved or annulled. If the partners are legally separated the court may make orders for financial provision and property adjustment as provided in Part 1 and 2 of Schedule 15 (Financial relief in the High Court or a county court etc.: Northern Ireland) to the Act.

749. *Paragraph 10* sets out the matters to which the court must have regard when exercising its powers under this Schedule, which are the same as those to be considered when making financial provision for civil partners in civil partnerships formed in Northern Ireland and for any children involved.

750. *Paragraph 11* establishes the restrictions on the court's powers when its jurisdiction to deal with the application arises only from the fact that the civil partnership home is situated in Northern Ireland. In these circumstances the court may make various orders including for lump sum payments, transfer of the property or sale of the property.

751. *Paragraph 12* provides for the court to make an order on terms agreed by the civil partners (a consent order).

752. *Paragraph 13* provides for the court to order transfer of tenancies of dwelling houses.

753. *Paragraph 14* applies certain provisions of Schedule 15 (Financial relief in the High Court or a county court etc.: Northern Ireland) to interim orders or orders for financial provision, property adjustment and pension sharing made under paragraphs 5 and 9 of this Schedule.

754. *Paragraph 15* provides for the avoidance of transactions designed to defeat claims under *paragraphs 5* and *9*. Where one of the civil partners (A) is granted leave to make an application for an order under paragraph 9 and the court is satisfied that the other civil partner (B) is, with the intention of defeating a claim by (A), about to deal with any property, it may make an order restraining (B) from doing so. *Paragraph 15* also provides that where one civil partner (A) is granted leave to make an application under *paragraph 9* or where an order has been made under *paragraph 5 or 9* and the other civil partner (B) has, with the intention of defeating a claim by (A), made a disposition, then the court may in certain circumstances set aside the disposition.

755. *Paragraph 16* provides circumstances in which it can be presumed, for the purposes of *paragraph 15*, that the person who disposed of or is about to dispose of property did so, or is about to do so, with the intention of defeating the other civil partner's claim.

Part 2 - Steps to prevent avoidance prior to application for leave under paragraph 4

756. Part 2 provides the court with powers to make such orders as it thinks fit restraining a party from making any disposition or transfer out of the jurisdiction intended to defeat the other party's prospective claim. The court may only make an order under this Part where the applicant intends to apply for leave to make an application for an order under *paragraph 9* as soon as he or she has been habitually resident in Northern Ireland for one year.

Part 3 - Supplementary

757. Part 3 clarifies the meaning of and defines various terms for the purposes of this Schedule and provides that the provisions relating to avoidance and prevention of

transactions are without prejudice to any power of the High Court to grant injunctions under section 91 of the Judicature (Northern Ireland) Act 1978.

Schedule 18: Housing and tenancies: Northern Ireland

758. Schedule 18 makes amendments to a range of enactments relating to housing and tenancies, in order to ensure equality of treatment between spouses and civil partners. This Schedule extends only to Northern Ireland.

759. *Paragraph 1* amends Article 14 of the Rent (Northern Ireland) Order 1978 which provides that on the making of an order for possession of a dwelling-house or at any time before the enforcement of such an order, the court, on application of the tenant or of the tenant's spouse if that spouse is occupying the dwelling-house as his or her residence, may stay or suspend enforcement of the order or postpone the date of possession. The amendment ensures that the court treats a tenant's civil partner in the same manner as a spouse in relation to applications for orders for possession.

760. *Paragraph 2* amends Schedule 1 to the Rent (Northern Ireland) Order 1978. This Schedule determines (for the purposes of tenancy succession) what person is the statutory tenant of a dwelling house at any time after the death of a person who, immediately before his death, was either a protected or statutory tenant. The amendment ensures that a civil partner is given the same rights as a spouse.

761. *Paragraph 3* amends Case 8 in Part 1 of Schedule 4 to the Rent (Northern Ireland) Order 1978 which sets out the grounds on which courts may make orders for possession of dwelling-houses let on or subject to protected or statutory tenancies. The amendment ensures that the civil partner of a landlord has the same rights as those of the landlord's spouse.

762. *Paragraph 4* amends Article 2A of the Housing (Northern Ireland) Order 1981 which provides a definition of the meaning of "member of a person's family" for the purposes of the Order. This paragraph amends Article 2A to provide that a person is a member of a person's family if he is the spouse or civil partner of that person, or if he and that person live together as husband and wife or as if they were civil partners. Paragraph 4 also amends Article 2A to provide that, for the purposes of Article 2A(1)(b), a relationship by marriage or civil partnership shall be treated as a relationship by blood.

763. *Paragraph 5* amends Article 24(3) of the Housing (Northern Ireland) Order 1983 which provides a definition of a member of a person's family for the purposes of Chapter 2 of Part 2 of the Order. This paragraph amends Article 24(3) to provide that a person is a member of another person's family if he is the spouse or civil partner of that person, or if he and that person live together as husband and wife or as if they were civil partners. Paragraph 5 also provides that a relationship by marriage or civil partnership shall be treated as a relationship by blood.

764. *Paragraph 6* deals with succession on the death of a tenant. It amends Article 26 of the Housing (Northern Ireland) Order 1983 which provides for qualified persons to succeed to a secure tenancy where the tenant dies. Article 26(2)(a) provides that a person is qualified to succeed to a such a tenancy if he occupied the dwelling as his only or principal home at the time of the tenant's death and he is the tenant's spouse. Article 26(3)(a) provides that where there is more than one person qualified to succeed the tenant, the tenant's spouse is to be preferred to another member of the tenant's family and Article 26 (4A) makes provision in respect of tenancies assigned under the Matrimonial Causes (Northern Ireland) Order 1978.

765. *Paragraph 6* amends Article 26(2)(a) to provide that a person is qualified to succeed to a secure tenancy if he occupied the dwelling as his only or principal home at the time of the

tenant's death and he is the tenant's spouse or civil partner and amends Article 26(3)(a) to provide that where there is more than one person qualified to succeed the tenant, the tenant's spouse or civil partner is to be preferred to another member of the tenant's family. Paragraph 6 also inserts a new Article 26 (4B) which makes provision in respect of tenancies assigned in pursuance of an order made under this Act.

766. *Paragraph 7* amends Article 32 of the Housing (Northern Ireland) Order 1983 which provides, *inter alia,* that a secure tenancy is not capable of being assigned unless the assignment is made in pursuance of an order made under the Matrimonial Causes (Northern Ireland) Order 1978. This paragraph inserts a new Article 32(1)(aa) which provides that a secure tenancy can also be assigned if the assignment is made in pursuance of an order made under this Act.

767. *Paragraph 8* amends Article 33(2)(a) of the Housing (Northern Ireland) Order 1983 which provides that where a secure tenancy is, on the death of the tenant, vested or otherwise disposed of in the course of the administration of the deceased tenant's estate, the tenancy ceases to be a secure tenancy unless the vesting or other disposal is in pursuance of an order made under the Matrimonial Causes (Northern Ireland) Order 1978. This paragraph inserts a new Article 33(2)(aa) to provide that such a tenancy will not cease to be a secure tenancy if the vesting or other disposal is in pursuance of an order made under this Act.

768. *Paragraph 9* makes provision in relation to subletting or assignments. It amends Article 94(2) of the Housing (Northern Ireland) Order 1983 which provides that certain protected tenancies are not capable of being assigned except in pursuance of an order made under the Matrimonial Causes (Northern Ireland) Order 1978. This paragraph amends Article 94(2) to ensure that such tenancies can also be assigned if the assignment is made in pursuance of an order made under this Act.

769. *Paragraph 10* makes amendment to Schedule 3 to the Housing (Northern Ireland) Order 1983 which sets out the grounds on which the court may order possession of a secure tenancy.

770. Ground 2A, provides a ground for possession where a dwelling house is occupied by a married couple, or by a couple living together as husband and wife, and one partner leaves the dwelling house because of violence by the other partner. *Paragraph 10* amends Ground 2A to provide a ground for possession where the occupants of such a dwelling are a married couple or a couple who are civil partners, or are a couple living together as husband and wife or living together as if they were civil partners.

771. *Paragraph 11* amends Article 3 of the Housing (Northern Ireland) Order 2003 which provides a definition of the meaning of "member of a person's family" for the purposes of the Order. The amendment provides that a person is a member of a person's family if he is the spouse or civil partner of that person, or if he and that person live together as husband and wife or as if they were civil partners. Paragraph 11 also amends Article 3 to provide that, for the purposes of Article 3(1)(b), a relationship by marriage or civil partnership shall be treated as a relationship by blood.

772. *Paragraph 12* amends Article 13 of the Housing (Northern Ireland) Order 2003 which provides that a person is qualified to succeed to an introductory tenancy if he occupied the dwelling as his only or principal home at the time of the tenant's death and he is the tenant's spouse. The amendment ensures that a tenant's civil partner is given the same rights as a tenant's spouse in relation to succession under an introductory tenancy.

773. *Paragraph 13* amends Article 14 of the Housing (Northern Ireland) Order 2003 which sets out the circumstances where an introductory tenant is a successor to the tenancy. These circumstances include the assignment of the tenancy to the tenant under family law. This paragraph inserts a new Article 14(2)(d) which provides that an introductory tenant is a successor to the tenancy where the tenancy was assigned to the tenant in pursuance of certain orders under this Act.

774. *Paragraph 14* makes amendment to Article 15 of the Housing (Northern Ireland) Order 2003 which provides for succession to an introductory tenancy where the tenant dies. Article 15(2) provides that where there is more than one person qualified to succeed the tenant, the tenant's spouse is to be preferred to another member of the tenant's family and Article 15 (3) makes provision in respect of tenancies vested or otherwise disposed of in pursuance of certain orders under family law. This paragraph amends Article 15(2) to provide that where there is more than one person qualified to succeed the tenant, the tenant's spouse or civil partner is to be preferred to another member of the tenant's family. It also inserts a new Article 15 (3)(a)(v) which makes provision in respect of tenancies vested or otherwise disposed of in pursuance of certain orders under this Act.

775. *Paragraph 15* amends Article 16 of the Housing (Northern Ireland) Order 2003 which provides that an introductory tenancy is not capable of being assigned except in pursuance of certain orders under family law. This paragraph inserts a new Article 16(2)(a)(v) to provide that an introductory tenancy may be assigned in pursuance of certain orders under this Act.

776. *Paragraph 16* amends Article 28 of the Housing (Northern Ireland) Order 2003 which provides definition of certain terms used in Part 3 of the Order. The term "partner" is defined as meaning a person's spouse or a person other than a spouse with whom a person lives as husband and wife. This paragraph amends the definition of "partner" to include a civil partner in the same context as a spouse.

Schedule 19: Family homes and domestic violence: Northern Ireland

Part 1 – Amendments of the Family Homes and Domestic Violence (Northern Ireland) Order 1998 (S.I. 1998/1071 (N.I. 6))

777. This Part extends the provisions relating to matrimonial homes and domestic violence contained within the Family Homes and Domestic Violence (Northern Ireland) Order 1998 ("the 1998 Order") so as to apply to civil partners as they apply to married persons.

778. Part 1 of the Schedule amends Articles 2 to 15, 20, 22, 24, 31, 33 and 39 of and Schedule 2 to the Family Homes and Domestic Violence (Northern Ireland) Order 1998. The amendments consist mainly of adding the words "civil partner", "civil partnership" and "civil partnership home", as appropriate, in order to extend the rights of spouses under those provisions to civil partners. Part 1 also amends references to "matrimonial home rights" to read "home rights", so that the description covers the rights of both married people and civil partners. The amendments provide for civil partners to apply for non-molestation orders and occupation orders, and grant civil partners the same rights to occupy the civil partnership home, as married people currently have to occupy the matrimonial home. The civil partner's right to occupy the civil partnership home will be a charge on the property. The amendments made to Schedule 2 will enable certain tenancies to be transferred on the dissolution of a civil partnership or following a declaration of nullity of a civil partnership.

Part 2 – Consequential amendments

779. This Part makes amendments consequential on the amendments to the 1998 Order in respect of the following enactments:

- Land Registration Act (Northern Ireland) 1970 (c. 18)

- Registration of Deeds Act (Northern Ireland) 1970 (c. 25)

- Land Acquisition and Compensation (Northern Ireland) Order 1973 (S.I. 1973/1896 (N.I. 21))

- Rent (Northern Ireland) Order 1978 (S.I. 1978/1050 (N.I. 20))

- Housing (Northern Ireland) Order 1983 (S.I. 1983/1118 (N.I. 15))

- Insolvency (Northern Ireland) Order 1989 (S.I. 1989/2405 (N.I.19))

Part 3 – Transitional arrangements

780. This Part provides that all references to rights of occupation and matrimonial home rights (within the meaning of the Family Law (Miscellaneous Provisions) (Northern Ireland) Order 1984 and the 1998 Order respectively) in any enactment, instrument and document shall be read, so far as is necessary for continuing the effect of the enactment, instrument or document as being or including a reference to home rights under the 1998 Order as amended by this Schedule. This Part also provides that all references to home rights before the Schedule is brought into force shall be read as including rights of occupation and matrimonial home rights without the amendments made by the Schedule. Therefore the rights conferred on civil partners by this Schedule will take effect from the date the Schedule is brought into force and are not retrospective.

781. This Part further provides that all references to a matrimonial charge (within the meaning of Article 5(1) of the 1984 Order and the 1998 Order) in any enactment, instrument or document shall be read, so far as is necessary for continuing the effect of the enactment, instrument or document as being or including a reference to a matrimonial or civil partnership charge under, or within the meaning of the 1998 Order as amended by this Schedule. This Part provides that all references to a matrimonial or civil partnership charge before the Schedule is brought into force shall be read as a matrimonial charge without the amendments made by the Schedule.

Schedule 20 – Meaning of overseas relationship: specified relationships

782. This Schedule lists the relationships in other countries or territories which are "specified relationships" for the purposes of section 212. Relationships falling within the descriptions in Schedule 20 come within the definition of an "overseas relationship" in section 212, but only if they are registered by two people of the same sex who are not already party to another civil partnership or lawful marriage. If these other requirements of section 212 are met, such relationships can therefore be treated as civil partnerships as set out in sections 215 to 218 (subject to meeting the requirements of those sections). The Schedule can be amended by subordinate legislation using the power contained in section 213.

Schedule 21 - References to step-children, etc. in Acts of Parliament

783. This Schedule lists the references in existing Acts to "step" relationships and "in-laws", to which section 246 applies. This Schedule may be amended under the power in section 247.

Schedule 22 - References to step-children, etc. in Northern Ireland legislation

784. This Schedule lists the references in existing Northern Ireland legislation to which the statutory interpretation provisions of section 246 apply. This Schedule may be amended under the power in section 248.

Schedule 23 – Immigration control and formation of civil partnerships

Part 1 - Introduction

785. Part 1 provides that where two people wish to register as civil partners of each other and one of them is subject to immigration control then the provisions set out in the Schedule will apply. Part 1 also sets out the circumstances in which the qualifying condition, referred to elsewhere in the Schedule, will be satisfied. The qualifying condition will be satisfied where the person subject to immigration control has an entry clearance granted expressly for the purpose of enabling him to form a civil partnership in the United Kingdom, has the written permission of the Secretary of State to form a civil partnership in the United Kingdom, or falls within a class specified by regulations. Part 1 provides the Secretary of State with a power to make regulations about applications for written permission to form a civil partnership. These regulations may, amongst other things, require a person seeking permission to make an application in writing and to pay a fee.

Part 2 – England and Wales

786. Part 2 provides that where the civil partnership is to be formed in England and Wales then each notice of proposed civil partnership must be given to a specified registration authority and must be delivered to the relevant individual in person by the two proposed civil partners. The relevant individual is such employee, officer or other person provided by the specified registration authority as is determined in accordance with regulations. A notice of proposed civil partnership cannot take effect unless the registration authority is satisfied by the production of specified evidence that the person subject to immigration control fulfils the qualifying condition set out in Part 1.

Part 3 – Scotland

787. Part 3 provides similar procedures to those in Part 2, which apply where the civil partnership is to be formed in Scotland and one of the proposed civil partners is subject to immigration control.

Part 4 – Northern Ireland

788. Part 4 provides similar procedures to those in Part 2, which apply where the civil partnership is to be formed in Northern Ireland and one of the proposed civil partners is subject to immigration control.

Schedule 24 – Social security, child support and tax credits

789. For the purpose of child support, social security and tax credits legislation amended, the intention is that, in general, couples in a civil partnership are treated in the same way as married couples and that same-sex couples who are not in a civil partnership but who are living together as if they were civil partners are treated in the same way as opposite-sex unmarried couples who are living together as husband and wife.

Part 1 – Amendments of the Child Support Act 1991 (c. 48) and Part 8 – Child Support Act 1995 (c. 34).

790. *Paragraphs 1 to 6 and 126 to 127* amend the Child Support Acts to ensure that civil partners are treated in the same way as members of a married couple. The amendments also ensure that a parent who is living together with a same-sex partner as if they were civil partners is treated, for the purposes of child support maintenance, in the same way as a parent who is living with an opposite-sex partner as if they were husband and wife. (For the

meaning of "living together as if they were civil partners", see commentary on *paragraphs 42 to 46*, below.)

Part 2 – Amendments of the Child Support (Northern Ireland) Order 1991 (S.I. 1991/2628 (N.I. 23))

791. *Paragraph 7* amends Article 3(2) of the Child Support (Northern Ireland) Order 1991 ("CSO 1991"). The amendments provide for persons who are or have been civil partners to be excluded from the definition of "child" for the purposes of CSO 1991 in the same way as persons who are or have been married.

792. *Paragraph 8* amends Article 10(11) of the CSO 1991 which concerns the role of the courts with respect to maintenance for children. The amendment inserts a reference to the Civil Partnership Act 2004.

793. *Paragraph 9* amends Article 17(7) of CSO 1991. This amendment extends the rule against self-incrimination, as it applies to married persons, to civil partners, where an inspector questions a person or requires that person to produce evidence in exercise of his powers under Article 17.

794. *Paragraphs 10 to 12* amend paragraph 6(5)(b) (old scheme) and 10C (new scheme) of Schedule 1 to CSO 1991. These definitions are central to the operation of the legislation and go directly to the purposes of the Order, which is the provision of child support maintenance. The amendments will ensure that same-sex civil partners and same-sex couples living together as if they were civil partners will be treated in the same way as opposite-sex couples living together in the same household. Paragraph 12 also amends Schedule 1 to the Child Support Pensions and Social Security Act (Northern Ireland) 2000 (c. 4 N.I.) in the same way.

Part 3 – Amendments of the Social Security Contributions and Benefits Act 1992 (c. 4)

795. *Paragraphs 13 to 54* amend the Social Security Contributions and Benefits Act 1992.

796. *Paragraph 13* amends the description in section 20 of category B retirement pension as a contributory benefit to reflect the fact that civil partners will be entitled like spouses (see commentary on *paragraphs 23 to 33* below).

797. *Paragraphs 14* and *15*, dealing with incapacity benefit, provide for taking account of contributions of a deceased civil partner and disregarding certain increases for civil partners in state retirement pension.

798. *Paragraphs 16 to 22* ensure that surviving civil partners are eligible (in the same way as spouses) for bereavement payment, bereavement allowance and widowed parent's allowance on the basis of their deceased civil partner's National Insurance contribution record. They also extend the rule that prevents certain bereavement benefits (and the widows' benefits which continue to be paid to women widowed before April 2001) from being paid if the survivor starts to live together as husband and wife with a person of the opposite sex to the situation where the survivor starts to live together with a person of the same sex as if they were civil partners. (For the meaning of "living together as if they were civil partners", see commentary on *paragraphs 42 to 46* below.) Further, they extend the rule that entitlement to these benefits ceases if the person remarries to cases where the person forms a new civil partnership.

799. *Paragraphs 23 to 33* and *51* extend state pension rights to civil partners. Currently, a married woman (but not a married man) can use her husband's National Insurance contribution record to qualify for a basic state pension when they have both reached state

pension age. Civil partners (like married men) will be able to qualify for these pensions when their civil partners who were born on or after 6 April 1950 reach state pension age. Because of the difference in state pension ages, this means that female civil partners will qualify from 2010 onwards and male civil partners from 2015 onwards.

800. Where a woman is widowed after reaching state pension age she can qualify for a state pension calculated as if her husband was entitled to it when he died, regardless of her husband's age on death. It consists of a basic pension plus additional pension (a percentage of SERPS depending on when the spouse reached pensionable age and 50 per cent of any State Second Pension). Until 2010 civil partners, like widowers, will only be able to receive these pensions if both spouses or civil partners are over state pension age when the first one dies. However, widowers and civil partners who reach pension age on or after 6 April 2010 will be able to qualify regardless of the age at which their wife or civil partner dies (i.e. on the same basis as widows).

801. Where a spouse is widowed before reaching pension age a state pension can be awarded if a widow or widower at any time in the past was entitled to a bereavement allowance or widowed parent's allowance when over age 45 but only as additional pension and, if aged 45 to 54 when widowed, it is reduced on a sliding scale. These provisions will apply to civil partners from the implementation date.

802. Where a marriage or civil partnership has ended, the contributions of the former spouse or civil partner may be substituted for the period of the marriage or civil partnership to allow a person to qualify for a basic state pension.

803. *Paragraph 34(a)* amends section 77(6)(a)(ii) so that where a child in respect of whom guardian's allowance is payable is not living with the beneficiary, any contributions made by the civil partner of the beneficiary count towards the cost of providing for the child if the beneficiary and his or her civil partner are living together.

804. *Paragraph 34(b)* extends the power in section 77(8)(a) to modify by regulations the circumstances in which the conditions of entitlement to guardian's allowance are satisfied in cases where a civil partnership has been dissolved.

805. *Paragraph 35* ensures that a woman's civil partner will be treated in the same way as her spouse would be for the purposes of determining whether adult dependency increases are payable with maternity allowance.

806. *Paragraphs 36* and *37* provide for civil partners to be treated in the same way as spouses for the purpose of determining whether adult dependency increases are payable with the state pension. This will apply from the date when the rules are equalised as between men and women in 2010.

807. *Paragraph 38* ensures that the provisions as to disqualification and suspension will apply to civil partners as they do to spouses.

808. *Paragraph 39* ensures that the rules set out in regulations that specify how to determine whether a person is maintaining another for the purposes of adult dependency increases will apply to civil partners as they do to spouses.

809. *Paragraph 40* provides for a voidable civil partnership which has been annulled to be treated for state pension purposes as a valid civil partnership which has been dissolved. This creates parity with the current position for marriage.

810. *Paragraph 41* amends the definition of relative to include a person related by civil partnership when determining whether a carer satisfies the conditions of entitlement for claiming carer's allowance.

811. *Paragraphs 42* to *46* amend the definition of terms relating to family membership within income support, housing and council tax benefits. In the case of a married or unmarried couple only one of them can claim these benefits and the other's needs and resources are also taken into account. For income support, benefit is only payable when neither one of the couple is in remunerative work (defined as 16 hours per week paid work for the claimant and 24 hours a week paid work for the claimant's partner). The amendments will ensure that civil partners are treated in the same way as married couples and that same-sex couples who are living together as if they were civil partners are treated in the same way as opposite-sex couples who are living together as husband and wife. Currently, unmarried couples who are living together as husband and wife are treated in the same way as married couples because otherwise they would benefit financially from choosing not to formalise their relationship. Similarly, the amendments ensure that a same-sex couple who are "living together as if they were civil partners" will be treated in the same way as a same-sex couple in a civil partnership. A same-sex couple will be regarded as "living together as if they were civil partners" for the purposes of the legislation if (but only if) they would be regarded as living together as husband and wife were they instead two people of the opposite sex. This definition is to ensure that the body of case law that applies to those living together as husband and wife will also apply to those living together as civil partners.

812. *Paragraph 47* amends section 143(5) to allow the child benefit regulations to be amended in due course to allow contributions made, or expenditure incurred, by one civil partner towards the cost of providing for the child to be treated as made or incurred by the other civil partner with whom he or she is residing. This is necessary because the regulations currently provide that where one of two spouses living together is making contributions, or incurring expenditure in respect of the child, that contribution or expenditure may be treated as made or incurred by the other spouse.

813. *Paragraph 48(2)* amends section 145A(2) so that where a child dies and within the prescribed period following the child's death the person entitled to child benefit in respect of the child also dies, the civil partner of the beneficiary, or if the beneficiary was a member of a cohabiting same-sex couple, the other member of the couple, will be entitled to child benefit for the remainder of the prescribed period.

814. *Paragraph 48(3)* defines for the purposes of section 145A(2) the terms "civil partnership" and "cohabiting same-sex couple".

815. *Paragraph 48(4)* inserts subsection 145A(6) which provides that two people of the same sex will be treated as living together as if they were civil partners if, but only if, they would be regarded as living together as husband and wife if they were instead two people of the opposite sex.

816. *Paragraph 49* amends the definition of "war widow's pension". These pensions will continue to act as qualifying benefits for the pensioners' Christmas bonus when they become available to surviving civil partners.

817. *Paragraph 50* inserts a reference to "civil partner" and "civil partnership" in subsection (4) of section 171ZL of the Social Security Contributions and Benefits Act 1992 to ensure civil partners are entitled to statutory adoption pay in the same way as spouses.

818. *Paragraphs 52* to *53* provide for account to be taken of civil partners or persons living together as if they were civil partners when determining increases of disablement pension or industrial diseases benefit or termination of industrial death benefit for widows.

819. *Paragraph 54* amends paragraph 3 of Schedule 9 to the Act so except where regulations otherwise provide, a person is excluded from entitlement to child benefit where the child is a civil partner.

Part 4 – Amendments to the Social Security Administration Act 1992 (c. 5)

820. *Paragraph 55* amends the definition of "couple" in section 2AA to align it with the new definition introduced into the Social Security Contributions and Benefits Act 1992 for the purposes of entitlement to the income-related benefits (see commentary on *paragraphs 42 to 46* above).

821. *Paragraph 56* extends to civil partners the special late claim provisions for bereavement benefits in cases where death is difficult to establish.

822. *Paragraph 57* extends the conditions under which mortgage interest payments are made within income support and jobseeker's allowance (income-based) to ensure that civil partners are treated in the same way as married couples and that same-sex couples who live together as if they were civil partners are treated in the same way as opposite-sex couples who live together as husband and wife.

823. *Paragraphs 58, 59* and *60* provide that the provisions relating to overlapping benefits and for the recovery of overpayments and social fund awards applicable to both members of a couple, regardless of which one is the claimant, will also apply to civil partners and same-sex couples who live together as if they were civil partners.

824. *Paragraph 61* provides that where maintenance payments are being collected on behalf of an income support or income-based jobseeker's allowance claimant, the same arrangements will apply to same-sex couples as currently apply to opposite sex couples. Where part or the whole of any payments are retained, they are disregarded in the calculation of the claimant's benefit.

825. *Paragraphs 62* and *63* extend the provisions on liability to maintain for income support and jobseeker's allowance (income-based) to civil partners. Where one spouse or civil partner claims, the other member of the couple may be required to make payments which offset some or all of the benefit paid unless or until the couple divorce or, as the case may be, dissolve their civil partnership.

826. *Paragraph 64* ensures that, like spouses, civil partners shall not be required to provide information which could incriminate their partner.

827. *Paragraph 65* amends the definition of "war widow's pension" for the purposes of allowing local authorities to disregard these pensions within the calculation of council tax benefit, to reflect the fact that surviving civil partners will be able to qualify for these pensions.

828. *Paragraph 66* applies the same annual uprating rules to civil partners awarded a state pension on the basis of their deceased partner's contributions as currently apply to spouses. Where a person has in payment an additional state pension on the basis of the contributions of a deceased civil partner as well as an additional state pension based on their own contributions, the uprating order shall not apply in respect of the contributions of the deceased civil partner where the civil partner died in the tax year preceding the tax year in which the uprating order comes into force and the person's final relevant tax year was an

earlier tax year. The uprating order shall not apply in respect of the contributions of the person where their final relevant tax year is the tax year preceding the tax year in which the uprating order comes into force and the deceased civil partner's final relevant year was an earlier tax year.

Part 5 - Amendments to the Social Security Contributions and Benefits (Northern Ireland) Act 1992 (c. 7)

829. *Paragraphs 67 to 106* amend the Social Security Contributions and Benefits (Northern Ireland) Act 1992.

830. *Paragraph 67* amends section 20 to provide a revised description of Category B Retirement Pension "payable to a person by virtue of the contributions of a spouse or civil partner".

831. *Paragraph 68* amends section 30A dealing with the entitlement conditions for incapacity benefit where a person is over pension age. It extends the provision whereby account may be taken of the contributions of a deceased spouse to a deceased civil partner.

832. *Paragraph 69* amends section 30B dealing with the rate of incapacity benefit where a person is over pension age and disregarding certain increases for spouses or civil partners in state retirement pension.

833. *Paragraph 70* amends section 36 to ensure that surviving civil partners are eligible (in the same way as spouses) for bereavement payment on the basis of their deceased civil partner's National Insurance contribution record. *Paragraph 70(3)* extends the rule that prevents bereavement payments benefits from being paid if the survivor is living together as husband and wife with a person of the opposite sex to the situation where the survivor is living together as if they were civil partners with a person of the same sex.

834. *Paragraph 71* amends section 36A(2) so that sections 39A to 39C (provisions relating to widowed parent's allowance and bereavement allowance) apply to civil partners as well as spouses.

835. *Paragraph 72* amends section 37 to extend the rule whereby entitlement to widowed mother's allowance (which continues to be paid to women widowed before April 2001) ceases if a widow remarries to the situation where a widow forms a civil partnership.

836. *Paragraph 73* amends section 38 to extend the rule whereby entitlement to widow's pension (which continues to be paid to women widowed before April 2001) ceases if a widow remarries to the situation where a widow forms a civil partnership.

837. *Paragraph 74* amends section 39A to ensure that surviving civil partners are eligible (in broadly the same way as spouses) for widowed parent's allowance on the basis of their deceased civil partner's National Insurance contribution record. In order to be entitled the surviving civil partner must be entitled to child benefit or responsible for a child of the family or a woman who is pregnant by artificial means and was living with her deceased civil partner at the time of her civil partner's death. *Paragraphs 74(5) and 74(6)* extend the rule that entitlement to widowed parent's allowance ceases if the survivor remarries, to cases where the survivor forms a new civil partnership. *Paragraph 74(7)* extends the rule that prevents widowed parent's allowance from being paid if the survivor is living together as husband and wife with a person of the opposite sex to the situation where the survivor is living together as if they were civil partners with a person of the same sex.

838. *Paragraph 75* amends section 39B to ensure that surviving civil partners where there are no dependant children are eligible (in the same way as spouses) for bereavement

allowance on the basis of their deceased civil partner's National Insurance contribution record. *Paragraphs 75(4) and 75(5)* extend the rule that entitlement to bereavement allowance ceases if the survivor remarries, to cases where the survivor forms a new civil partnership. *Sub-paragraph (6)* extends the rule that prevents bereavement allowance from being paid if the survivor is living together as husband and wife with a person of the opposite sex to the situation where the survivor is living together as if they were civil partners with a person of the same sex.

839. *Paragraph 76* amends section 39C to ensure that weekly bereavement benefits will be calculated in the same way for surviving civil partners as for surviving spouses.

840. *Paragraph 77* amends section 46 to ensure that where a deceased civil partner dies under pension age additional pension payable with widowed parent's allowance or state pension is calculated in the same way as for spouses.

841. *Paragraph 78* amends section 48 so that where a marriage or civil partnership has terminated, the contributions of the former spouse or civil partner may be substituted for the period of the marriage or civil partnership to allow a person to qualify for a basic state pension. Where a person has been married or formed a civil partnership more than once, this applies only to the last marriage or civil partnership.

842. *Paragraph 79* amends section 48A. Currently, a married woman (but not a married man) can use her husband's National Insurance contribution record to qualify for a lower rate (60 per cent) basic state pension when they have both reached state pension age. Amendments to this section ensure that civil partners (like married men) will be able to qualify for these pensions when their civil partners or wives who were born on or after 6 April 1950 reach state pension age. Because of the difference in state pension ages, this means that female civil partners will qualify from 2010 onwards and male civil partners from 2015 onwards. Where one spouse or civil partner dies after qualifying for these pensions, the rate increases to the full standard rate of basic pension plus at least half of any additional pension to which the deceased spouse or civil partner was entitled.

843. *Paragraph 80* amends section 48B to provide that civil partners who reach pension age on or after 6 April 2010 will be able to qualify for a state pension by virtue of the contributions of their deceased civil partner, consisting of a basic pension plus additional pension (a percentage of SERPS depending on when the spouse reached pensionable age and 50 per cent of any State Second Pension).

844. *Paragraph 81* amends section 48BB to provide for civil partners whose partners die before reaching pension age to be able to receive a state pension at any time if in the past they were entitled to a Bereavement Allowance or Widowed Parent's Allowance when over age 45 and have not married or formed a civil partnership following the death. This is payable only as additional pension and, if age 45 to 54 when bereaved, it is reduced on a sliding scale. (These provisions will apply to civil partners from the implementation date).

845. *Paragraph 82* amends section 51 to provide for civil partners to be able to receive a state pension based on their deceased civil partner's contribution record if both civil partners are over state pension age when the first one dies. This provision will apply to civil partners who reach pensionable age between the implementation date and 5 April 2010. Thereafter section 48B applies.

846. *Paragraph 83* amends section 51A so that where a civil partner is entitled to a reduced-rate category A state pension and a category B (lower rate) state pension, the category A entitlement can be topped-up to the rate of a full category B (lower rate) state pension.

847. *Paragraph 84* amends section 52 so that where a civil partner is entitled to a reduced-rate category A state pension and a category B state pension payable by virtue of a deceased civil partner's contribution record, the category A entitlement can be topped-up to the rate of a full standard category B basic state pension and any additional pension can be added up to the prescribed maximum.

848. *Paragraph 85* amends section 60 so that where a civil partner dies as a result of an industrial injury or industrial disease and he has an incomplete contribution record, the contribution conditions are taken to be satisfied for the purpose of his surviving civil partner's entitlement to any bereavement benefit or category B state pension.

849. *Paragraph 86* amends section 61A so that civil partners and surviving civil partners are treated in the same way as spouses, widows and widowers for the purposes of contributions paid in error.

850. *Paragraph 87* amends section 62 to ensure that the regulations that keep the graduated retirement benefit scheme in place may be amended to provide for surviving civil partners to be able to inherit, like spouses, half of any graduated retirement benefit to which their deceased civil partner was entitled, if they are both over pensionable age when the death occurs.

851. *Paragraph 88(a)* amends section 77(6)(a)(ii) so that where a child in respect of whom guardian's allowance is payable is not living with the beneficiary, any contributions made by the civil partner of the beneficiary count towards the cost of providing for the child if the beneficiary and their civil partner are living together.

852. *Paragraph 88(b)* extends the power in section 77(8)(a) to modify by regulations the circumstances in which the conditions of entitlement to guardian's allowance are satisfied in cases where a civil partnership has been dissolved.

853. *Paragraph 89* amends section 82 to ensure that a woman's civil partner will be treated in the same way as her spouse for the purposes of determining whether adult dependency increases are payable with maternity allowance.

854. *Paragraph 90* amends section 83A to provide for civil partners to be treated in the same way as spouses for the purposes of determining whether adult dependency increases are payable with the state pension, from the date when the rules are equalised as between men and women in 2010.

855. *Paragraph 91* amends section 85 to provide for adult dependency increases to be payable with category A retirement pension in respect of an adult childminder who is not the civil partner of the pensioner. (Provision is made only in respect of category A retirement pension because civil partners will not be able to qualify for category C retirement pensions as they are for people who were already over pensionable age in 1948).

856. *Paragraph 92* amends section 113 to ensure that the provisions as to disqualification and suspension will apply to civil partners as they do to spouses.

857. *Paragraph 93* amends section 114 to ensure that the rules set out in regulations that specify how to determine whether a person is maintaining another for the purposes of adult dependency increases will apply to civil partners as they do to spouses.

858. *Paragraph 94* amends section 120 to provide for a voidable civil partnership which has been annulled to be treated for state pension purposes as a valid civil partnership which has been dissolved. This creates parity with the current position for marriage.

859. *Paragraph 95* amends the definition of "relative" in section 121 to include a person related by civil partnership when determining whether a carer satisfies the conditions of entitlement for claiming Carer's Allowance. *Paragraph 88(3)* inserts a new definition of "living together" in section 121 to ensure that, for the purposes of social security benefits, a couple who are "living together as if they were civil partners" will be treated in the same way as a couple in a civil partnership. A same-sex couple will be regarded as "living together as if they were civil partners" for the purposes of the legislation if (but only if) they would, if of opposite sexes, be regarded as living together as husband and wife.

860. *Paragraph 96* amends section 123 by replacing references to "married or unmarried couple" with references to "couple". Together with paragraph 92 which inserts a definition of "couple", these amendments ensure that same-sex couples will be treated in the same way as married couple and opposite-sex unmarried couples living together as husband and wife for the purposes of entitlement to Income Support. In the case of a couple only one of them can be entitled to Income Support and the other's needs and resources are also taken into account. Benefit is only payable when neither one of the couple is in remunerative work (defined as 16 hours per week paid work for the claimant and 24 hours a week paid work for the claimant's partner).

861. *Paragraph 97* amends section 125 to ensure that where one or both members of a same-sex couple are involved in a trade dispute Income Support will be calculated in the same way as for a married couple or an opposite-sex unmarried couple living together as husband and wife.

862. *Paragraph 98* amends section 126 to ensure that on return to work following involvement in a trade dispute same-sex couples will be treated the same as married couples or opposite-sex unmarried couples living together as husband and wife for the purposes of income support.

863. *Paragraph 99* inserts a new definition in section 133 so that for the purpose of Part 7 (income-related benefits) the term "couple" includes married couples, opposite-sex unmarried couples living together as husband and wife and same-sex couples who are civil partners or living together as if they were civil partners.

864. *Paragraph 100* amends section 139(5) to allow the child benefit regulations to be amended in due course to allow contributions made, or expenditure incurred, by one civil partner towards the cost of providing for the child to be treated as made or incurred by the other civil partner with whom he or she is residing. This is necessary because the regulations currently provide that where one of two spouses living together is making contributions, or incurring expenditure in respect of the child, that contribution or expenditure may be treated as made or incurred by the other spouse.

865. *Paragraph 101(2)* amends section 141A(2) so that where a child dies and within the prescribed period following the child's death the person entitled to child benefit in respect of the child also dies, the civil partner of the beneficiary, or if the beneficiary was a member of a cohabiting same-sex couple, the other member of the couple, will be entitled to child benefit for the remainder of the prescribed period.

866. *Paragraph 101(3)* defines for the purposes of section 141A(2) the terms "civil partnership" and "cohabiting same-sex couple".

867. *Paragraph 101(4)* inserts subsection 141A(6) which provides that two people of the same sex will be treated as living together as if they were civil partners if, but only if, they

would be regarded as living together as husband and wife if they were instead two people of the opposite sex.

868. *Paragraph 102(2)* amends section 146 so that the definition of "war widow" reflects the fact that certain war pensions will become available to surviving civil partners and they will continue to act as qualifying benefits for the pensioners' Christmas bonus. *Paragraph 102(3)* amends section 146 so that references to "couple" in Part 10 (Christmas bonus) include same-sex couples.

869. *Paragraph 103* inserts a reference to "civil partner" and "civil partnership" in subsection (4) of section 167ZL to ensure civil partners are entitled to statutory adoption pay in the same way as spouses.

870. *Paragraph 104* amends Schedule 4A to provide that the calculation of state second pension for surviving civil partners will be the same as for surviving spouses.

871. *Paragraph 105* amends Schedule 7 to provide for account to be taken of civil partners or two persons of the same sex living together as if they were civil partners when determining increases of disablement pension or termination of industrial death benefit for widows.

872. *Paragraph 106* amends paragraph 3 of Schedule 9 to the Act so except where regulations otherwise provide, a person is excluded from entitlement to child benefit where the child is a civil partner.

Part 6 – Amendments of the Social Security Administration (Northern Ireland) Act 1992 (c. 8)

873. *Paragraphs 107 to 117* amend the Social Security Administration (Northern Ireland) Act 1992.

874. *Paragraph 107* amends the definition of "couple" in section 2AA to align it with the new definition introduced into the Contributions and Benefits Act for the purposes of entitlement to the income-related benefits (see commentary on paragraphs 42 to 46 above). This extends the conditionality/work-focussed interview provisions applicable for partners to same-sex couples.

875. *Paragraph 108* amends section 3 to extend to civil partners the special late claim provisions for bereavement benefits in cases where death is difficult to establish.

876. *Paragraph 109* amends section 13A to extend the conditions under which mortgage interest payments are made within income support and jobseeker's allowance (income-based) to ensure that same-sex couples are treated in the same way as married couples and opposite-sex unmarried couples living together as husband and wife.

877. *Paragraph 110* amends section 69 so that provisions relating to the recovery of overpayments applicable to both members of a couple, regardless of which one is the claimant, will also apply to civil partners.

878. *Paragraph 111* amends section 71 so that provisions relating to overlapping benefits applicable to both members of a couple, regardless of which one is the claimant, will also apply to same-sex couples.

879. *Paragraph 112* amends section 72A to provide that where maintenance payments are being collected on behalf of an income support or income-based jobseeker's allowance claimant, the same arrangements will apply to same-sex couples as currently apply to married couples and opposite-sex unmarried couples who are living together as husband and wife.

Where part or the whole of any payments are retained, they are disregarded in the calculation of the claimant's benefit.

880. *Paragraph 113* amends section 74 so that provisions relating to the recovery of social fund awards applicable to both members of a couple, regardless of which one is the claimant, will also apply to same sex-couples.

881. *Paragraphs 114 and 115* amend sections 100 and 102 to extend the provisions on liability to maintain for income support and jobseeker's allowance (income-based) to civil partners. Where one spouse or civil partner claims, the other member of the couple may be required to make payments which offset some or all of the benefit paid unless or until the couple divorce or, as the case may be, dissolve their civil partnership.

882. *Paragraph 116* amends section 103B to ensure that, like spouses, civil partners will not be required to provide information which could incriminate their partner.

883. *Paragraph 117* amends section 136 to apply the same annual up-rating rules to civil partners awarded a state pension on the basis of their deceased partner's contributions as currently apply to spouses. Where a person has in payment an additional state pension on the basis of the contributions of a deceased civil partner as well as an additional state pension based on their own contributions, the up-rating order shall not apply in respect of the contributions of the deceased civil partner where the civil partner died in the tax year preceding the tax year in which the up-rating order comes into force and the person's final relevant tax year was an earlier tax year. The up-rating order shall not apply in respect of the contributions of the person where their final relevant tax year is the tax year preceding the tax year in which the up-rating order comes into force and the deceased civil partner's final relevant year was an earlier tax year.

Part 7 – Amendments of the Jobseekers Act 1995 (c. 18)

884. *Paragraphs 118 to 121, 123 and 124* amend the definition of terms relating to family membership within the Jobseekers Act 1995 in line with those for other income-related benefits (see *paragraphs 42 to 46*). For jobseeker's allowance there are additional effects of being treated as a couple. Where either the claimant or their partner was born after 28th October 1957 and is 18 and over and neither is responsible for children in certain circumstances, then they are required to make a claim for jobseekers allowance as a "joint-claim couple". There are sanctions implications for joint-claim couples where one member of the couple does not comply with jobseekers directions requiring them to attend opportunities to improve their job prospects. These provisions will apply in the same way to same-sex couples who are civil partners or "living together as if they were civil partners".

885. *Paragraph 122* extends the provisions that currently allow for the recovery of spousal maintenance where an award of jobseeker's allowance has been made to that spouse to cover civil partners in the same circumstances.

886. *Paragraph 125* substitutes the term "couple" for "married or unmarried couple" in Schedule 1 to the Jobseekers Act 1995. This has the effect of extending the power contained in paragraph 9C(1) to include same-sex couples. The paragraph 9C(1) power allows regulations to be made which can provide for situations where a couple which was not previously a joint-claim couple to become a joint-claim couple.

Part 8 – Amendments of the Child Support Act 1995 (c. 34)

887. See note under Part 1.

Part 9 – Amendments of the Child Support (Northern Ireland) Order 1995 (S.I. 1995 / 2702 (N.I. 13))

888. *Paragraphs 128* and *129* amend Article 4(7) of the Child Support (Northern Ireland) Order 1995. These amendments are to definitions so as to bring same-sex couples who are civil partners or living together as if they were civil partners within the scope of Article 4, which provides for child maintenance bonus (repealed by the Child Support, Pensions and Social Security Act (Northern Ireland) 2000, so they relate to the old scheme only).

Part 10 – Amendments of the Jobseekers (Northern Ireland) Order 1995 (S.I. 1995/2705 (N.I. 15))

889. *Paragraphs 130 to 137* amend the Jobseekers (Northern Ireland) Order 1995.

890. *Paragraph 130* amends Article 2 so that definitions of "couple" etc. are brought in line with those for the other income-related benefits.

891. *Paragraphs 131 – 134, 136 and 137* amend the definition of "joint-claim couple". For jobseeker's allowance there are additional effects of being treated as a couple. Where either the claimant or their partner was born after 28th October 1957 and is 18 and over and neither is responsible for children in certain circumstances, then they are required to make a claim for jobseekers allowance as a "joint-claim couple". There are sanctions implications for joint-claim couples where one member of the couple does not comply with jobseekers directions requiring them to attend opportunities to improve their job prospects. These provisions will apply in the same way to same-sex couples who are civil partners or "living together as if they were civil partners".

892. *Paragraph 135* amends Article 25 to extend the provisions that currently allow for the recovery of spousal maintenance where an award of jobseeker's allowance has been made to that spouse to cover civil partners in the same circumstances.

Part 11 – Amendments of the Social Security Act 1998 (c. 14)

893. *Paragraph 138* amends section 72 of the Social Security Act 1998 to modify the definition of "lone parent". Section 72 provides for regulations to be made to end the provision whereby a lone parent receives a higher rate of child benefit, these regulations contain transitional and savings provisions whereby certain people continue to receive this higher rate. The effect of this amendment is that any parent who is living with another person as their civil partner, or living with another person as if they were that person's civil partner, will cease to be treated as a lone parent.

Part 12 - Amendments of the Social Security (Northern Ireland) Order 1998 (S.I. 998/1506 (N.I. 10))

894. *Paragraph 139* amends Article 68 of the Social Security (Northern Ireland) Order 1998, to modify the definition of "lone parent". Article 68 provides for regulations to be made to end the provision whereby a lone parent receives a higher rate of child benefit, these regulations contain transitional and savings provisions whereby certain people continue to receive this higher rate. The effect of this amendment is that any parent who is living with another person as their civil partner, or living with another person as if they were that person's civil partner, will cease to be treated as a lone parent.

Part 13 – Amendments of the State Pension Credit Act 2002 (c. 16)

895. *Paragraphs 140 to 143* ensure entitlement to state pension credit on the same basis as spouses and opposite-sex couples living together as husband and wife for, respectively, civil

partners and same-sex couples who are "living together as if they were civil partners"; and amends the definition of terms relating to family membership within the State Pension Credit Act 2002 in line with those for other income-related benefits (see *paragraphs 42 to 46*). *Sub-paragraphs (3) and (5)* of *paragraph 142* amend the definitions of "foreign war widow's or widower's pension" and "war widow's or widower's pension" to recognise that surviving civil partners will be able to receive these pensions.

Part 14 - Amendments of the Tax Credits Act 2002 (c. 21)

896. *Paragraph 144 (2)* amends section 3(3)(a) of the Tax Credits Act 2002 by replacing existing references to a married or unmarried couple with a single reference to a "couple". This will provide that joint tax credit claims may be made by same-sex couples in the same way as joint claims by married and unmarried opposite-sex couples.

897. *Paragraph 144(3)* deletes subsections (5) and (6) in section 3 of the Tax Credits Act, which respectively define a "married couple" and an "unmarried couple", and replaces them with a new subsection (5A) to define the term "couple". This definition includes married and unmarried opposite-sex couples and civil partnerships in which the civil partners are neither formally separated nor separated and likely to remain so permanently. The definition also extends to same-sex couples in which the parties are not civil partners but are living together as if they were civil partners.

898. *Paragraphs 145 and 146* amend various sections in the Tax Credits Act.

899. Section 4 allows for detailed rules about tax credit claims to be set out in regulations. In particular, subsection (1)(g) provides that in certain circumstances, the regulations enable one member of a married or unmarried couple to be treated as acting on behalf of the other member when making a joint claim, for example when responding to an end-of-year notice to renew a tax credit award. These regulations are in the Tax Credits (Claims and Notifications) Regulations 2002 (S.I. 2002 No. 2014, as amended by S.I. 2003 No. 3240). Subsection (1)(g) is amended to allow the regulations to be extended in due course to provide that a claim made by one party in a couple, whether opposite-sex or same-sex, is to be treated in prescribed circumstances as also made by the other party in that couple.

900. Section 11 provides for the elements making up the working tax credit to be set out in regulations. By virtue of subsection (6)(b) and (c) respectively, a working tax credit award may include an element for being a member of a married or unmarried couple or for being a lone parent who is not a member of a married or unmarried couple. These elements are described as the "second adult element" and the "lone parent element" in regulations 3(1), 11 and 12 of the Working Tax Credit (Entitlement and Maximum Rate) Regulations 2002 (S.I. 2002 No. 2005, as amended by S.I. 2003 No. 701 and S.I. 2003 No. 2815). Subsection (6)(b) is amended so that entitlement to the second adult element may extend to being a member of a same-sex couple. Subsection (6)(c) is amended to refer to a person not being a member of a couple, whether opposite-sex or same-sex, but who is responsible for a child or qualifying young person.

901. Section 17 provides that the Inland Revenue should send recipients of a tax credit award a notice after the end of each tax year. The notice requires the recipients to confirm that the circumstances affecting their entitlement (such as the number of children, whether a recipient is disabled, and the level of income) are as stated in the notice or, if different, to say how they differ. This must be done within the time limit specified in the notice. Subsection (10)(b) enables regulations to be made setting out the circumstances in which one member of a married or unmarried couple is taken to be acting for the other in responding to the notice.

The regulations are in the Tax Credits (Claims and Notifications) Regulations 2002, referred to above. Subsection (10)(b) is amended to refer to members of a couple, whether opposite-sex or same-sex, so that appropriate changes may be made in due course to the regulations.

902. Section 24 provides that payment of a tax credit award must be made to the person to whom that award has been made. Subsection (2) provides that in the case of a married or unmarried couple receiving a joint tax credit award, regulations are to prescribe to whom payment is to be made. These regulations are in the Tax Credits (Payments by the Board) Regulations 2002 (S.I. 2002 No. 2173). Subsection (2) is amended to add a reference to an award made to members of a couple, whether opposite-sex or same-sex, to enable appropriate changes to be made to the regulations in due course.

903. Section 32 provides that penalties may be imposed on a person (whether the tax credit claimant or an employer) who fails to comply with a request by the Inland Revenue to supply information or evidence in connection with a tax credit claim. Subsection (2) provides for an initial penalty of £300 followed by a further penalty of up to £60 a day for each day on which the failure to supply information or evidence continues after the imposition of the initial penalty. Subsection (6) provides that the penalties to be imposed on the members of a married or unmarried couple are not to exceed the aggregate limits contained in subsection (2). Also, if both members of a married or unmarried couple fail to notify the Inland Revenue of changes in circumstances which may reduce their tax credit award, then the aggregate amount of the penalty imposed on that couple must not exceed £300. Subsection (6) is amended so that the same penalty provisions will apply, when appropriate, in respect of tax credit claims made jointly by a same-sex couple.

904. *Paragraph 147 (2)* inserts a definition of "couple" in the list of terms in the new subsection (1) of section 48. This refers to the new subsection (5A) of section 3 of the Tax Credits Act inserted by paragraph 144(3) of this Schedule. The paragraph also deletes the definitions of a "married couple" and "unmarried couple" currently in section 48.

905. *Paragraph 147(3)* inserts a new subsection (2) in section 48 of the Tax Credits Act. It provides that two people of the same sex will be treated as living together as if they were civil partners if, but only if, they would be regarded as living together as husband and wife if they were instead two people of the opposite sex.

Part 15 – Amendments of the State Pension Credit Act (Northern Ireland) 2002 (c. 14 (N.I.))

906. *Paragraphs 148 to 151* amend the State Pension Credit Act (Northern Ireland) 2002.

907. *Paragraphs 148 to 151* ensure entitlement to state pension credit on the same basis as spouses and opposite-sex couples living together as husband and wife for, respectively, civil partners and same-sex couples who are "living together as if they were civil partners"; and amends the definition of terms relating to family membership within the State Pension Credit Act (Northern Ireland) 2002 in line with those for other income-related benefits.

908. *Paragraph 150(3) and (5)* amends the definitions of "foreign war widow's or widower's pension" and "war widow's or widower's pension" to recognise that surviving civil partners will be able to receive these pensions.

Schedule 25 – Amendment of certain enactments relating to pensions

Paragraph 1 – Fire Services Act 1947 (c. 41)

909. Section 26 of the Fire Services Act 1947 gives the Secretary of State power, by order, to bring into operation a Firemen's Pension Scheme to provide for pensions, allowances and

gratuities to be paid to persons employed as members of fire brigades or to their widows, children and dependants. The current Scheme is in the Firemen's Pension Scheme Order 1992, S.I. 1992/129, as amended. *Paragraph 1* extends section 26 to include a member of a fire brigade's surviving civil partner. It also clarifies the position in relation to widowers, by substituting the words "surviving spouse" for "widow".

Paragraph 2 - House of Commons Members' Fund Act 1948 (c. 36)

910. Section 4 of the House of Commons Members' Fund Act 1948 gives the trustees of the fund powers to make periodical or other payments to former members of the House of Commons or to their widows, widowers and orphan children, having regard to their circumstances. *Paragraph 2* extends this to include a surviving civil partner of a former member.

Paragraph 3 - Parliamentary and Other Pensions Act 1972 (c. 48)

911. Section 27(2)(a) of the Parliamentary and Other Pensions Act 1972 makes provision for the payment of pensions to the widow, widower and any eligible children of a former Prime Minister or Speaker of the House of Commons. *Paragraph 3* extends this to include the surviving civil partner of a former Prime Minister or Speaker.

Paragraph 4 - Theatres Trust Act 1976 (c. 27)

912. Section 3(d)(iii) of the Theatres Trust Act 1976 gives the trustees power to enter into agreements with insurance (or other) companies to provide gratuities or pensions to a Trust employee, his widow, family and dependants. *Paragraph 4* extends this to include an employee's surviving civil partner.

913. It also clarifies the existing law in relation to widowers by substituting the words "surviving spouse" for "widow" to ensure that it is clear that the same arrangements apply to surviving spouses of both male and female employees.

Schedule 26 – Amendment of certain enactments relating to the armed forces

914. This Schedule amends a number of statutory provisions relating to the armed forces. These provisions deal variously with the pension rights of Service personnel and of employees of Service charities, and of the spouses and surviving spouses of such personnel and employees; appeals in relation to such rights; the application of the property of deceased Service personnel; financial compensation in respect of service by members of the reserve and auxiliary forces; and appeals on behalf of deceased persons convicted by courts-martial. Each provision is amended so that it applies to a civil partner as it applies to a spouse, to civil partnership as it applies to marriage, and to a surviving civil partner as it applies to a surviving spouse.

Schedule 27 - Minor and consequential amendments

915. This Schedule amends various pieces of primary legislation to include civil partners as appropriate.

Paragraph 1 - Explosive Substances Act 1883 (c. 3)

916. *Paragraph 1* extends to civil partners the provision in section 6(2) of the Explosive Substances Act 1883 that a witness in any inquiry set up under section 6 is not excused from answering any question that might incriminate his or her husband or wife.

Paragraph 2 - Partnership Act 1890 (c. 39)

917. *Paragraph 2* amends section 2 of the Partnership Act 1890 which sets out certain rules to be taken into account when determining whether a business partnership exists or not. Rule 3(c) prevents surviving spouses or children of deceased partners from being regarded as partners merely because they receive payments from the partnership after the death. The amendment extends this provision so that the rule will also apply to surviving civil partners.

Paragraph 3 - Law of Distress Amendment Act 1908 (c. 53)

918. The Law of Distress Amendment Act 1908 protects certain tenants, lodgers and other persons in specified circumstances against the acts of landlords who might otherwise seize the goods of tenants when rent is in arrears. . Section 4 sets out a list of goods to which the 1908 Act does not apply. The list includes the goods of the husband or wife of the tenant whose rent is in arrears. *Paragraph 3* extends the exclusion to the goods belonging to the civil partner of a tenant.

Paragraph 4 - Census Act 1920 (c. 41)

919. *Paragraph 4* amends the Schedule to the Census Act 1920 which sets out the particulars which may be required during a census. Paragraph 5 of the Schedule provides for information relating to a person's condition as to marriage, relation to head of family and issue born in marriage to be collected. The amendment ensures that information may also be collected in connection with a person's condition as to civil partnership.

Paragraphs 5 and 6 - Trustee Act 1925 (c. 19)

920. *Paragraph 5* amends section 31(2)(i) of the 1925 Act which deals with the trusts upon which income accumulated during a person's infancy is to be held in certain cases where the person reaches the age of 18 or marries. *Paragraph 6* amends section 33 which relates to the holding of income on protective trusts for the benefit of any person. The amendment replaces references to "wife or husband" in section 33(1)(ii) by "spouse or civil partner".

Paragraph 7 – Law of Property Act 1925 (c. 20)

921. *Paragraph 7* amends section 205(1)(xxi) of the Law of Property Act 1925 which defines "purchaser" to include a purchaser in good faith for "valuable consideration". Valuable consideration is further defined as including marriage. This paragraph provides that the definition of valuable consideration shall be changed to include civil partnership in addition to marriage.

Paragraph 8 - Judicial Proceedings (Regulation of Reports) Act 1926 (c. 61)

922. *Paragraph 8* amends section 1 of the Judicial Proceedings (Regulation of Reports) Act 1926 to ensure that proceedings relating to the dissolution, annulment or separation of civil partners are subject to the same reporting restrictions as apply in relation to proceedings for divorce, nullity or judicial separation in relation to a marriage. The paragraph also removes references to proceedings for restitution of conjugal rights, which are obsolete. The remedy of restitution of conjugal rights was repealed by the Matrimonial and Property Act 1970.

Paragraph 9 – Population (Statistics) Act 1938 (c. 12)

923. Paragraph 9 amends paragraph 2 of the Schedule to the Population (Statistics) Act 1938 which provides for the following information to be collected when a death is registered - whether the deceased was single, married, widowed or divorced and the age of the surviving spouse, if any, of the deceased. The amendments ensure that the age of the surviving civil

partner, if any, of the deceased may be collected, together with information about whether the deceased was a civil partner or a former civil partner.

Paragraph 10 – Landlord and Tenant (Requisitioned Land) Act 1942 (c. 13)

924. *Paragraph 10* extends the definition of "member of the family" (in relation to any tenant) in section 13(1) to include civil partner.

Paragraph 11 – Limitation (Enemies and War Prisoners) Act 1945 (c. 16)

925. *Paragraph 11* adds section 51(2) of the Civil Partnership Act 2004 (which prevents a nullity order being made on certain grounds in England and Wales unless proceedings were instituted within 3 years from formation of the civil partnership) to the list of statutes of limitation in section 2 of the Limitation (Enemies and War Prisoners) Act 1945. The effect is that the rules in that Act (which suspend the operation of limitation periods where a person is an enemy or was detained in enemy territory) apply in the same way as they would in relation to proceedings for nullity of marriage.

Paragraph 12 - Statistics of Trade Act 1947 (c. 39)

926. *Paragraph 12* amends section 10 of the Statistics of Trade Act 1947 which provides for information to be collected from persons entering or leaving the United Kingdom by air to ensure that where information may be collected relating to marriage, it may also be collected in relation to civil partnerships.

Paragraphs 13 to 17 - Marriage Act 1949 (c. 76)

927. *Paragraphs 13* and *17* amend section 1 of and Schedule 1 to the Marriage Act 1949. Currently, section 1 and Schedule 1 prohibit or restrict marriage between people related within specified degrees by parentage, descent or marriage. Schedule 1 to the Civil Partnership Act 2004 provides for parallel prohibitions and restrictions to apply to civil partnerships. *Paragraphs 13* and *17* of this Schedule provide for the extension of the prohibitions and restrictions that apply to marriage to include civil partnership.

928. Section 27 of the Marriage Act 1949 sets out the information to be recorded on a notice of marriage in respect of the couple. Section 28A sets out the evidence that a superintendent registrar may require the person giving the notice of marriage to produce. One of the items of information and one of the pieces of evidence is that relating to the marital status of the person giving notice of marriage. The amendments made by *paragraphs 14* and *15* amend these two sections so that information may also be recorded and evidence required where a person wishing to give a notice of marriage has previously formed a civil partnership.

929. *Paragraph 16* amends section 78(1) (interpretation) of the Marriage Act 1949 to make clear that the term "child", when used in the Act to express a relationship, applies to persons over, as well as persons under, the age of 18.

Paragraph 18 - Maintenance Orders Act 1950 (c. 37)

930. The Maintenance Orders Act 1950 concerns the enforcement of maintenance orders as between the various jurisdictions of the United Kingdom. *Paragraph 18* amends section 16(2)(a) so that maintenance orders made in each of the three United Kingdom jurisdictions (England and Wales, Scotland and Northern Ireland) in respect of civil partners and children of the family can be enforced in the other United Kingdom jurisdictions in the same way as maintenance orders made in respect of married couples under that Act. The amendments also add references to maintenance orders made in respect of civil partners to the list of orders to which the provisions of the Maintenance Orders Act 1950 apply.

Paragraph 19 – Births and Deaths Registration Act 1953 (c. 20)

931. *Paragraph 19* extends the definition of "relative" in section 41 of this Act to include relatives by civil partnership as well as by marriage. This will qualify civil partners and those related to them to give information concerning a death to a registrar of births and deaths, providing the civil partner meets the prescribed conditions in order to give this information.

Paragraph 20 – Pharmacy Act 1954 (c. 61)

932. Section 17(c) of the Pharmacy Act 1954, provides that the Council of the Royal Pharmaceutical Society of Great Britain may make provision from the Society's benevolent fund for the relief of distressed persons including members or former members of the Society, persons registered as pharmaceutical chemists or registered chemists and druggists under the Act, widows, orphans and other dependants of deceased members of the Society. The amendment to the Pharmacy Act made by *paragraph 20* replaces the reference to widows with surviving spouses and surviving civil partners.

Paragraph 21 - Registration of Births, Deaths and Marriages (Special Provisions) Act 1957 (c. 58)

933. Section 1 of the Registration of Births, Deaths and Marriages (Special Provisions) Act 1957 confers power to provide by Order in Council for the recording of births, deaths and marriages among the armed forces outside the United Kingdom. *Paragraph 21* extends the Act so as to apply also to the recording of civil partnerships.

Paragraph 22 – Maintenance Orders Act 1958 (c. 39)

934. This Act enables orders made in a High Court or county court to be registered in a magistrates' court and orders made in a magistrates' court to be registered in the High Court. *Paragraph 22* amends sections 4(5A) and 4(5B) of the 1958 Act which apply section 60(4) to (11) of the Magistrates' Courts Act 1980 regarding the variation of maintenance orders, disregarding certain provisions of specified Acts which by this amendment will include the Civil Partnership Act. It also amends section 4(6B) which excludes variations of certain registered orders made under Part III of the Matrimonial and Family Proceedings Act 1984 so that the exclusion will be extended to the variation of certain registered orders made under Schedule 7 to the Civil Partnership Act.

Paragraph 23 - Offices, Shops and Railway Premises Act 1963 (c. 41)

935. The Offices, Shops and Railway Premises Act 1963 lays down a number of requirements relating to the health and safety of persons employed to work in office or shop premises and in certain railway premises. Section 2(1) excludes any premises where the only people employed to work are the husband, wife, parent, grandparent, son, daughter, grandchild, brother or sister of the employer. *Paragraph 23* extends this list to cover civil partners.

Paragraphs 24 and 25 - Industrial and Provident Societies Act 1965 (c. 12)

936. A member of an industrial and provident society registered under the Industrial and Provident Societies Act 1965 can request that, when they die, any property they may have in the society be transferred to a nominated person. However, under section 23, a member is permitted to nominate an officer or a servant of the society only if they are the member's spouse, parent, child, sibling, nephew or niece. *Paragraphs 24* and *25* extend this list to include the member's civil partner.

937. The 1965 Act also provides that, where a member of an industrial and provident society marries, any nomination made previously is revoked so that on the death of the member the property formerly subject to the nomination belongs to the estate of the deceased member. These paragraphs make corresponding provision for civil partners, so that where a member of such a society forms a civil partnership, any previous nomination is revoked.

938. Under section 25, where a member of an industrial and provident society dies leaving property of not more than £5000 in the society, in certain circumstances the society must deal with that property in accordance with a direction from the Treasury unless the member is survived by a child, parent, widow or widower. These paragraphs extend this list to include the member's surviving civil partner.

Paragraph 26 - Criminal Appeal Act 1968 (c. 19)

939. The Criminal Appeal Act 1968 sets out a system of appeals against verdicts and sentences in criminal proceedings. Section 44A of the Act provides that, where the appellant or potential appellant has died, the appeal may be begun or continued by a person approved by the Court of Appeal. Such approval may be given to the deceased's widow or widower, without their needing to show a substantial financial or other interest in the determination of the appeal. *Paragraph 26* allows approval to be given to a surviving civil partner in the same way.

Paragraphs 27 and 28 - Theft Act 1968 (c. 60)

940. *Paragraphs 27* and *28* amend sections 30 and 31 of the Theft Act 1968 to ensure that civil partners are treated in the same way as spouses under that Act. Section 30 ensures that the Act applies in relation to spouses and their property just as it would apply if they were not married, although (subject to certain exceptions) a person may not be charged with the theft of property belonging to their spouse unless the proceedings are instituted by or with the consent of the Director of Public Prosecutions. Section 31 provides that a person is not excused from answering any question put, or complying with any order made, in certain proceedings relating to property or trusts, by reason that to do so may incriminate that person or their spouse of an offence under the Theft Acts 1968 or 1978. However no statement or admission made by a person in these circumstances is admissible in evidence in proceedings against that person or (unless they married after the making of the statement or admission) their spouse, for an offence under the Theft Acts 1968 or 1978. The same approach will apply to civil partners.

Paragraph 29 – Domestic and Appellate Proceedings (Restriction of Publicity) Act 1968 (c. 63)

941. Section 2 of the Domestic and Appellate Proceedings (Restriction of Publicity) Act 1968 lists certain proceedings to which the publicity restrictions in the Judicial Proceedings (Regulation of Reports) Act 1926 are extended, subject to certain modifications. *Paragraph 29* extends the list to cover proceedings under Part 9 of Schedule 5 to the Civil Partnership Act 2004 (financial provision in cases of failure to maintain) and section 58 of the Act (declarations in relation to a civil partnership). The amendment ensures that civil partners benefit from similar protections as apply to spouses.

Paragraph 30 - Civil Evidence Act 1968 (c. 64)

942. The Civil Evidence Act 1968 deals with the giving of evidence in legal proceedings other than criminal proceedings. Section 14 of the 1968 Act currently provides privilege against incrimination for a husband and wife, by giving each of them a right not to answer a question if to do so would tend to expose their spouse to criminal proceedings. *Paragraph 30*

extends such privilege to civil partners by substituting "spouse and civil partner" for "husband and wife".

Paragraph 31 - Gaming Act 1968 (c. 65)

943. *Paragraph 31* amends Paragraph 35A(8)(a) of Schedule 2 to the Gaming Act 1968, adding civil partners to the definition of "associate" for the purpose of assessing who controls a corporate body. This ensures that the Gaming Board will consider the voting power of the husband, wife, or civil partner of the holder of a certificate of consent.

Paragraph 32 - Medicines Act 1968 (c. 67)

944. The Medicines Act 1968 makes provision for the regulation of medicinal products in the United Kingdom. Section 114(2) makes it an offence to fail to comply with a requirement imposed, or to provide assistance or information reasonably required, by a person duly authorised by an "enforcement authority" to take certain enforcement action under section 112 of the Act. However section 114(4) prevents a person being required to answer any question or give any information if to do so might incriminate that person or their spouse. *Paragraph 32* extends this provision, so that there is no requirement to answer a question or provide information where to do so might incriminate the person's civil partner.

Paragraph 33 - The Employers' Liability (Compulsory Insurance) Act 1969 (c.57)

945. The Employers' Liability (Compulsory Insurance) Act 1969 requires employers to insure against their liability for personal injury to their employees. Insurance is not required however where the employee is a specified relation of the employer. *Paragraph 33* extends this list of relations in section 2(2)(a) of the Act to include a civil partner of the employee.

Paragraph 34 - Administration of Justice Act 1970 (c. 31)

946. *Paragraph 34* amends Schedule 8 to the Administration of Justice Act 1970 to extend the definition of maintenance orders for the purposes of Part II of that Act and the Maintenance Orders Act 1958 to include an order for periodical or other payments made under Schedules 5, 6, or 7 of the Civil Partnership Act.

Paragraph 35 - Attachment of Earnings Act 1971 (c. 32)

947. *Paragraph 35* adds orders made under Schedules 5 and 6 to the Civil Partnership Act to the list of maintenance orders to which the provisions of the Attachment of Earnings Act 1971 apply. This ensures that maintenance orders in cases involving civil partners will be enforceable by means of attachment of earnings orders in the same way as other maintenance orders.

Paragraph 36 - Criminal Damage Act 1971 (c. 48)

948. Section 9 of the Criminal Damage Act prevents a statement or admission made in certain proceedings from being used as evidence, in proceedings for an offence under the Act, against the person who made it or their spouse. Paragraph 36 extends the same protection against incrimination to the person's civil partner.

Paragraph 37 - Immigration Act 1971 (c. 77)

949. *Paragraph 37* amends the Immigration Act 1971. Section 3 of the 1971 Act provides that a person is liable to deportation if another person to whose family he or she belongs is or has been ordered to be deported. Section 5 of the 1971 Act states that, for the purposes of deportation, a person (A) is to be regarded as belonging to the family of another person (B) if A is B's spouse or child under the age of eighteen. *Paragraph 37* amends section 5 of the

1971 Act to add that A is to be regarded as belonging to the family of B if A is B's civil partner.

Paragraphs 38 and 39 - Local Government Act 1972 (c. 70)

950. Sections 95 and 96 of the Local Government Act 1972 are part of the regime imposed by that Act regarding the registration and declaration of pecuniary interests of members of local authorities, and certain other bodies, including Transport for London. The regime established by the 1972 Act no longer applies to local authorities, having been replaced by a new regime for the regulation of conduct and ethical standards of members of local authorities introduced by the Local Government Act 2000. However, the new regime does not apply to members of Transport for London, who remain subject to the 1972 Act.

951. Section 95 of the Local Government Act 1972 provides that in certain circumstances a pecuniary interest of a member's spouse must be treated as an interest of the member and must be declared. *Paragraph 38* amends section 95 to provide that a pecuniary interest of a member's civil partner shall, in the same circumstances as currently apply in the case of a spouse, be deemed to be an interest of the member.

952. Section 96 of the Local Government Act 1972 makes provision in relation to the giving of written notice by a member of his pecuniary interests (including those of his or her spouse). *Paragraph 39* amends section 96 to apply these provisions to the interests of a member's civil partner.

Paragraphs 40 to 46 - Matrimonial Causes Act 1973 (c. 18)

953. *Paragraphs 40 to 46* of the Schedule amend the Matrimonial Causes Act 1973. *Paragraphs 40* and *41* amend sections 11 and 14 to ensure that a marriage will be void if at the time of the marriage either party was already a civil partner. *Paragraphs 42 to 45* extend the provisions of the Matrimonial Causes Act so that where certain entitlements and obligations are affected by remarriage, they will also be affected by the formation of a civil partnership. *Paragraph 46* inserts subsection (3A) in section 52 of the Act (interpretation) to clarify that a reference to the formation of a civil partnership includes a civil partnership which is void or voidable.

Paragraph 47 - Fair Trading Act 1973 (c. 41)

954. *Paragraph 47* amends section 30(6) of the Fair Trading Act 1973 to extend the privilege against incriminating one's spouse to civil partners, where answers to questions are sought relating to contraventions of orders made under section 22. Although section 22 has been repealed by the Enterprise Act 2002 the two orders made under that section are preserved by that Act and therefore so are the enforcement provisions.

Paragraph 48 - Slaughterhouses Act 1974 (c. 3)

955. Section 10 of the Slaughterhouses Act 1974 provides for the temporary continuance of a slaughterhouse or a knacker's yard licence upon the death of the holder. The continuance is either for 2 months or a longer period granted by the local authority and is for the benefit of a personal representative widow or any other family member. *Paragraph 48* adds "surviving civil partner" to the list of people to whom a licence shall temporarily enure upon the death of the licence holder.

Paragraph 49 - Health and Safety at Work Act 1974 (c. 37)

956. Section 20(7) of the Health and Safety at Work Act 1974 provides that any statement taken by an inspector using the power to require information as set out in section 20(2)(j) is

inadmissible as evidence if presented in proceedings against that person or the husband or wife of the person providing the statement. *Paragraph 49* extends the same protection against incrimination to the person's civil partner.

Paragraphs 50 and 51 - Consumer Credit Act 1974 (c. 39)

957. Section 165(3) of the Consumer Credit Act 1974 states that a person cannot be required to answer any question or give any information if to do so might incriminate that person or (where that person is married) the husband or wife of that person. *Paragraph 50* extends this provision, so that there is no requirement to answer questions or provide information where to do so might incriminate the person's civil partner.

958. Part II of the Consumer Credit Act (CCA) 1974 classifies consumer credit and consumer hire agreements. The term "associate" appears in the provisions defining a number of these transactions: running-account and fixed–sum credit (section 10); small agreements (section 17); and linked transactions (section 19).

959. Part III of the CCA 1974 deals with the principles of licensing. Section 25 sets out various matters which should be taken into account by the Office of Fair Trading in deciding whether an applicant is a fit person to carry on licensed activities. One of these is the conduct not only of the applicant but of, amongst others, the applicant's associates.

960. The word "associate" is defined in section 184 of the CCA 1974 and embraces certain forms of business association and relatives. "Relative" is defined in subsection (5) and includes former and reputed husbands and wives and children born outside wedlock, step-children and adopted children.

961. *Paragraph 51* extends the meaning of "associate" to civil partners and to those relationships created by the formation of a civil partnership, which mirror those created by marriage. It extends the definition of "relative" at subsection (5) to include former civil partners, and also, for the purposes of the subsection, allows that a relationship will be established as if any illegitimate child, step-child or adopted child had been a child born within a civil partnership, as well as in wedlock.

Paragraph 52 - Friendly Societies Act 1974 (c. 46)

962. In the case of most types of friendly society registered within the meaning of the Friendly Societies Act 1974, under section 66, a member can request that, when they die, a sum payable by the society on their death be paid to a nominated person. *Paragraph 52* provides that the civil partner of a member can be nominated even where that nominee is an officer or servant of the society.

963. Section 66 also provides that, where a member of a registered friendly society marries, any nomination made previously is revoked so that on the death of the member any sums due from the society become part of the estate of the deceased member. Paragraph 52 also makes corresponding provision for civil partners, so that where a member of such a society forms a civil partnership, any previous nomination is revoked.

Paragraph 53 - Rehabilitation of Offenders Act 1974 (c. 53)

964. If a person has become a rehabilitated person in accordance with the provisions of the Rehabilitation of Offenders Act 1974, limitations are placed upon evidence that can be admitted and questions which that person can be required to answer, in relation to spent convictions. An exception is made to this general principle so that evidence relating to spent convictions can be admitted or required in proceedings relating to the marriage of a minor.

Paragraph 53 amends section 7(2)(c) of the Act so that it applies equally in relation to the formation of a civil partnership by a minor.

Paragraph 54 – Sex Discrimination Act 1975 (c. 65)

965. *Paragraph 54* amends the definition of "near relative" in section 82(5) of the Sex Discrimination Act to include civil partners and relatives of civil partners. This is relevant for the housing provisions in sections 29 to 32 of this Act which make it unlawful to discriminate in relation to the disposal or management of premises, or in relation to giving consent for the assignment of a lease or for sub-letting. Sections 31(2) and 32(1) provide an exception for small dwellings occupied by the alleged discriminator and/or a near relative where there is other accommodation in addition to that occupied by the alleged discriminator and/or his near relative which he shares with other persons residing on the premises who are not members of his household.

Paragraph 55 – Race Relations Act 1976 (c. 74)

966. *Paragraph 55* amends the definition of "near relative" in section 78(5) of this Act to include civil partners and relatives of civil partners. This affects housing discrimination provisions (sections 20 to 22 of the Race Relations Act as amended) which have the same effect as those in sections 29 to 32 of the Sex Discrimination Act 1975 (see note on *paragraph 54* above).

Paragraph 56 - Criminal Law Act 1977 (c. 45)

967. *Paragraph 56* amends section 2 of the Criminal Law Act 1977 to ensure that civil partners benefit from the same exemption from liability for the offence of conspiracy that currently applies to a spouse.

Paragraphs 57 and 58 - Domestic Proceedings and Magistrates Courts Act 1978 (c. 22)

968. *Paragraphs 57 and 58* amend sections 4 and 35 of the Domestic Proceedings and Magistrates Courts Act 1978 so that where certain financial obligations and entitlements are affected by remarriage, they will, by these amendments, also be affected by the formation of a civil partnership.

Paragraph 59 – Interpretation Act 1978 (c. 30)

969. *Paragraph 59* inserts a new entry into Schedule 1 to the Interpretation Act 1978. Under sections 5 and 23 of the Interpretation Act 1978 if an expression listed in Schedule 1 is used in any Act or subordinate legislation it is presumed to have the meaning given in Schedule 1 unless the contrary intention appears from the Act or subordinate legislation in question. The amendment to Schedule 1 means that references in future legislation to "civil partnership" or "civil partner" will be interpreted by reference to the Civil Partnership Act without need for express definition.

Paragraph 60 - Protection of Children Act 1978 (c. 37)

970. Section 1A of the Protection of Children Act 1978 concerns cases where a defendant, charged with an offence involving an indecent photograph of a child under section 1 of the Act, proves that at the relevant time the child was aged 16 or over and was either married to the defendant or living with the defendant as a partner in an enduring family relationship. In such cases, where the evidence raises an issue as to the child's consent, section 1A provides that the defendant is not guilty unless it is proved that the child did not so consent and the defendant did not reasonably believe that the child consented. Where the offence is one of possession with a view to the photograph being shown or distributed, section 1A provides

that the defendant is not guilty unless it is proved that the showing or distributing was to a person other than the child. *Paragraph 60* amends section 1A of the Protection of Children Act 1978 to ensure that the same provisions apply if the defendant and the child were civil partners of each other, so that they are treated in the same way as spouses.

Paragraph 61 – Credit Unions Act 1979 (c. 34)

971. Under section 1(6) of the Credit Unions Act 1979, a credit union may provide that a person who resides in the same household as, and is a relative of, a member of the credit union may be automatically entitled to become a member of the credit union. Section 31(1) of the Credit Unions Act 1979 (interpretation) defines a relative to include a spouse (including a former or reputed spouse) and certain relations and in-laws of a spouse. *Paragraph 61* extends the definition of a "relative" in section 31(1) of the Credit Unions Act so as to include civil partners (including former civil partners) and their relations and in-laws.

Paragraphs 62 and 63 - Estate Agents Act 1979 (c. 38)

972. Section 27(1) of the Estate Agents Act 1979 makes it an offence for a person to obstruct certain authorised officers. Section 27(4) provides that nothing in subsection (1) requires a person to answer any question or give any information if to do so might incriminate that person or that person's husband or wife. *Paragraph 62* amends section 27(4) to extend it so that a person will not be required, by section 27(1), to answer any question or give any information that might incriminate that person's civil partner.

973. Under the Estate Agents Act 1979, estate agents are required to make full disclosure to their clients of any personal interest, whether direct or indirect, so that their clients are aware of any potential conflict of interest. This personal interest can include those of any associate of theirs or the estate agent. "Associate" is defined in section 32 of the Act and includes spouses or relatives. The amendments made by para*graph 63* include civil partners or relatives by civil partnership within the definition of section 32.

Paragraphs 64 and 65 - Magistrate's Courts Act 1980 (c. 43)

974. Section 59 of the Magistrates' Courts Act 1980 sets out the powers of a magistrates' court to determine the means by which certain periodical payments are made. Subsection (7) sets out certain cases where the court must order that payments be made to the designated officer for a magistrates' court unless satisfied that it is undesirable to do so. *Paragraph 64* makes amendments to add orders made under Schedule 6 to the Civil Partnership Act 2004 (financial relief in magistrates' courts etc.) to the list of maintenance orders to which subsection (7) applies. This ensures that maintenance orders under Schedule 6 to the Civil Partnership Act are treated in the same way as maintenance orders under Part I of the Domestic Proceedings and Magistrates' Courts Act 1978.

975. *Paragraph 65* amends the definition of family proceedings in section 65 of the 1980 Act extending the definition to cover certain proceedings under Schedules 2, 5 and 6 to the Civil Partnership Act. These amendments are consequential upon the creation of the relationship of civil partner and upon the classification of proceedings arising from civil partnerships as family proceedings.

Paragraph 66 - Disused Burial Grounds (Amendment) Act 1981 (c. 18)

976. The purpose of the Disused Burial Grounds (Amendment) Act 1981 is to amend the Disused Burial Grounds Act 1884 to enable buildings to be erected on certain disused burial grounds with appropriate safeguards. Sections 4 and 8 of the 1981 Act make provision for a relative of a person whose remains are interred to claim compensation for the loss of burial

rights in certain circumstances. *Paragraph 66* amends section 9 of the 1981 Act to extend the definition of "relative" include the spouse or civil partner.

Paragraph 67 - Forgery and Counterfeiting Act 1981 (c. 45):

977. *Paragraph 67* amends the Forgery and Counterfeiting Act 1981 adding certified copies of entries relating to civil partnerships to the list of instruments in section 5(5) of the Act. This means that the possession of false certified copies, or of equipment for making them, will be an offence. Section 5(5) already applies to false marriage certificates.

Paragraphs 68 to 70 – Supreme Court Act 1981 (c. 54)

978. *Paragraph 68* amends section 18(1) of the Supreme Court Act 1981 so that restrictions on appeal following the making of a decree nisi absolute in divorce or nullity proceedings are to apply in the same way to final dissolution or nullity orders made in civil partnership cases under Chapter 2 of Part 2 of the Civil Partnership Act 2004.

979. *Paragraph 69* amends section 72 of the Supreme Court Act 1981 so that a person will not be able to refuse to make a statement or admission because to do so might incriminate his or her civil partner. The same obligations regarding giving evidence will apply to civil partners as to married people.

980. *Paragraph 70* amends paragraph 3 of Schedule 1 to the Supreme Court Act 1981 to reflect the classification of proceedings relating to civil partnerships as family proceedings for the purposes of allocating business to the Family Division of the High Court. The amendment adds certain proceedings arising from civil partnerships to the list of proceedings assigned to the Family Division of the High Court. These specified proceedings are to be treated as family proceedings in the same way as the corresponding proceedings arising from marriage are treated as family proceedings.

Paragraphs 71 to 78 – British Nationality Act 1981 (c. 61)

981. *Paragraphs 71 to 78* make consequential amendments to the British Nationality Act 1981. The effect is to place civil partners in the same position as spouses in terms of eligibility to acquire or resume British nationality by registration or naturalisation and the ability to renounce British nationality. Thus:

- An applicant for naturalisation who is the civil partner of a British citizen or a British overseas territories citizen will be subject to the less onerous requirements, in terms of residence etc, that currently apply in the case of husbands and wives of British citizens and British overseas territories citizens (sections 6(2) and 18(2) and paragraphs 4(d) and 8(d) of Schedule 1);

- A person seeking to resume British nationality, having previously renounced it pre-1983, may rely on his or her civil partner's connections with the United Kingdom or, as the case may be, with a British overseas territory (sections 10(2)(b) and 22(2)(b));

- A person who is or has been a civil partner will be able to renounce British nationality notwithstanding that he or she is still a minor (section 12(5)); and

- Provisions relating to the registration as a British citizen or British overseas territories citizen of a minor whose parents' marriage has been terminated will include corresponding references to the termination of the parents' civil partnership (sections 3(6)(a) and 17(6)(a)).

Paragraph 79 - Forfeiture Act 1982 (c. 34)

982. Section 3 of the Forfeiture Act 1982 Act lists the provisions under which financial provision will not be affected by the forfeiture rule. *Paragraph 79* amends section 3 of the Act to add references to the variation of periodical payments orders and maintenance orders in Schedule 5 to the Civil Partnership Act and the provisions for variation of periodical allowances in respect of marriages and civil partnerships in Scotland. These orders will have the same exemption from the forfeiture rule as orders made in relation to marriage.

Paragraphs 80 to 85 - Representation of the People Act 1983 (c. 2)

983. These *paragraphs* make amendments to the Representation of the People Act 1983 to provide for civil partners to be treated in the same way as married couples. For example, the amendments provide the same treatment as spouses for the civil partners of service personnel in relation to continuing voter registration whilst serving outside the UK; a civil partner will be treated in the same way as a husband/wife for the purpose of attending the delivery of nomination papers where his or her spouse or civil partner is standing as a candidate; to assist his or her disabled spouse or civil partner to cast a vote; or to act as a proxy voter for the spouse or civil partner.

Paragraph 86 - Mental Health Act 1983 (c. 20)

984. *Paragraph 86(a)* adds a reference to the civil partner of the patient to the list of individuals named in section 12 of the Mental Health Act 1983 who may not provide a medical recommendation for the purposes of an application for compulsory admission to hospital of a patient for assessment or treatment under the Act.

985. *Paragraph 86(b)* adds a reference to the civil partner of the patient to the definition of close relative in section 25C of the Mental Health Act 1983. A close relative may not provide a written recommendation about a patient for the purposes of an application for aftercare under supervision.

Paragraphs 87 and 88 – Mobile Homes Act 1983 (c. 34)

986. *Paragraphs 87* and *88* amend the Mobile Homes Act 1983, which applies to any agreement under which an occupier is entitled to station a mobile home on land forming part of a protected site, and to occupy the mobile home as his only or main residence. Such occupiers are given statutory security of tenure by the Act. The amendments ensure that surviving civil partners are entitled to succeed to the agreement on the same basis as widows and widowers.

Paragraph 89 - Dentists Act 1984 (c. 24)

987. Section 41 of the Dentists Act 1984 provides that where a dentist dies, his widow may continue to carry on the business for three years. The amendment to the 1984 Act reflects existing practice of treating "widow" as including "widower" by referring to surviving spouses, and also adds surviving civil partners to this provision.

Paragraphs 90 to 96 – Matrimonial and Family Proceedings Act 1984 (c. 42)

988. *Paragraph 90* amends section 12 of the Matrimonial and Family Proceedings Act 1984 so that in respect of applications for financial relief following overseas divorces, no application may be made if the applicant either remarries or forms a subsequent civil partnership.

989. *Paragraphs 91 to 96* insert amendments to enable civil partnership proceedings to be designated as family business and for the Lord Chancellor to allocate courts to deal with civil partnership proceedings.

990. *Paragraph 91* amends section 32 to add a definition of civil partnership causes to the defined terms used in Part V of the 1984 Act.

991. *Paragraph 92* inserts new sections 36A to 36D. The new section 36A makes provision for the jurisdiction of county courts in civil partnership causes, so that the Lord Chancellor may by order designate any county court as a "civil partnership proceedings county court". Section 36B makes provision for the civil partnership proceedings county courts to have jurisdiction to deal with financial relief and protection of children in respect of civil partnership causes. Section 36C allows for court rules to confer jurisdiction on civil partnership proceedings county courts to consider agreements made between civil partners in respect of civil partnership proceedings. Section 36D provides for the Lord Chancellor to assign circuit judges to exercise the jurisdiction of civil partnership proceedings county courts.

992. *Paragraph 93* amends section 38(3) of the Matrimonial and Family Proceedings Act 1984 to provide for the High Court to give directions for civil partnership causes to be transferred from the High Court to a county court where appropriate.

993. *Paragraph 94* amends section 39(2) of the 1984 Act to enable civil partnership causes to be transferred to the High Court from a county court.

994. *Paragraph 95* amends section 40(4)(b) of the 1984 Act to allow orders made in respect of civil partnership causes to be enforced in the High Court.

995. *Paragraph 96* amends section 42 of the 1984 Act to enable civil partnership causes to be dealt with by the principal registry of the Family Division where appropriate and for the same jurisdiction and powers of enforcement to be available in the principal registry of the Family Division as in a county court.

Paragraphs 97 and 98 - Police and Criminal Evidence Act 1984 (c. 60)

996. Section 80 of the Police and Criminal Evidence Act 1984 sets out the circumstances in which the spouse of a person who is charged in proceedings, shall be compellable to give evidence. *Paragraph 97* amends section 80 to ensure that a civil partner of a person who is charged in proceedings will be compellable in the same circumstances.

997. Section 80A of the 1984 Act provides that the failure of the spouse of a person charged in any proceedings to give evidence shall not be made the subject of any comment by the prosecution. *Paragraph 98* amends section 80A so that it applies equally where a civil partner fails to give evidence in the same circumstances.

Paragraphs 99 to 105 and 128 – Companies Act 1985 (c. 6) and 1989 (c. 40)

998. *Paragraphs 99 to 105* and *128* ensure that, in relation to the provisions of the Companies Acts of 1985 and 1989 specified in the Schedule, civil partners are to be treated in the same way as spouses of directors.

999. Under the Companies Act provisions persons with a notifiable interest in shares should notify the company. Section 203 of the Companies Act 1985 deems a person to be interested in shares in which his spouse is interested. *Paragraph 99* extends this obligation to civil partners.

1000. Section 323 of the 1985 Act contains a prohibition on directors dealing in share options of his or her own company. Section 327 applies the prohibition to the wife or husband of a director. *Paragraph 100* extends the prohibition to the civil partner of a director.

1001. Section 328 of the 1985 Act requires directors to disclose shareholdings in their own company. Section 328 treats the interests of a wife or husband of a director as an interest of that director. *Paragraph 101* extends this to civil partners of directors.

1002. Part X of the 1985 Act contains a number of provisions designed to enforce fair dealing by directors. A number of these provisions apply to persons connected with a director. Section 346 defines " connected person" to include spouse. *Paragraph 102* extends this definition to include civil partners.

1003. Section 430E of the 1985 Act disregards shares held by the associate of an offeror in certain circumstances (relating to takeover offers). Where an offeror is an individual, "associates" includes spouses, and this definition will be extended by *paragraph 103* to include civil partners.

1004. *Paragraphs 104* and *105* amend section 742A of and Schedule 7 to the Companies Act 1985. Section 742A deals with the meaning of the term "offer to the public" in relation to shares and debentures. Schedule 7 sets out the matters to be dealt with in a directors' report. The amendments ensure that civil partners are treated in the same way as spouses.

1005. *Paragraph 128* defines "associate" to include civil partner as well as spouse for the purposes of the Companies' Act 1989.

Paragraphs 106 to 108 - Enduring Powers of Attorney Act 1985 (c. 29)

1006. The Enduring Powers of Attorney Act 1985 provides that where an enduring power of attorney is created, the power shall not be revoked by the subsequent mental incapacity of the person creating it. *Paragraph 106* amends section 3(5)(a) of the Act, which enables an attorney to make gifts of a seasonal nature or at a time, or on an anniversary, of a birth or marriage on behalf of the mentally incapacitated person, so that it also extends to the time or anniversary of the formation of a civil partnership. *Paragraph 107* amends the provisions in Schedule 1 to the Act which require an attorney, before he applies for the power to be registered (which he is required to do when he considers that the donor is or is becoming mentally incapable), to notify relatives of the person who created the enduring power of attorney, so as to include civil partners in the list of relatives so entitled. *Paragraph 108* states that *paragraphs 106 and 107* apply in relation to the enduring powers of attorney created both before and after the passing of the Civil Partnership Act.

Paragraph 109 - Food and Environment Protection Act 1985 (c. 48)

1007. Paragraph 2A(1) of Schedule 2 to the Food and Environment Protection Act 1985 provides that an officer may require a person to answer questions and to sign a declaration of the truth of his answers. Subparagraph (4) provides that a person is not to be excused from complying with a requirement under subparagraph (1) on the grounds that to do so might incriminate him or his spouse of an offence. *Paragraph 109* amends Schedule 2 to extend this provision to civil partners.

Paragraph 110 - Child Abduction and Custody Act 1985 (c. 60)

1008. *Paragraph 110* amends section 24A of the Child Abduction and Custody Act 1985 to ensure civil partners are treated in the same way as spouses for the purposes of this section which concerns the power to order the disclosure of a child's whereabouts.

Paragraph 111 - Airports Act 1986 (c. 31)

1009.*Paragraph 111* amends section 20(6)(b) of the Airports Act 1986 to extend the scope of the "employees' share scheme", which encourages or facilitates the holding of shares or debentures in a public airport company. As well as the spouses and surviving spouses, a future scheme provided for under this provision will need to extend to the civil partners and surviving civil partners of the employees or former employees of the company.

Paragraphs 112 to 122 - The Insolvency Act 1986 (c. 45)

1010.The Insolvency Act 1986 contains various provisions protecting creditors from fraud and attempting to ensure a proper *pari passu* distribution amongst creditors. These provisions allow certain transactions, including transactions involving close family and other associated persons, entered into by a debtor or company prior to the onset of insolvency proceedings to be undone or adjusted.

1011.*Paragraphs 112 to 121* make consequential amendments to the 1986 Act to ensure that where a person is adjudged bankrupt, the person's civil partner is to have the same rights and liabilities as the spouse of a bankrupt has at present. Amendments are made to certain anti-abuse and avoidance provisions in the Act to ensure that transactions involving civil partners entered into prior to the onset of insolvency proceedings are treated in the same way as transactions involving spouses.

1012. *Paragraph 122* amends the definition of "associate" in the 1986 Act so that the relevant anti-avoidance provisions cover a civil partner in the same way as a spouse.

Paragraph 123 – Building Societies Act 1986 (c. 53)

1013.*Paragraph 123* amends the definition in section 70 of the Building Societies Act 1986 of a person "connected with" a director of a building society to ensure that directors' civil partners are subject to the same prohibitions and requirements as directors' spouses.

Paragraphs 124 and 125 – Family Law Act 1986 (c. 55)

1014.*Paragraph 124* amends subsection (2) of section 33 of the Family Law Act 1986 to add a reference to a civil partner. This amendment provides that a person will not be able to refuse to disclose information about the whereabouts of a child because to do so might incriminate either the person or his or her civil partner. The amendment places the same restriction on a civil partner as is already placed upon a husband or wife.

1015.*Paragraph 125* amends section 50, which currently applies only to divorce, annulment and remarriage, so that when a dissolution or annulment of a civil partnership granted in any part of the United Kingdom is not recognised elsewhere, that fact will not prevent or render invalid in that part a subsequent marriage or civil partnership.

Paragraph 126 - Consumer Protection Act 1987 (c. 43)

1016.Section 47(2) of the Consumer Protection Act 1987 provides for a privilege against self-incrimination and incrimination of spouses where answers to questions or information are sought under the enforcement provisions of the Act. *Paragraph 126* amends section 47(2) to extend the privilege to civil partners.

Paragraph 127 - Criminal Justice Act 1988 (c. 33)

1017.Section 160A of the Criminal Justice Act 1988 concerns cases where a defendant, charged with an offence involving an indecent photograph of a child under section 160 of the Act, proves that at the relevant time the child was aged 16 or over and was either married to the defendant or living with the defendant as a partner in an enduring family relationship. In such cases, where the evidence raises an issue as to the child's consent, section 160A provides that the defendant is not guilty unless it is proved that the child did not so consent and the defendant did not reasonably believe that the child consented. *Paragraph 127* amends section 160 to ensure that the same provisions apply if the defendant and the child were civil partners of each other, so that they are treated in the same way as spouses.

Paragraph 128 – Companies Act 1989 (c. 40)

1018.See note on *paragraphs 99* to *105* above.

Paragraphs 129 to 132 - Children Act 1989 (c. 41)

1019.*Paragraph 129* makes an amendment to section 8 of the Children Act 1989 to add proceedings under Schedule 5 (financial relief in the High Court and county court) and Schedule 6 (Financial relief in magistrates' courts) to the Civil Partnership Act 2004 to the definition of family proceedings for the purposes of the Children Act contained in section 8(4) of the Act. This ensures proceedings under the Civil Partnership Act are treated as family proceedings for the purposes of the Children Act in the same way as proceedings involving married people.

1020.Paragraphs 130 to 132 provide that the same restrictions placed on people seeking to be excused from complying with requests to assist in the recovery of children or requirements to give evidence in cases involving the care of children on the grounds of self-incrimination or incrimination of a husband or wife also apply to the incrimination of a civil partner.

1021.*Paragraph 130* amends section 48(2) to provide that no person may be excused from complying with a requirement to assist in the recovery of a child who may be in need of emergency protection on the ground that complying might incriminate his or her civil partner of an offence.

1022.*Paragraph 131* amends section 50(11) to provide that no person may be excused from complying with any request made in connection with an order for recovery of an abducted child on the ground that complying might incriminate his or her civil partner of an offence.

1023.*Paragraph 132* amends section 98(1) and (2) to provide that no person shall be excused from giving evidence in proceedings regarding care or protection of a child on the ground that giving evidence could incriminate his or her civil partner of an offence.

Paragraphs 133 and 134 - Local Government and Housing Act 1989 (c. 42)

1024.Section 19 of the Local Government and Housing Act 1989 is linked to the regime imposed by the Local Government Act 1972 regarding the registration and declaration of pecuniary interests of members of local authorities, and certain other bodies, including Transport for London. The regime established by the 1972 Act no longer applies to local authorities, having been replaced by a new regime for the regulation of conduct and ethical standards of members of local authorities introduced by the Local Government Act 2000. However, the new regime does not apply to members of Transport for London, who continue to be subject to the 1972 Act and to the related provisions in the Local Government and Housing Act 1989.

1025.Section 19 of the 1989 Act gives the Secretary of State powers to make regulations regarding the interests, including the indirect pecuniary interests, of members of local authorities (including members of Transport for London). The definition of an indirect pecuniary interest in section 19(7) includes an interest which may arise through a member's spouse. *Paragraph 133* amends section 19 to provide that an indirect pecuniary interest arising through a member's civil partner will be treated in the same way as one arising through a member's spouse.

1026. Section 69 of the 1989 Act sets out the circumstances in which a company can be said to be under the influence of a local authority. In order to determine this, it may be necessary to establish whether a person is associated with the local authority. Subsection (5) sets out how a person may be associated with a local authority. Subsection (6) gives the Secretary of State power to provide by order that a person may also be associated with a local authority if he or she is at that time the spouse of, or carries on business in partnership with, a person who is associated with the authority by virtue of subsection (5)(a) (he or she is a member of the authority). *Paragraph 134* amends section 69 to insert a reference to civil partner to ensure civil partners are treated in the same way as spouses.

Paragraph 135 - Opticians Act 1989 (c. 44)

1027. Section 29 of the Opticians Act 1989 provides that where an optician dies, his widow may continue to carry on the business for three years. The amendment to the 1989 Act reflects the existing practice of treating "widow" as including "widower" by referring to surviving spouses, and also adds surviving civil partners to this provision.

Paragraph 136 - Food Safety Act 1990 (c. 16)

1028. Section 43 of the Food Safety Act 1990 allows, on death of the registration holder/licensee, for the continuation of the registration or licence granted for food premises in accordance with regulations made under the Act. Currently this applies to the deceased licence or registration holder's personal representative, widow or any other member of his family for a period of three months beginning with his death or for such longer period as the enforcement authority may allow. *Paragraph 136* amends the Food Safety Act to enable surviving civil partners to benefit from the same rights accorded to personal representatives, and other members of the deceased's family.

Paragraphs 137 and 138 - Courts and Legal Services Act 1990 (c. 41)

1029. *Paragraph 137* amends section 10 of the Courts and Legal Services Act 1990 to insert a reference to proceedings under Schedule 6 to the Civil Partnership Act (financial relief in the magistrates' court) to the list of proceedings defined as family proceedings in magistrates' courts. This amendment is consequential upon the classification of proceedings arising from civil partnerships as family proceedings and will facilitate the handling of these proceedings in the magistrates' court.

1030. *Paragraph 138* amends Section 58A of the 1990 Act to add references to proceedings for dissolution, nullity and separation of civil partners, and proceedings for financial relief under Schedules 5, 6 and 7 to the Civil Partnership Act to the list of proceedings for which conditional fee agreements are not permissible.

Paragraph 139 – Broadcasting Act 1990 (c. 42)

1031. Broadcasting legislation requires the provision of television and radio services to be licensed. Under the media ownership rules in this legislation, certain persons and their "associates" are disqualified from holding broadcasting licences. The effect of this paragraph is to amend that legislation so that, where a husband or wife is regarded as an "associate" for these purposes under the current legislation, civil partners are also to be so regarded

Paragraph 140 - Local Government Finance Act 1992 (c. 14)

1032.*Paragraph 140(1)* makes changes to local government finance legislation. *Paragraph 140(1)* amends section 9(1)(a) of the Local Government Finance Act 1992 to provide that civil partners will be jointly and severally liable for council tax in the same way as married couples.

1033.*Paragraph 140(2)* amends section 9(3) of the 1992 Act to provide that, for the purposes of defining civil partners for that section, they are of the same sex and either civil partners of each other or are not in a civil partnership but who are living together as if they were civil partners.

1034.*Paragraph 140(3)* amends section 18(1)(b) of the 1992 Act to provide a regulation making power to deal with a case where a civil partner dies who was liable as a civil partner to pay council tax. A regulation making power already exists in section 18(1)(b) in relation to a person who dies who was liable as a spouse under section 9 of the Act to pay council tax.

Paragraph 141 –to 142 – Friendly Societies Act 1992 (c. 40)

1035.*Paragraph 141* amends section 77 of the Friendly Societies Act 1992 which concerns the information to be disclosed in a friendly society's balance sheet as regards the society's appointed actuary, and that actuary's spouse, children or stepchildren. It extends the disclosure provision in subsection 3(a) to include the civil partner of an actuary as well as the spouse.

1036.*Paragraph 142* amends the meaning of "associate" in section 119A of the 1992 Act to include a civil partner as well as a wife or husband.

1037.Among the activities that a friendly society incorporated under the 1992 may conduct is the provision of insurance policies that pay out a sum of money on marriage or the birth of a child. *Paragraph 143* amends Schedule 2 to the 1992 Act to allow incorporated friendly societies to provide insurance policies that pay out in the event of formation of a civil partnership.

Paragraphs 144 to 146 - Trade Union and Labour Relations Act 1992 (c. 52)

1038.*Paragraph 144* amends section 23 of the 1992 Act in order to give a civil partner the same rights as the husband or wife of a trade union member. Section 23 provides for restriction on enforcement of awards against certain property held by trade unions. This includes property comprised in a separate fund maintained for the purpose only of providing provident benefits, including "a payment in discharge or aid of funeral expenses on the death of a member or the wife of a member or a provision for the children of a deceased member".

1039.*Paragraph 145* amends section 241 of the 1992 Act in order to give a civil partner the same protection as the husband or wife of a person. Section 241 relates to intimidation or annoyance in connection with industrial action. It provides that a person commits a criminal offence if, with a view to compelling another person to abstain from doing or to do an act which that person has a legal right to do or abstain from doing, he wrongfully and without legal authority uses violence to or intimidates that person or his wife or children.

1040.*Paragraph 146* amends section 292 of the 1992 Act in order to give a surviving civil partner the same rights as widow or widower of a person. Section 292 provides for the continuation of employment tribunal proceedings in the event of the death of an employee or employer by a personal representative. It provides that where there is no personal representative tribunal proceedings may be instituted or continued by such other person as the employment tribunal may appoint, being either, the widower, widow, child, father mother, brother, or sister of the employee.

Paragraph 147 – Charities Act 1993 (c. 10)

1041.*Paragraph 147* amends Schedule 5 to the Charities Act 1993. It ensures that the definition of "connected person" includes the civil partner (and any corporate body or institution in which they have an interest) of a person connected with a charity. The spouse (or corporate body or institution in which they have an interest) of such a person is already included in the definition.

Paragraph 148 – Pension Schemes Act 1993 (c. 48)

1042.*Paragraph 148* amends the Pension Schemes Act 1993 to allow pension schemes to secure their liability to provide benefits in respect of a pension credit with the consent of a surviving civil partner.

Paragraph 149 – Pension Schemes (Northern Ireland) Act 1993 (c. 49)

1043.*Paragraph 149* amends the Pension Schemes (Northern Ireland) Act 1993 to allow pension schemes to secure their liability to provide benefits in respect of a pension credit with the consent of a surviving civil partner.

Paragraph 150 - Disability Discrimination Act 1995 (c. 50)

1044.Section 23 of the Disability Discrimination Act specifies circumstances in which section 22, relating to discrimination in relation to the disposal of premises, does not apply in certain cases where the "relevant occupier" resides on small premises. Section 23 (6) defines the "relevant occupier" for the purposes of this section as the person who has the power to dispose of premises or the person whose consent or licence is required to dispose of the premises, or a "near relative" of this person. "Near relative" is defined in section 23(7). *Paragraph 150* extends the definition of "near relative" to include a civil partner or a relative by civil partnership. It also replaces the definition of partner so that it includes a reference to two people of the same sex who are not civil partners of each other but are living together as if they were civil partners.

Paragraph 151 - Employment Rights Act 1996 (c. 18)

1045.*Paragraph 151* amends subsection (3)(a) of section 57A of Employment Rights Act to include a civil partner as a dependant for the purposes of an employee's entitlement to time off for dependants. This ensures that an employee will be able to take time off work to deal with certain emergencies involving a dependant who is a civil partner, just as an employee may currently take time off work to deal with an emergency involving a spouse.

Paragraph 152 - Family Law Act 1996 (c. 27)

1046.*Paragraph 152* makes an amendment to add proceedings under Schedule 5 (financial relief in the High Court or a county court etc) and Schedule 6 (financial relief in magistrates' court etc.) to the Civil Partnership Act to the proceedings for which it is possible for the Lord Chancellor to provide for separate representation in section 64 of the Family Law Act 1996.

Paragraph 153 – Trusts of Land and Appointment of Trustees Act 1996 (c. 47)

1047.*Paragraph 153* amends paragraph 3 of Schedule 1 to the 1996 Act which concerns family charges. It extends the categories of land becoming charged voluntarily or in consideration of marriage so that it includes land charged in consideration of the formation of a civil partnership.

Paragraph 154 - Civil Procedure Act 1997 (c. 12)

1048. Section 7(7) of the Civil Procedure Act 1997 preserves the right of a person to refuse to do anything on the ground that to do so might tend to expose him or his spouse to proceedings for an offence or recovery of a penalty. *Paragraph 154* amends the Civil Procedure Act 1997 to extend this right by inserting a reference to a "civil partner" after the reference to "spouse."

Paragraph 155 - National Minimum Wage Act 1998 (c. 39)

1049. Section 14(1)(b) and (c) of the National Minimum Wage Act 1998 provides that an officer acting for the purposes of the 1998 Act shall have power for the performance of his duties to require a relevant person to furnish him with certain information. Section 14(2) presently provides that a person shall not be required under section 14(1)(b) or (c) to answer any question or furnish any information which might incriminate the person or, if married, the person's spouse. *Paragraph 155* amends section 14(2) to provide equal protection to a person in a civil partnership.

Paragraph 156 - Access to Justice Act 1999 (c. 22)

1050. *Paragraph 156* makes an amendment inserting a reference to proceedings for financial relief under Schedule 6 to the Civil Partnership Act 2004 (financial relief in the magistrates courts etc) after the reference to parallel legislative provisions relating to marriage in Schedule 2 to the Access to Justice Act 1999. The amendment provides that proceedings under Schedule 6 to the Civil Partnership Act are eligible for funding under the Community Legal Service in the same way as parallel proceedings in respect of marriage.

Paragraphs 157 to 161 – Welfare Reform and Pensions Act 1999 (c. 30)

1051. *Paragraphs 157 to 161* make a number of changes to the Welfare Reform and Pensions Act 1999 such that certain provisions which relate to pension sharing orders will apply where a civil partnership is dissolved or annulled. These amendments are made to the provisions concerning the supply of information, the charges which can be made in relation to earmarking orders, and the activation and implementation of pension sharing.

Paragraphs 162 to 163 - Immigration and Asylum Act 1999 (c. 33)

1052. *Paragraph 162* amends the Immigration and Asylum Act 1999 by inserting a new section, section 24A, which establishes a duty to report suspicious civil partnerships to the Home Office. Section 24A(1) places the duty to report, where there are reasonable grounds for suspecting a civil partnership will be a sham civil partnership, on those registration authorities to whom notice of proposed civil partnership is given under section 8 of the present Act; any person who attests a declaration under section 8; a district registrar who receives a notice under section 88; and a registrar who receives a notice under section 139.

1053. Subsection (2) of 24A also applies the duty to report where two people register as civil partners of each other under Part 2, 3 or 4 of the Act if before, during or immediately after they do so the registrar has reasonable grounds for suspecting the civil partnership is, or will be, a sham civil partnership.

1054. Subsection (3) of 24A establishes the duty to report to the Secretary of State without delay and in such form and manner as may be prescribed by regulations. Subsection (4) sets out who is to make the regulations. Subsection (5) defines the term "sham civil partnership" and subsection (6) defines the term "registrar".

1055. *Paragraph 163* is consequential.

Paragraph 164 - Representation of the People Act 2000 (c. 2)

1056.*Paragraph 164* makes amendments to the Representation of the People Act 2000 to provide that civil partners are treated in the same way as married couples with regard to the rights and obligations of spouses, husbands and wives in electoral legislation pertaining to voting by proxy.

Paragraphs 165 - 166 - Financial Services and Markets Act 2000 (c. 8)

1057.*Paragraph 165* amends section 422 (controller) of the Financial Services and Markets Act 2000 (c.8). It ensures that a civil partner will be treated in the same way as a spouse by adding reference to a civil partner in the definition of "associate" in section 422(4)(a) of the Act.

1058.*Paragraph 166* amends *Paragraph 16* (qualifying persons) of Schedule 11 to the Financial Services and Markets Act 2000. It ensures that a civil partner or surviving civil partner of a relevant employee will be treated in the same way as a wife, husband, widow or widower of such an employee by adding reference to a civil partner and surviving civil partner in the definition of "qualifying person" in *paragraph 16(2)* of Schedule 11 to the Act.

Paragraph 167 - Land Registration Act 2002 (c. 9)

1059.Section 125(2) of the Land Registration Act 2002 provides that no evidence obtained under subsection (1) of the provision is admissible in any criminal proceedings against the person from whom it was obtained or that person's spouse. *Paragraph 167* extends this privilege to that person's civil partner by amending section 125(2).

Paragraphs 168 and 169 - Enterprise Act 2002 (c. 40)

1060.*Paragraph 168* amends section 127 (associated persons) of the Enterprise Act 2002. It ensures that a civil partner will be treated the same way as a spouse by adding references to civil partners in the definition of an "associated person", including relatives, in sections 127(4)(a) and (c) and 127 (6) of the Act. These definitions are relevant to determining whether "enterprises have ceased to be distinct" (i.e. there has been a merger) and what business activities can be made the subject of certain remedial action as a result of a merger or market investigation.

1061.*Paragraph 169* amends section 222(10) to extend the definition of "associate" to civil partners and their relatives. Civil partners and their relatives will therefore be treated as "associate persons" in the same way as spouses and their relatives when orders are sought to enforce consumer protection legislation against people who control companies.

Paragraph 170 - Licensing Act 2003 (c. 17)

1062.*Paragraph 170* amends section 101 of the Licensing Act 2003 to provide that a civil partner will be treated in the same way as a spouse when determining whether an individual is an associate of another person for the purposes of section 101.

Paragraph 171 - Local Government Act 2003 (c. 26)

1063.*Paragraph 171* amends paragraph 2(1)(a) of Schedule 4 to the Local Government Act 2003. It provides that a person shall be disqualified from being a member of the Valuation Tribunal Service ("VTS") if he is the civil partner of an employee of the VTS. This mirrors the provision that exists for spouses.

Paragraph 172 - Courts Act 2003 (c. 39)

1064.*Paragraph 172* amends section 76 of the Courts Act 2003 (dealing with the scope of the Family Procedure Rules) to add a reference to "civil partnership proceedings county court (within the meaning of Part 5 of the Matrimonial and Family Proceedings Act 1984)" after the reference to "divorce county court". This amendment will facilitate the drafting of rules for proceedings arising from civil partnerships and will enable the same rules committee to consider these rules together with the rules for family proceedings generally.

Paragraphs 173 to 175 – Sexual Offences Act 2003 (c. 42)

1065.*Paragraphs 173 to 175* amend sections 23, 28 and 43 of the Sexual Offences Act 2003 to include a reference to civil partners where there are currently only references to persons who are lawfully married. At present, sections 23, 28 and 43 provide that an offence will not be committed under sections 16 to 19, 25 and 26 and 38 to 41 respectively, of the 2003 Act where a person (B) is 16 years or over and (A) and (B) are lawfully married. Those sections also provide that the defendant must prove that A and B were lawfully married at the time. These amendments provide that an offence will not be committed under these sections where person B is 16 years or over and A and B are civil partners of each other and replace references to "were lawfully married at the time" with "were at the time lawfully married or civil partners of each other.".

Schedule 28 – Consequential amendments: Scotland

1066.This Schedule sets out consequential amendments that will be required to Scottish primary legislation to take account of the new relationship of civil partners. The amendments pick up instances where spouses have a particular right or responsibility and where it is appropriate that this also apply to civil partners.

Part 1 – Amendments of the Succession (Scotland) Act 1964 (c. 41)

1067.The Succession (Scotland) Act 1964 sets out the rights that spouses have under the law of succession (i.e. the law which governs how property is, on the death of its owner, handed over to those who succeed to it). This section amends references to spouses throughout the Succession (Scotland) Act 1964 to include reference to civil partners. This, coupled with section 131, has the effect of providing civil partners with the same rights of succession as spouses.

Part 2 – Amendments of the Family Law (Scotland) Act 1985 (c. 37)

1068.This section addresses the financial provision which should be made when a civil partnership ends. It makes amendments to the Family Law (Scotland) Act 1985 to include reference to civil partners. The amendments mean that civil partners should be treated in the same way as spouses in determining the rights and responsibilities to financial provision following dissolution of a civil partnership. It further provides that any child brought up in a civil partnership as a child of the family can be financially provided for following the breakdown of the civil partnership. This part of the Act is easiest read in conjunction with the Family Law (Scotland) Act 1985.

Part 3 – Amendments of the Bankruptcy (Scotland) Act 1985 (c. 66)

1069.This section amends the Bankruptcy (Scotland) Act 1985 to ensure that civil partners are recognised in the same way as spouses.

Part 4 – Miscellaneous amendments

1070.This part amends various pieces of primary legislation to include civil partners as appropriate.

Schedule 29 – Minor and consequential amendments: Northern Ireland

1071.This Schedule amends various pieces of Northern Ireland legislation to include civil partners as appropriate. The amendments contained within this Schedule extend to Northern Ireland only.

Paragraph 1 – Interpretation Act (Northern Ireland) 1954 (c. 33 (N.I.))

1072.*Paragraph 1* amends section 46(2) of the Interpretation Act (Northern Ireland) 1954 to include a definition of a civil partnership.

Paragraphs 2 and 3 – Trustee Act (Northern Ireland) 1958 (c. 23 (N.I.))

1073.*Paragraph 2* amends section 32(3)(a) of the 1958 Act. That section relates to trustees' powers to apply income for maintenance and to accumulate surplus income during a minority. Sub-paragraph (i) refers to the marriage of the infant for whom the income is held. This is amended to refer to either the marriage or civil partnership of such person. *Paragraph 2* also amends section 34 of the 1958 Act which relates to the holding of income on protective trusts for the benefit of any person. The reference to husband or wife is amended to include spouse or civil partner.

Paragraphs 4 and 5 – Perpetuities Act (Northern Ireland) 1966 (c. 2 (N.I.))

1074.*Paragraph 4* amends section 3(4) and (5) of the Perpetuities Act (Northern Ireland) 1966 which makes provision in relation to dispositions of interests in circumstances where there is uncertainty as to remoteness. The references to "spouse" are amended to include civil partners.

1075.Section 5 of the 1966 Act makes provision in relation to dispositions which are conditional upon the death of a surviving spouse. *Paragraph 5* amends references to "spouse" contained within section 5 of the 1966 Act to include civil partners.

Paragraph 6 – Office and Shop Premises Act (Northern Ireland) 1966 (c.26 (N.I.))

1076.The Office and Shop Premises Act (Northern Ireland) 1966 lays down a number of requirements relating to the health, safety and welfare of persons employed to work in office or shop premises. Section 2(1) of the 1966 Act provides that office or shop premises where only the employer's relatives work are exempted from the scope of the 1966 Act. *Paragraph 6* amends section 2(1) of the 1966 Act to include civil partners in the definition of an employer's relatives.

Paragraphs 7 and 8 - Maintenance and Affiliation Orders Act (Northern Ireland) 1966 (c. 35 (N.I.))

1077.*Paragraph 7* amends section 10(2) of the Maintenance and Affiliation Orders Act (Northern Ireland) 1966 which defines a "maintenance order" for the purposes of the 1966 Act. The amendment provides that orders made under particular provisions of the Civil Partnership Act 2004 are included within this definition.

1078.Section 13 of the 1966 Act makes provision in relation to the variation of orders registered in courts of summary jurisdiction. *Paragraph 8* amends section 13(5A) & (7B) of the 1966 Act to ensure that particular orders made under the Civil Partnership Act 2004 are treated in the same manner as those made under the corresponding provisions of the

Domestic Proceedings (NI) Order 1980 and the Matrimonial and Family Proceedings (NI) Order 1989.

Paragraph 9 – Census Act (Northern Ireland) 1969 (c.8 (N.I.))

1079.Paragraph 5 of the Schedule to the Census Act (Northern Ireland) 1969 sets out matters in respect of which particulars may be required for the purposes of a census. *Paragraph 9* amends the Schedule to the 1969 Act to provide that particulars may be required in respect of a person's condition as to a civil partnership for the purposes of a census.

Paragraph 10 – Theft Act (Northern Ireland) 1969 (c. 16 (N.I.))

1080.*Paragraph 10* amends section 29(1) of the Theft Act (Northern Ireland) 1969 which makes provision in relation to the effect of the 1969 Act on civil proceedings and rights. The amendment allows for civil partners to be treated in the same manner as spouses in relation to the 1969 Act in so far as self-incrimination is concerned in relation to an offence under the 1969 Act.

Paragraphs 11 and 12 – Industrial and Provident Societies Act (Northern Ireland) 1969 (c. 24 (N.I.))

1081.*Paragraph 11* amends section 22 of the 1969 Act. That section makes provision for members of registered societies to nominate persons to become entitled to any property in the society. A nomination will not be valid if the nominee is an officer of the society unless that person is a spouse or family of the member. The reference in section 22(2) to husband and wife is amended to include spouse or civil partner. Section 22(6) is amended to ensure that any nomination is revoked by the marriage or civil partnership of a member.

1082.*Paragraph 12* amends the definition of "member of the family" in section 101 of the 1969 Act to include a spouse and civil partner.

Paragraph 13 – Land Registration Act (Northern Ireland) 1970 (c.18 (N.I.))

1083.Schedule 11 to the Land Registration Act (Northern Ireland) 1970 sets out various matters which are required to be registered in the Statutory Charges Register. *Paragraph 13* amends Schedule 11 to the 1970 Act to provide that orders made under paragraph 59(2) of Schedule 15 to the Civil Partnership Act 2004 must also be registered in the Statutory Charges Register.

Paragraphs 14 and 15 – Leasehold (Enlargement and Extension) Act (Northern Ireland) 1971 (c.7 (N.I.))

1084.*Paragraph 14* amends section 1 of the 1971 Act which makes provision in relation to a person's general right to acquire a fee simple or to obtain an extension of a lease. The reference in section 1 to a spouse is amended to include a civil partner.

1085.*Paragraph 15* amends section 19 which relates to restrictions on a person's right to extend a lease or to acquire a fee simple. The reference to a spouse in section 19 is amended to include a civil partner.

Paragraph 16 – Civil Evidence Act (Northern Ireland) 1971 (c. 36 (N.I.))

1086.Section 10 of the Civil Evidence Act (Northern Ireland) 1971 provides that a person has a right to refuse to answer incriminating questions in legal proceedings if those questions would tend to expose that person or his/her spouse to proceedings for a criminal offence. *Paragraph 16* amends section 10 of the 1971 Order to ensure that the privilege against incrimination of a spouse is extended to civil partners.

Paragraphs 17 and 18 – Local Government Act (Northern Ireland) 1972 (c. 9 (N.I.))

1087.*Paragraph 17* amends section 30(6) of the 1972 Act which provides a list of persons who are considered to be in a "relevant family relationship". Under certain circumstances councillors must disclose such relationships to the council. References to "husband" and "wife" have been amended to include civil partners in the same context.

1088.*Paragraph 18* amends section 146(2) of the 1972 Act which makes provision in relation to the pecuniary interests of spouses living together. References to spouses are amended to include civil partners. The provisions amended are intended to remove any conflict of interest between councillors and the work of the council.

Paragraph 19 - Employers' Liability (Defective Equipment and Compulsory Insurance) (Northern Ireland) Order 1972 (S.I. 1972/963 (N.I. 6))

1089.The Employers' Liability (Defective Equipment and Compulsory Insurance) (Northern Ireland) Order 1972 requires employers to insure against their liability for personal injury to their employees. Insurance is not required however where the employee is a specified relation of the employer. *Paragraph 19* extends the list of relations identified by article 6(a) of the Employer's Liability Order to include a civil partner of the employee and any other relationships formed by virtue of a civil partnership.

Paragraph 20 – Births and Deaths Registration (Northern Ireland) Order 1976 (S.I. 1976/1041 (N.I. 14))

1090.*Paragraph 20* extends the definition of "relative" in Article 2(2) of the 1976 Order to include relatives by civil partnership as well as by marriage. This will qualify civil partners and those related to them to give information concerning a death to a registrar of births and deaths, providing the civil partner meets the prescribed conditions in order to give this information.

Paragraph 21 – Sex Discrimination (Northern Ireland) Order 1976 (S.I. 1976/1042 (N.I. 15))

1091.*Paragraph 21* amends the definition of "near relative" in Article 2(6) of the 1976 Order to include civil partners and relatives of civil partners. This is relevant for the housing provisions in Articles 30 to 33 of the 1976 Order which make it unlawful to discriminate in relation to the disposal or management of premises, or in relation to giving consent for the assignment of a lease or for sub-letting. Article 33 provides an exception for small dwellings occupied by the alleged discriminator and/or a near relative where there is other accommodation in addition to that occupied by the alleged discriminator and/or his near relative which he shares with other persons residing on the premises who are not members of his household.

Paragraph 22 – Pharmacy (Northern Ireland) Order 1976 (S.I. 1976/ 1213 (N.I. 22))

1092.*Paragraph 22* amends Article 3(3)(e)(iii) of the Pharmacy (Northern Ireland) Order 1976 which sets out the objectives of the Pharmaceutical Society of Northern Ireland. The amendment ensures that a civil partner of a deceased member of the Society is treated in the same manner as a widow and may receive financial relief.

Paragraph 23 – Criminal Damage (Northern Ireland) Order 1977 (S.I. 1977/426 (N.I. 4))

1093.Article 11 of the Criminal Damage (Northern Ireland) Order 1977 makes provision in relation to the giving of evidence in connection with offences under the 1977 Order.

Paragraph 23 amends Article 11 of the 1977 Order to ensure that civil partners are treated in the same manner as husbands and wives.

Paragraphs 24 to 26 – Judicature (Northern Ireland) Act 1978 (c.23)

1094.Section 31(7)(b) of the Judicature (Northern Ireland) Act 1978 provides that the High Court's powers in relation to the remittal and removal of proceedings to a county court do not apply to applications under section 17 of the Married Women's Property Act 1882. *Paragraph 24* amends section 31(7)(b) so that the High Court's powers of removal and remittal do not apply to applications made under provisions in the Civil Partnership Act 2004 corresponding to section 17 of the 1882 Act.

1095.Section 35(2)(e) of the 1978 Act provides that the Court of Appeal may not hear an appeal from specific orders or judgements made by the High Court in relation to a marriage. *Paragraph 25* amends section 35(2) of the 1978 Act so that appeals may not lie to the Court of Appeal from particular orders or judgements made by the High Court in relation to a civil partnership.

1096.Section 94A of the 1978 Act makes provision in relation to proceedings where the privilege against incrimination of self or spouse is withdrawn. *Paragraph 26* amends section 94A to ensure that a civil partner has the same rights as a spouse in relation to this privilege.

Paragraph 27 – Health and Safety at Work (Northern Ireland) Order 1978 (S.I. 1978/ 1039 (N.I. 9))

1097.Article 22(7) of the Health and Safety at Work (Northern Ireland) Order 1978 provides that no answer given by a person (upon questioning by an inspector) shall be admissible in evidence against that person or the husband or spouse of that person in any proceedings. *Paragraph 27* amends Article 22(7) of the 1978 Order by extending it to those in a civil partnership.

Paragraphs 28 to 33 - Matrimonial Causes (Northern Ireland) Order 1978 (S.I. 1978/1045 (N.I. 15))

1098.*Paragraphs 28* to *33* of the Schedule amend the Matrimonial Causes (Northern Ireland) Order 1978. Amendments to Articles 13 and 17 ensure that a marriage will be void if at the time of the marriage either party was already a civil partner. Provisions of the Matrimonial Causes (Northern Ireland) Order dependent upon marriage or remarriage are extended so as to be dependent upon marriage, remarriage or upon the formation of a civil partnership.

Paragraph 34 – Rehabilitation of Offenders (Northern Ireland) Order 1978 (S.I. 1978/ 1908 (N.I. 27))

1099.*Paragraph 34* amends Article 8(2)(c) of the Rehabilitation of Offenders (Northern Ireland) Order 1978 to provide that, despite a person's rehabilitation, his or her previous convictions may be considered in relation to proceedings relating to a minor's marriage or civil partnership.

Paragraph 35 – Criminal Appeal (Northern Ireland) Act 1980 (c. 47)

1100.Section 47A of the Criminal Appeal (Northern Ireland) Act 1980 sets out the circumstances in which an appeal may be begun or continued (by any person approved by the Court of Appeal) notwithstanding that the appellant or potential appellant has died. *Paragraph 35* amends Section 47A(3)(a) of the 1980 Act to include civil partners in the category of persons who may be approved by the Court of Appeal to take an appeal.

Paragraphs 36 to 38 – County Courts (Northern Ireland) Order 1980 (S.I. 1980/ 397 (N.I. 3))

1101.*Paragraph 36* inserts a new Article 10(3A) into the County Courts (Northern Ireland) Order 1980 to provide that, in relation to the general civil jurisdiction of county courts, a county court which is not a civil partnership proceedings county court shall not have jurisdiction to hear civil partnership causes except as otherwise provided in the Civil Partnership Act 2004.

1102.Article 14 of the 1980 Order sets out a county court's jurisdiction in relation to equitable matters, including applications under section 17 of the Married Women's Property Act 1882. *Paragraph 37* amends Article 14 to extend this jurisdiction to applications made under provisions in the Civil Partnership Act 2004 corresponding to section 17 of the 1882 Act.

1103.Article 39 of the 1980 Order makes provision in relation to the capacity of parties to institute and continue proceedings. *Paragraph 38* amends Article 39 of the 1980 Order to provide that proceedings shall not abate by reason of the registration of a civil partnership by any party where the cause of action survives or continues.

Paragraphs 39 and 40 - Domestic Proceedings (Northern Ireland) Order 1980 (S.I. 1980/563 (N.I. 5))

1104.*Paragraphs 39* and *40* amend the Domestic Proceedings (Northern Ireland) Order 1980 to provide that where entitlements to maintenance and other financial support are affected by remarriage, they will, by these amendments, also be affected by the formation of a civil partnership.

Paragraphs 41 to 52 – Judgements Enforcement (Northern Ireland) Order 1981 (S.I. 1981/ 226 (N.I. 6))

1105.Articles 4,6 & 7 of the Judgements Enforcement (Northern Ireland) Order 1981 set out the various orders and judgements to which the 1981 Order does and does not apply. *Paragraphs 41* to *43* amend these articles so that the 1981 Order also applies to orders made under provisions of the Civil Partnership Act 2004.

1106.Articles 25, 32, 33, 36, 38 & 44 of the 1981 Order make provision in relation to the seizure of property for the purposes of enforcing judgements. By virtue of these articles a debtor's spouse is to be treated in the same manner as the debtor. *Paragraphs 44* to *49* amend these articles to provide that a debtor's civil partner is treated in the same way as a debtor's spouse for the purposes if the 1981 Order.

1107.Articles 96A, 98 & 107 of the 1981 Order set out the powers of the High Court and divorce county courts in relation to periodical maintenance orders. *Paragraphs 50* to *52* of this Schedule amend these articles to ensure that the High Court and civil partnership proceedings county courts have the same powers in relation to such maintenance orders made under provisions in the Civil Partnership Act 2004.

Paragraphs 53 and 54– Legal Aid, Advice and Assistance (Northern Ireland) Order 1981 (S.I. 1981/228 (N.I. 8))

1108.*Paragraph 53* amends Article 14(4) of the Legal Aid, Advice and Assistance (Northern Ireland) Order 1981 to ensure that when a person's resources are being assessed the resources of that person's spouse or civil partner are treated as those of that person.

1109.*Paragraph 54* amends Part 1 of Schedule 1 to the 1981 Order which lists proceedings for which legal aid may be given. The amendment provides that legal aid may be given for certain civil partnership proceedings.

Paragraphs 55 to 61 – Magistrates' Courts (Northern Ireland) Order 1981 (S.I. 1981/ 1675 (N.I. 26))

1110.Articles 85, 86, 88, 98, 99, 143 & 164 of the Magistrates' Courts (Northern Ireland) Order 1981 make provision for the powers of the court in relation to various provisions of the Domestic Proceedings (Northern Ireland) Order 1980 relating to maintenance orders. Paragraphs 55 to 61 amend these particular articles of the 1980 Order to provide that they apply equally to the provisions in the Civil Partnership Act 2004 corresponding to those in the 1980 Order.

Paragraph 62 – Criminal Attempts and Conspiracy (Northern Ireland) Order 1983 (S.I. 1983/ 1120 (N.I. 13))

1111.*Paragraph 62* amends Article 10 of the Criminal Attempts and Conspiracy (Northern Ireland) Order 1983 which provides that a person is exempt from liability for conspiracy if the person with whom he or she agreed is his or her spouse. The amendment provides that the reference to a spouse in this Article also includes a civil partner.

Paragraph 63 – Forfeiture (Northern Ireland) Order 1982 (S.I. 1982/ 1082 (N.I. 14))

1112.Article 5 of the Forfeiture (Northern Ireland) Order 1982 provides that applications for financial maintenance made under particular provisions of the Matrimonial Causes (Northern Ireland) Order 1978 are not subject to the forfeiture rule. *Paragraph 63* amends Article 5 of the 1982 Order so that applications for financial provision made under the corresponding provisions of the Civil Partnership Act 2004 are also exempt from the forfeiture rule.

Paragraph 64 – Family Law (Miscellaneous Provisions) (Northern Ireland) Order 1984 (S.I. 1984/1984 (N.I. 14))

1113.*Paragraph 64* provides for amendments to Article 18 of the Family Law (Miscellaneous Provisions) Order. Currently Article 18 prohibits or restricts eligibility for marriage between people related within specific degrees by parentage, descent or marriage. Schedule 12 to the Act provides for parallel prohibitions and restrictions to apply to civil partnerships between people who are related within the same degrees by parentage, descent, marriage or civil partnership. Paragraph 64 provides for the extension of the prohibitions and restrictions that already apply to marriage so as to include relationships by civil partnership.

Paragraphs 65 and 66 – Credit Unions (Northern Ireland) Order 1985 (S.I. 1985/1205 (N.I. 12))

1114.Article 3 of the Credit Unions (Northern Ireland) Order 1985 provides that in order to qualify for registration as a credit union, a society must restrict its membership to persons who fulfil certain qualifications. Under Article 3(6) of the 1985 Order a credit union may make rules allowing a member of a member's family automatically to fulfil membership qualifications if they are part of the same household as the member. *Paragraph 65* extends the definition of a "member of the family" in article 2(2) of 1985 Order so as to include civil partners (including former civil partners) and their relations and in-laws. *Paragraph 65* also inserts a definition of a civil partner to include a former civil partner in article 2(2) of the 1985 Order.

1115.Article 17 of the 1985 Order provides that a registered society's member may not nominate an officer of the society to become entitled to their property upon their death unless the officer is related to the member. *Paragraph 66* amends Article 17 of the 1985 Order to include civil partners within the class of persons who are deemed to be related to the member.

Paragraph 67 - Mental Health (Northern Ireland) Order 1986 (S.I. 1986/595 (N.I. 4))

1116.*Paragraph 67* adds "civil partner" to the list of individuals named in the Mental Health (Northern Ireland) Order 1986 who may not provide a medical recommendation for the purposes of an application for compulsory admission to hospital of a patient for assessment or treatment under the Order.

Paragraphs 68 to 75 and 90 – Companies (Northern Ireland) Order 1986 (S.I. 1986/1032 (N.I. 6)) and 1990 (S.I. 1990/593 (N.I.))

1117.*Paragraphs 68* to *75* and *90* ensure that, in relation to the provisions of the Companies Orders of 1986 and 1990 specified in the Schedule, civil partners are to be treated in the same way as spouses.

1118.Article 10A of the 1986 Order provides that an offer of shares in or debentures of a private company is to be regarded as a domestic concern of the persons giving or receiving it if it is made to (among others) the widow or widower of a former member or employee of that company. *Paragraph 68* amends Article 10A(3)(iii) so that surviving civil partners are treated in the same way as surviving spouses.

1119.Article 11 of the 1986 Order sets out those persons who may participate in an "Employees' share scheme". *Paragraph 69* amends Article 11 of the 1986 Order so that an employee's civil partner is entitled to participate in the scheme in the same way as an employee's spouse.

1120.Under the Companies Order provisions persons with a notifiable interest in shares should notify the company. Article 211 of the Companies (Northern Ireland) Order 1986 deems a person to be interested in shares in which his spouse is interested. *Paragraph 70* extends this obligation to civil partners.

1121.Article 331 of the 1986 Order contains a prohibition on directors dealing in share options of his or her own company. Article 335 applies the prohibition to the wife or husband of a director. *Paragraph 71* extends the prohibition to the civil partner of a director.

1122.Article 332 of the 1986 Order requires directors to disclose shareholdings in their own company. Article 336 treats the interests of a wife or husband of a director as an interest of that director. *Paragraph 72* extends this to civil partners of directors.

1123.Part XI of the 1986 Order contains a number of provisions designed to enforce fair dealing by directors. A number of these provisions apply to persons connected with a director. Article 354 defines " connected person" to include spouse. *Paragraph 73* extends this definition to include civil partners.

1124.Article 423E of the 1986 Order disregards shares held by the associate of an offeror in certain circumstances (relating to takeover offers). Where an offeror is an individual, "associates" includes spouses, and this definition will be extended by paragraph 74 to include civil partners.

1125.*Paragraph 90* defines "associate" to include civil partner as well as spouse for the purposes of the Companies' Order 1990.

Paragraphs 76 to 78 – Enduring Powers of Attorney (Northern Ireland) Order 1987 (S.I. 1987/ 1627 (N.I. 16))

1126.Article 5(5) of the Enduring Powers of Attorney (Northern Ireland) Order 1987 enables an attorney to make gifts of reasonable value out of a donor's property at the time or anniversary of a marriage. *Paragraph 76* extends Article 5(5) so that an attorney may also make such gifts at the time or on the anniversary of the registration of a civil partnership.

1127.*Paragraph 77* amends paragraph 2(1) of Schedule 1 to the 1987 Order to include civil partners in the list of relatives who are entitled to receive notification of an attorney's intention to apply to register the instrument creating the power of attorney.

Paragraph 79 – Matrimonial and Family Proceedings (Northern Ireland) Order 1989 (S.I. 1989/677 (N.I. 4))

1128.*Paragraph 79* amends Article 16 so that in respect of applications for financial relief following overseas divorces, no application may be made if the applicant either remarries or forms a subsequent civil partnership.

Paragraphs 80 to 87 - The Insolvency (Northern Ireland) Order 1989 (S.I. 1989/2405 (N.I. 19)

1129.The Insolvency (Northern Ireland) Order 1989 contains various provisions protecting creditors from fraud and attempting to ensure a proper *pari passu* distribution amongst creditors. These provisions allow certain transactions, including transactions involving close family and other associated persons, entered into by a debtor or company prior to the onset of insolvency proceedings to be undone or adjusted. *Paragraph 80* amends the definition of "associate" in the 1989 Order so that the relevant anti-avoidance provisions cover a civil partner in the same way as they would if the civil partner were a spouse.

1130.*Paragraphs 81* to *87* amend various articles of the 1989 Order to provide that the civil partner of a debtor or a bankrupt is subject to the same treatment as the spouse of such persons for the purposes of the 1989 Order.

Paragraphs 88 and 89 – Police and Criminal Evidence (Northern Ireland) Order 1989 (S.I. 1989/ 1341 (N.I. 12))

1131.Article 79 of the Police and Criminal Evidence (Northern Ireland) Order 1989 makes provision in relation to the compellability of the spouse of an accused person to give evidence against the accused. *Paragraph 88* amends Article 79 of the 1989 Order to ensure that a civil partner of an accused person is treated in the same manner as a spouse.

1132.Article 79A of the 1989 Order provides that the failure of husband or wife of a person charged in any proceedings to give evidence in the proceedings shall not be made the subject of any comment in the prosecution. *Paragraph 89* amends Article 79A so that the failure of an accused person's civil partner to give evidence shall also not be the subject of comment in the prosecution.

Paragraph 91 – Food Safety (Northern Ireland) Order 1991 (S.I. 1990/ 762 (N.I. 7))

1133.Article 42 of the Food Safety (Northern Ireland) Order 1991 provides that the registration or licensing of food premises may continue after the death of any person who was registered or held a licence in respect of such premises for the benefit of that person's widow. *Paragraph 91* amends this reference to "widow" to include spouses and civil partners.

Paragraph 92 – Industrial Relations (Northern Ireland) Order 1992 (S.I. 1992/807 (N.I. 5))

1134.Article 23 of the Industrial Relations (Northern Ireland) Order 1992 makes provision in relation to the recovery of sums awarded in proceedings involving trade unions and employers' associations. Article 23(3) of the 1992 Order provides that "provident benefits" include (amongst other things) a payment in discharge or aid of funeral expenses on the death of a member or the wife of a member. *Paragraph 92* amends Article 23(3) of the 1992 Order by adding a reference to "spouse or civil partner" so that a member's civil partner has the same rights as those of his/her spouse.

Paragraph 93 – Pension Schemes (Northern Ireland) Act 1993 (c.49)

1135.Section 97E of the Pension Schemes (Northern Ireland) Act 1993 makes provision in relation to the discharge of liability where pension credits or alternative benefits were secured by insurance policies or annuity contracts. *Paragraph 93* amends section 97E to provide that civil partners are treated in the same manner as spouses.

Paragraph 94 – Family Law (Northern Ireland) Order 1993 (S.I. 1993/ 1576 (N.I. 6))

1136.*Paragraph 94* amends Article 12 of the Family Law (Northern Ireland) Order 1993 to provide that rules of court made under this article shall treat sums payable under the legal aid scheme in relation to defined matrimonial causes in the same manner as those sums payable in respect of corresponding civil partnership causes.

Paragraphs 95 to 100 – Children (Northern Ireland) Order 1995 (S.I. 1995/ 755 (N.I. 2))

1137.Article 8(4) of the Children (Northern Ireland) Order 1995 provides a definition of "family proceedings" for the purposes of the 1995 Order. *Paragraph 95* amends the definition in Article 8(4) to include specified civil partnership proceedings.

1138.*Paragraph 96* amends Article 50 of the 1995 Order to provide that a court may not make a care order or a supervision order in respect of any child who has reached the age of 16 and is married or in a civil partnership.

1139.Article 67 of the 1995 Order provides that a person must comply with a court's requirement to disclose any information relating to a child's whereabouts in relation to an emergency protection order. *Paragraph 97* amends Article 67(2) to provide that a person is not excused from complying with this requirement on the ground that complying might incriminate that person and his/her spouse or civil partner.

1140.Article 69 of the 1995 Order provides that a person may be required, by virtue of a Recovery Order, to disclose information relating to a child's whereabouts. *Paragraph 98* amends Article 69(11) to provide that a person is not excused from complying with this requirement on the ground that to do so would incriminate his/her spouse or civil partner.

1141.*Paragraph 99* amends Article 166 of the 1995 Order so that, with regard to appeals, proceedings in divorce county courts are treated in the same manner as proceedings in civil partnership proceedings county courts.

1142.*Paragraph 100* amends Article 171 of the 1995 Order to provide that, in applications for orders under the 1995 Order, no person shall be excused from giving evidence on the ground that to do so might incriminate him or his spouse or civil partner of an offence.

Paragraph 101 – Trade Union and Labour Relations (Northern Ireland) Order 1995 (S.I. 1995/ 1980 (N.I. 12))

1143.Article 125 of the Trade Union and Labour Relations (Northern Ireland) Order 1995 provides for criminal offences in relation to the intimidation or annoyance of any person or his wife or children. *Paragraph 101* amends Article 125 of the 1995 Order to provide that a civil partner has the same rights as a spouse for the purposes of the 1992 Order.

Paragraphs 102 and 103 – Employment Rights (Northern Ireland) Order 1996 (S.I. 1996/1919 (N.I. 16))

1144.Article 85A of the Employment Rights (Northern Ireland) Order 1996 provides that an employee is entitled to take a reasonable amount of time off work in order to provide necessary assistance or make arrangements in respect of a dependant. *Paragraph 102* amends Article 85A(3)(a) of the 1996 Order to include civil partners in the list of dependants.

1145.Article 248(5) of the 1996 Order provides that, where an employee or employer has died, tribunal proceedings may be instituted or continued by any appropriate person that the court may appoint (including a widow or widower). *Paragraph 103* amends Article 248(5)(b) of the 1996 Order so that a bereaved civil partner has the same rights as that which belongs to a widow or widower.

Paragraph 104 – Registration of Clubs (Northern Ireland) Order 1996 (S.I. 1996/ 3159 (N.I. 23))

1146.Paragraph 11 of Schedule 1 to the Registration of Clubs (Northern Ireland) Order 1996 exempts a club member's husband or wife from the restriction which applies in relation to the number of times a non-member can be admitted to a club in a twelve month period. *Paragraph 104* amends paragraph 11 of Schedule 1 to the 1996 Order so that a member's civil partner is also exempt from this restriction in the same way as a member's spouse.

Paragraph 105 – Race Relations (Northern Ireland) Order 1997 (S.I. 1997/869 (N.I. 6))

1147.*Paragraph 105* amends the definition of "near relative" in Article 23(7) of this Order to include civil partners and relatives of civil partners. This affects housing discrimination provisions (Articles 22 to 24 of the Race Relations (Northern Ireland) Order as amended) which have the same effect as those in Articles 30 to 33 of the Sex Discrimination (Northern Ireland) Order 1976.

Paragraphs 106 and 107 – Fair Employment and Treatment (Northern Ireland) Order 1998 (S.I. 1998/3162 (N.I. 21))

1148.*Paragraph 106* amends the meaning of "near relative" in Article 30(7) of this Order to include civil partners and relatives of civil partners.

1149.*Paragraph 107* amends the interpretation of a "connected person" to include civil partners.

Paragraphs 108 to 112 - Welfare Reform and Pensions (Northern Ireland) Order 1999 (S.I. 1999/ 3147 (N.I. 11))

1150.The Welfare Reform and Pensions (Northern Ireland) Order 1999 makes provision in relation to pension sharing orders over shareable state scheme rights upon a divorce or nullity of a marriage. *Paragraphs 108* to *112* amend the 1999 Order to ensure that these provisions are applied in the same way on the dissolution or nullity of a civil partnership.

1151.*Paragraph 108* amends Article 21 of the 1999 Order to provide that pension information must be supplied in connection with the dissolution of a civil partnership just as it must be supplied in connection with a divorce.

1152.Article 22 of the 1999 Order allows persons responsible for pension arrangements to recover prescribed charges relating to earmarking orders made in relation to a marriage. *Paragraph 109* amends Article 22 so that it applies to earmarking orders made in relation to a civil partnership.

1153.Article 25 of the 1999 Order makes provision in relation to the activation of pension sharing orders. *Paragraph 110* amends Article 25 to provide that pension sharing orders made in relation to a civil partnership are dealt with in the same manner as those made in connection with a marriage.

1154.Article 31 of the 1999 Order makes provision in relation to the implementation period required for a pension credit to be effected in relation to a marriage. *Paragraph 111* amends Article 31 to ensure that pension credits to be effected in relation to a civil partnership are subject to the same implementation period.

1155.Article 45 of the 1999 Order provides for the activation of benefit sharing in relation to pension sharing orders made in connection with a marriage. *Paragraph 112* extends the scope of Article 45 so that it also applies to pension sharing orders made in connection with a civil partnership.

Paragraph 113 – Housing (Northern Ireland) Order 2003 (S.I. 2003/ 412 (N.I. 2))

1156.Article 85 of the Housing (Northern Ireland) Order 2003 sets out disposals of property which are deemed to be "exempt disposals" for the purposes of grant applications. *Paragraph 113* amends Article 85 of the 2003 Order to provide that disposals made in pursuance of orders made under particular provisions of the Civil Partnership Act 2004 are also exempt disposals.

Paragraphs 114 and 115 – Marriage (Northern Ireland) Order 2003 (S.I. 2003/ 413 (N.I. 3))

1157.Article 5 of the Marriage (Northern Ireland) Order 2003 provides that a registrar has the power to require evidence in relation to various matters, including the marital status of any party to a marriage notice. *Paragraph 114* amends Article 5 so that a registrar may require evidence as to a person's civil partnership status.

1158.*Paragraph 115* amends Article 6(6)(b) of the 2003 Order to provide that a legal impediment will be deemed to exist in relation to a marriage where either party is or was already married or in a civil partnership.

Paragraph 116 – Access to Justice (Northern Ireland) Order 2003 (S.I. 2003/ 435 (N.I. 10))

1159.Article 39 of the Access to Justice (Northern Ireland) Order 2003 provides that family proceedings cannot be the subject of an enforceable conditional fee agreement. This paragraph amends the definition of "family proceedings" for the purposes of Article 39 to include certain proceedings under the Civil Partnership Act 2004.

1160.Paragraph 2(d) of Schedule 2 to the 2003 Order sets out various proceedings (including proceedings under the Domestic Proceedings (Northern Ireland) Order 1980) in relation to which the Northern Ireland legal services commission may fund representation services.

Paragraph 116 amends Schedule 2 to the 2003 to include proceedings under the Civil Partnership Act 2004 corresponding to those under the 1980 Order.

Paragraph 117 – Firearms (Northern Ireland) Order 2004 (S.I. 2004/ 702 (N.I. 3))

1161.*Paragraph 117* amends the definition of "relative" contained within Article 2(2) of the Firearms (Northern Ireland) Order 2004 to include civil partners. This provides that civil partners are treated in the same manner as spouses for the purposes of the 2004 Order.

Schedule 30 – Repeals and revocations

1162.This Schedule contains repeals and revocations of the specified provisions of various Acts which have been superseded by or made redundant by the provisions of the Act.

TERRITORIAL APPLICATION: WALES

1163.The Act does not raise any general issues concerning devolution to Wales. The Act confers two powers on the National Assembly for Wales, in relation to matters falling within its functions: the power in section 247(3)(c) by order to amend Schedule 21 (references to stepchildren etc.) and the power in section 259(2) by order to make further provision in connection with civil partnership.

COMMENCEMENT

1164.All substantive provisions of the Act are to come into force by commencement orders. These orders will be made by the Secretary of State, except for the Scottish provisions, which will be made by the Scottish Ministers and the Northern Ireland provisions, which will be made by the Department of Finance and Personnel, both after consulting the Secretary of State. The Secretary of State must also consult the Scottish Ministers or the Department of Finance and Personnel before commencing certain other provisions.

HANSARD REFERENCES

1165.The following table sets out the dates and Hansard references for each stage of the Act's passage through Parliament.

Stage	Date	Hansard Reference
House of Lords: Presentation and First Reading	30th March 2004	Vol. 659 (no. 63), Col 1176
House of Lords: Second Reading	22nd April 2004	Vol. 660 (no. 71), Col 387 - 433
House of Lords: Grand Committee First Day	10th May 2004	Vol. 661 (no. 80), Col. GC1 – GC60
House of Lords: Grand Committee Second Day	12th May 2004	Vol. 661 (no. 82), Col. GC115 – GC180
House of Lords: Grand Committee Third Day	13th May 2004	Vol. 661 (no. 83), Col. GC181 – GC238
House of Lords: Grand Committee Fourth Day	17th May 2004	Vol. 661 (no. 84), Col. GC239 – GC334
House of Lords: Grand Committee Fifth Day	25th May 2004	Vol. 661 (no. 90), Col. GC449 – GC526
House of Lords: Report	24th June 2004	Vol. 662 (no. 104), Col 1354 – 1391; 1406 - 1462
House of Lords:	1st July 2004	Vol. 663 (no. 109), Col 391 -

Third Reading		430
House of Commons: First Reading	5th July 2004	
House of Commons: Second Reading	12th October 2004	Vol. 425 (no. 135), Col 174 - 257
House of Commons: Standing Committee	19th, 21st, 26th October 2004	SC - D
House of Commons: Remaining stages	9th November 2004	Vol. 426 (no. 152), Col 724 - 815
Lords' Consideration of Commons' Amendments	17th November 2004	Vol. 666 (no. 156), Col 1449 - 1530

Royal Assent – 18th November 2004
    House of Lords Hansard Vol. 666 (no. 157) Col 1659
    House of Commons Hansard Vol. 426 (no. 158) Col 1518

Printed in the UK by The Stationery Office Limited
under the authority and superintendence of Carol Tullo, Controller of
Her Majesty's Stationery Office and Queen's Printer of Acts of Parliament.

12/2004   993065   19585